D0294617

£4.77 ~ /₩

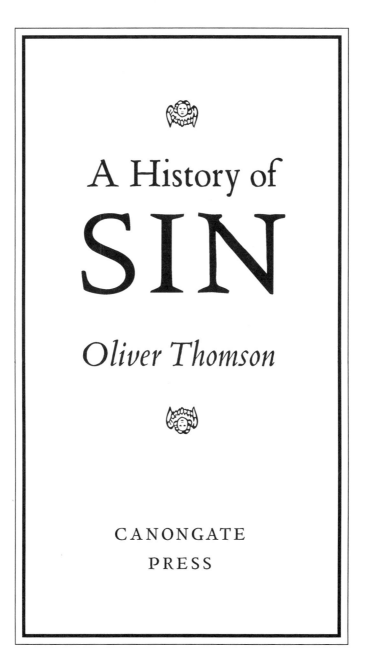

A History of
SIN

Oliver Thomson

CANONGATE
PRESS

Acknowledgments

The author wishes to express his appreciation of those who have helped or
tolerated the production of this book over and beyond the call of duty: his
wife and family, Alasdair Gray and Angela Mullane of Dog & Bone,
Lorraine McCann of Canongate.

First published in Great Britain in 1993 by
Canongate Press
14 Frederick Street
Edinburgh EH2 2HB

British Library Cataloguing-in-Publication Data
A catalogue record for this book is available on request from
the British Library.

ISBN 0 86241 406 7

Typeset by The Electronic Book Factory Ltd, Cowdenbeath, Fife, Scotland
Printed and bound by Biddles, Guildford, Surrey

Preface

F OR SOME REASON the study of moral history has not been a particularly fashionable subject, yet the need for people to understand how moral codes evolve in both the past and present is obvious. In retrospect we may regard many moralities as downright wicked—those that blessed genocide, human sacrifice, torture, infanticide, drugs, prostitution and many other habits now unacceptable to our own codes.

Histories have been written of the law and of criminal behaviour. There are also individual studies of many of the corporate crimes of mankind such as slavery and torture, but there have been few attempts at a broad historical view of the peaks and troughs of moral fashions through the ages. The great pioneering work was E.H. Lecky's *History of European Morals from Augustus to Charlemagne*, first published in 1906. Since then most historians have steered clear of such an approach except perhaps for the French, particularly Ariés and Duby with their four-volume *A History of Private Life*. Constitutional and economic histories are safer because they deal with concrete evidence; examinations of foreign policy, administration, warfare or material life are easier because they are based on official documents or archaeological evidence. Moral history by its nature depends on flimsier source material. There are risks of misinterpretation, of subjective judgements, and this book does not pretend to be immune from such difficulties, or to contain any information which is not already available in existing specialist studies.

The intention of this study is to look at the history of sin from five points of view. First, what are the factors of time and place which help to create moral climates and ethical codes? Why do we find that what is regarded as good or evil can be quite different amongst different peoples in different eras? What causes these differences, and how (if at all) do they relate to any absolute standards of good or evil?

Second, what effect in turn do changing moral codes and attitudes have on the events of history, on the life and happiness of nations? While a moral code may be a product of its time, the result of socio-economic pressures, once it is established it may subsequently inflict reciprocal pressures which can influence events radically.

Third, it is important to examine the functioning of morality in different periods, the nature of moral leadership offered by the great moral thinkers and codifiers, the structure of ethical systems, the motivation offered to the people, the components and characteristics of the systems. This will in turn lead back to history and an examination of how some moral systems contained features which by almost any of our recent standards are extremely immoral. The fascist ethic included genocide, the Spartans blessed infanticide, the Jesuits believed in torture, the Puritans in burning witches, the followers of Hassan i Suffah or the IRA in assassination. Great corporate crimes are often committed in the name of virtue. Actual deviations from the moral conventions of each era, the myriad acts of anti-social behaviour are much less our concern than the vast numbers of acts of cruelty to which societies and conventions have given their blessing.

Fourth, we may find evidence of the typical life-expectancy of moral codes, signs of the reactive ebb and flow of strictness and permissiveness in successive generations, like the rise and fall of hemlines. Throughout much of history it can be argued that the fundamental morality of the vast silent majority of subsistence peasants changed hardly at all, but it was the changeable moral codes of the fashion-conscious minority which often created instability and misery for the rest.

Finally, it may be useful in a historical context to look at the particular moral problems of the late twentieth century, possibly to compare it with periods of similar moral stress or crisis in the past and put some of our current dilemmas in some kind of perspective.

Accordingly, this study is divided into three parts: the first is an attempted analysis and classification of moral codes, their background, functions, attributes and peculiarities. The second part comprises historical examples, and the third is a tentative review of moral directions towards the end of the twentieth century seen in their long-term historical context. We can begin with some self-evident premises: that the level of moral consciousness of peoples and leaders is one of the most important factors in governing their conduct and therefore in controlling the destinies of history. Attitudes to war, violence, the family, property, work and human rights are of fundamental importance, they vary considerably, and there has been less historical study of them than there should be.

To avoid breaking up the narrative the use of footnotes has been avoided, but readers interested in pursuing references or quotations can do so by referring to the bibliography. It will be noticed that in many cases reference is made to historians of several generations ago rather than the most up-to-date historical scholars. This is because men like Gibbon, Macaulay, Lecky and Finlay took a broader view of history and were not afraid to indulge in moral commentary, whereas today's researchers tend to prefer statistics and objectivity.

Contents

PART TWO: A History of Sin

List of Illustrations

PART ONE

The Nature of Moralities

Who else but Nature whispers to us of personal hatreds, venge-
ances, wars, in fact all the everlasting motives for murder? . . . it
is impossible for murder ever to outrage Nature.

de Sade

Justice is the interest of the stronger.

Plato

I can't change conditions. I just meet them without backing up.

Al Capone

The present moral crisis is due among other things to the demand
for a moral code which shall be intellectually respectable.

R. Niebuhr

Remove prostitutes from human affairs and you will destroy
everything with lust.

St Augustine

Many of the worst crimes of history have been committed by
men who had a strong sense of duty.

Nowell-Smith

They honestly consider they are doing the right thing.

*(E.W. Elkington, 1907,
on New Guinea cannibals)*

1) THE GENESIS OF MORALITIES

> Their sense of right and wrong springs from the unconscious roots of social feeling and is therefore unreasoned, compulsive and strong.
>
> Kroeber

In 1705 Bernard Mandeville, a London doctor of French parentage but born and brought up in Holland, wrote a remarkable poem called 'The Grumbling Hive', which was later republished under the title of 'The Fable of the Bees'. In this fable the hive became wealthy, happy and powerful so long as the individual bees were greedy, ambitious and corrupt, but when the bees were converted to a less selfish morality, their empire began to collapse. The bees

> Flew into a hollow tree
> Blest with content and honesty.

Mandeville was neither the first nor last philosopher to draw attention to the difference between personal and national morality, but probably no one has used such wit and simplicity to underline the alternative objectives of man-made moral systems.

The current century has seen the gradual, worldwide emergence from the codes of the great religions, often without firm or clear-cut philosophies to put in their place. The problems attending on this we shall come to later, but as a starting point it will be useful first to review the way in which moral systems emerge.

While there are fundamentalists from most religions who would still argue that their codes are the results of divine decree, it is probably now fair to suggest that the vast majority of people recognise that moral codes are man-made: they are rules of behaviour thought out by groups of people or individuals to make existence more pleasant for the majority.

This implied artificiality does not mean that morality is unnatural or that man without a moral code is necessarily bad. After all, signs of moral behaviour are found in animals. The fossils of sabre-toothed tigers indicate that they looked after wounded members of their own group, and there is a species of caterpillar in which members of the group sacrifice their lives to warn their fellows of impending danger. Hebb observed that

> If a chimpanzee is eating and he sees another chimpanzee begging for food he feels compelled to give some of his food away, even though he shows clear signs of anger and irritation.

Similarly, mother monkeys spank those of their young who bully others.

3

Male ursine seals attack their own females if they fail to take proper care of their young.

At the time of primitive man there were early signs that each society developed its own moral code. As Redfield put it,

> Each precivilized society was held together by largely undeclared but continually realised ethical conceptions.

Malinowski, the great anthropologist, studied the relationships of primitive peoples paddling large communal canoes in the Trobriand Islands. He observed how mutual obligations evolved into a moral code: the man who failed to dig in with his paddle was the butt of better paddlers. This is one of the foundations of morality.

Commenting on the instincts of the working man in the twentieth century, Richard Hoggart noted:

> "Ah like fair dealings" may seem to be an inadequate guide to the cosmos and can be self-righteous, but said sincerely by a middle-aged man after a hard life it can represent a considerable triumph over difficult circumstances.

These are the basic features of moral behaviour, what G.K. Chesterton called 'the dumb certainties of existence'. Or, as Anthony Storr put it:

> It can be assumed that from the very beginning of life there is present a drive towards self-realisation, towards finding one's own identity as a person and that this is as powerful a force as sex itself.

The combined wisdom of the zoologists and anthropologists suggests therefore, in Robertson's words, that 'primary morality must have been on animal lines', while Sherrington commented that 'biology cries the individual for itself' but it is 'altruism that seems as yet Nature's noblest product'.

Philosophers and theologians, however, have sometimes preferred the pessimistic view of man as naturally immoral or at best amoral. St Augustine of Hippo was the pioneer of the concept of original sin (he had a very rakish youth), and Spinoza was one of many following a similar line:

> If men were born free they would so long as they remained free have absolutely no conception of good or evil.

At this stage, philosophical arguments about the nature of morality are neither relevant or meaningful. What is self-evident is that the majority of societies have needed and therefore created some form of moral code as a basis for their communal life. We may not all agree with or find particularly moral the rules they chose, but a pattern of behavioural control always does seem to emerge, even if sometimes at an apparently lower level than at others.

We also find in larger societies a whole series of moral sub-systems, separate codes for warriors, priests, mothers and innumerable small groups. In a modern community there is not only the main broadly accepted set of standards for the whole nation, or group of nations, but there are business codes, hospital codes, school codes, army codes, union codes, sports codes, even criminal codes.

Another fact which seems obvious is that moral codes not only vary but have life spans; their popularity and credibility first rise, then later fall. Sometimes they may be rejuvenated by fresh thinking, they may disappear and then return, but they do have some kind of life cycle, and when they are on the wane people experience what is loosely called a moral crisis. E.H. Carr describes the lack of direction thus:

> When we lose the comfortable formulas that have hitherto been our guides amidst the complexities of existence we feel like we are drowning in the sea of facts until we find a new foothold or learn to swim.

This study does not pretend to prove the existence of absolute moral values or to disprove them, but rather to chronicle the techniques, skills and effort which have led to apparently successful ethical systems, in other words systems under which there appears to have been a reasonable level of human happiness, contentment and mental stability. It will also draw attention to those moral systems which have become overtly deviant, obsessive, fanatical, cruel and which have led to human misery and degradation.

2)   THE CAUSES OF MORAL DIFFERENCES

> Which will give greater happiness to its possessor, justice or injustice?
>
> Aristotle, *Ethics*

It is clear that different types of external pressures help to forge different types of morality. To quote some extreme examples from areas of harsh environment, the moral code of the Thuggee tribe in India regarded murder by strangulation of non-Thuggee men (not women) as a virtue. A Sioux did not win his adult feather until he had killed another man, nor a Dyak his wife till he had a head, nor a Naga his tattoo till he had a scalp. In post-depression Germany, several senior ss officers won promotion for their skill in genocide. Violence has surprisingly often been blessed by moral codes, but usually it could be argued as the outcome of population pressures and a violent society where life-expectancy was short or life itself of lesser value than other considerations.

In all, history demonstrates that definitions of good and evil habits have been substantially different in different situations, but in each example the pressure on the individual was to follow the ethic of his own people, however that ethic might be regarded in comparison with other more generally accepted moralities. 'Man', said R.S. Peters, 'is a rule following animal.' But the rules change according to the pressures, ambitions and ideas of those who invent them and who have to persuade the rest to follow, hence Stevenson's maxim:

> Morality is persuasion.

And the persuasion is made easier because most people do not want to think it out for themselves. Edward de Bono comments:

> The objective is to stop thinking. Basically people hate having to think about decisions because it is mentally taxing. There is a fundamental preference for automatic decision making based on patterns.

Actual freedom to make decisions is a painful burden, as was observed by Bergson, Jean Paul Sartre and the existentialists. Codes of packaged morality which remove this pain are therefore convenient, desirable and useful. In W.R. Whyte's formula, 'Good values are values that allow groups to interact benevolently on one another and individuals within them.' But since social environments alter, so can the nature of values and goodness. Westermarck's position that

> Moral concepts relate to industry and society: right and good are neither natural, innate or intuitive, only implanted by social pressures . . .

compares with Karl Marx's statement that

> The hand mill gives us a society with a feudal lord, the steam mill gives us a society with an industrial capitalist.

So moral codes tend to relate to the societies in which they grow, and while there may be an absolute standard, views of right and good have nevertheless at times varied considerably. There are several recognisable factors in this process which are worth looking at briefly.

The first is that economic circumstances, the availability of food and other supplies have a demonstrable effect on moral standards. For instance, a shortage usually induces some form of co-operative sharing or rationing, even amongst chimpanzees. This is the moral foundation of a sharing attitude which makes a virtue out of abstinence, cultivates the morality of conservation, and encourages an equal distribution of nature's benefits even to the weaker members of a society. There are many examples where extreme shortage has had a contrary effect, with panic, hoarding and material élitism in their stead, but whichever the effect it can be traced back to the same cause. In the one type of code we find that poverty is not a disgrace, in the other type it probably is; in the first mendicancy may be respectable, in the second prestige attaches to wealth and ostentation; in the first selflessness may be rewarded hereafter, in the second it is imbecilic.

On the other hand a relative overabundance of material goods tends to condone wastage, discourage conservation, make sharing unimportant, to provide instead moral respectability for over-indulgence, and encourage inequality of distribution and exploitation. It is a characteristic of relatively wealthy groups in history that bribery becomes acceptable behaviour, as it was in imperial Rome, China, the French *ancien régime* and medieval Byzantium.

We get a hint of the contrasting attitude in a few initial examples. The Republican Roman prided himself on light eating, but a few hundred years later the comic hero of imperial Rome, Trimalchio, made himself vomit so that he could eat more, and the Emperor Vitellius supposedly consumed millions' worth of food in nine months. Mohammed rated the three most important human activities prayer, fasting and alms-giving, but his later Ottoman followers showed substantially less restraint. Buddha, Lao Tsu, and Socrates all preached restraint of the appetites. In the Renaissance, the Restoration, the 'naughty nineties', the 'gay twenties', such people would have been regarded as spoilsports, at least in the upper levels of society, where the value attached to material comforts led Loelia, Duchess of Westminster, to remark that

> Anyone seen on a bus after the age of thirty has been a failure in life.

Shortages sometimes decrease, sometimes increase the level of aggression. In the frozen north the people fought nature rather than each other—as Gibbon commented, 'the Arctic tribes alone among the sons of man are ignorant of war and unconscious of human blood'. And the Eskimo ethic involved rigid patterns of behaviour linked to the dangers of their existence and the difficulties of hunting. But amongst the Ik in Africa the hardships and pressures of dispossession bred violence. As the old proverb had it, 'The hunter commands but the farmer entreats.'

A related socio-economic influence is the population balance of the sexes. In medieval Belgium there developed the concept of the beguinages, lay nunneries to use up the spare female population. In twelfth-century England it has been calculated that warfare led to a huge surplus of women, hence to a huge lowering in the value attached to women in general and prostitutes in particular: it was said that a woman could be bought for 'a packet of lace needles'. Examples will be found in other periods, and there are other biological factors which have influenced moral attitudes: the arrivals of syphilis in the 1490s and AIDS in the 1980s both caused reassessment of a permissive trend. Inevitably, societies where women's work skills were as economically valuable as men's tended to produce a society with greater equality of the sexes, whereas if male skills predominated women suffered loss of status.

The second major causal factor in the creation of moral attitudes is the nature of power in a society. For instance in societies where men on horseback were the dominating physical force, the ethics imposed on the whole of their people tended to be those associated with cavalry throughout the ages, a kind of horse-borne élitism, with special privileges required for their expensive and time-consuming battle practice in return for brief moments of dashing bravery. From Genghis Khan to Lord Cardigan of the Light Brigade, from Prince Rupert to Billy the Kid, men on horses have always expected their own ethic, usually a ruthless one, to be adopted by all around them. The longbow accounted for a healthy deviation in English moral history, and more recently the tank has delivered the final body-blow to equestrian élitism. By contrast the periods of history which were dominated by infantry produced different attitudes: the egalitarian togetherness of classical Greece, the tight discipline and self-effacing ethos required by the foot legions of Rome, the lessening of class barriers in Europe between 1914 and 1918 and the first requirement of American blacks to fight for their country in 1917. Another example of physical weapons producing a new ethos has been the advent of piracy, coinciding with advances in ship construction: the Cilician pirates of 60 BC, the Vikings of the early eighth century, the Elizabethan privateers, all justified marine robbery as a basic way of life accompanied by various other codes of semi-normal group control.

Each successive source of wealth has also had its influence, because the controllers of wealth would use it to help instil the kind of ethic most likely to maintain that wealth. So cotton made a virtue out of slavery in America and child labour in Lancashire, oil made a virtue out of speed. The British East India Company, for cash flow reasons, regarded it as ethical to promote the opium trade to China. A peasant community produces a morality with an emphasis on the nuclear family as a production unit, while a cottage industry economy also enhances the role of motherhood and rearing productive children; commerce throughout the ages has produced the bourgeois morality of thrift; a high technology economy produces a very different ethic, with the accent on acute competitiveness; a consumer-orientated economy encourages an ethic which encourages self-indulgence, makes a virtue out of personal vanity. In a society where musicians, actors or sporting heroes are the most admired personalities then the mores typical of those professions are likely to be imitated by the majority who admire them.

The fourth area of pressure on ethical development is the nature of political power. Monarchy, for instance, tends to require a moral code which gives priority to obedience and reverence as virtues, emphasises loyalty, selfless devotion to the state, and stratified levels of material rewards. Bismarck defined the Prussian virtues as 'honour, loyalty, obedience and valour which shape the army from the officer corps to the youngest recruit'. We will see numerous examples of imperial moralities of this kind, in which the worst sins are treason or cowardice, the greatest good to kill or die for the motherland. Even suicide has been a virtue in many military regimes from Sparta and Rome to Japan and Hanoi. Platonic homosexuality was turned into a virtue by Epaminondas, the Theban general of the fourth century BC, to get better results from his army of male pairs, and a not dissimilar ethic was encouraged by some Japanese shoguns, and by Admiral Donitz in the Third Reich. Drug-taking was made acceptable by the Ottoman Empire for their janissary warriors, just as heavy drinking was allowed to make life bearable for Nelson's sailors and Wellington's soldiers. Throughout history we shall find how in the main it has suited kings and tyrants to encourage the macho virtues, and sometimes democracies have had to follow suit in order to survive.

The fifth moral conditioner is prejudice or tradition, the residue of the previous generation or two's morality passed on to the next. Racial feelings, class or other genetic superiorities, pride in colour, caste or creed, tend to be inculcated at an early age, so they pass readily from one generation to the next. Ulster Protestants, Bengali Sikhs and Palestinian Shiites all inherit generations of paranoia. Anti-Semitism can be shown lurking beneath the surface, raising its ugly head then re-submerging for a generation, ready for the next. Long-term prejudices of this kind tend to foster an ethic which justifies violence and persecution, rejects the servile virtues.

One complex example of an ethic created by a mixture of external passions and historical prejudices was that of the Yąnomamö people of North Brazil, which included perpetual warfare, female infanticide, wife-beating, polygyny and gang rape, a self-perpetuating mess of acute stress. Psychological pressures exerted on a generation of children can re-surface twenty years later as a paranoid reaction affecting many attitudes. The German children of 1918 were the opinion leaders of 1938; the Russian Kulak children of 1936 were the mentally scarred misfits of the 1950s.

Since, as we have seen, every moral code is an expression of how the leading group in a society finds it most convenient for itself that the majority should behave, it is clear that morality is a form of management by objectives. In a fragile military situation you require a self-effacing military ethic and a lust for glory; in a tough economic period you need to turn austerity into a virtue; in a labour-intensive economy you need a strong work ethic, and so on. So moral codes can be classified by their objectives: survival of a government, military aggression and success, economic stability, religious propriety. The state function of morality has tended to fascinate the philosophers from Plato through Macchiavelli to Nietzsche. The complications have always arisen when they tried to prove in philosophical terms something which has always been a day-to-day political reality, thus creating unnecessarily potent ideologies with a tendency to self-destruct.

A moral code can therefore be defined as a system of ethical standards by which a given society controls the behaviour of its members and motivates them to attain its objectives. It is a process of group psychological control usually providing a much broader framework of manipulation than is embodied just in the legal code of that particular society. In such a society a rebel against the code will be considered an immoral person, even if subsequent investigators judge the rebel to be right and the society wrong. In terms of judging such moralities it is essential to bear in mind the background pressures and circumstances which prevailed at the time and place. Moral codes are still moral codes even if they contain evil precepts, but they are open to criticism and comparison, just as religions and political systems can be criticised against absolute standards of effect on human well-being.

3)   THE RAW MATERIALS OF MORALITIES

All men's appetites have a tendency to promote both the private and the public good . . .

Bishop Butler

There are probably five main components in human nature which form the raw material for the development of moral codes: compassion, love of family, the desire for co-operative self-defence, the desire for approval and a preference for easy decision making.

Compassion may not be universal: its level in different human beings depends a great deal on their upbringing, treatment and emotional

maturity, but without question it exists in sufficient quantities in most societies, particularly amongst women, to form the backbone of moral development. It may in some periods be blunted or suppressed by hardships, disasters or conflicting obsessions. The lives of the seventeenth-century slave-traders for instance show how normal men could quickly become used to inflicting appalling treatment on slaves; the monks of the Spanish Inquisition, the guards in Nazi concentration camps were quite easily trained by their masters to be obedient implements of mass sadism. Compassion may disappear for half a generation, but it usually seems to come back to restore even unbalanced societies to a relatively even keel.

Love of family, husband-wife and parent-child relationships, tend to be strong enough to withstand tremendous buffeting and to remain the toughest nucleus of most moral codes. Physiologically, this was necessitated by the slow maturing of human young who, even in primitive societies, could not become independent before the age of about ten.

Even though in many eras and in many countries marriages have tended to be arranged rather than based on spontaneous attraction, the family bond has more often been a success than a failure. It may occasionally be disrupted in permissive or obsessive periods, but it always comes back in some recognisable form. It is sometimes resented, particularly by recent feminists who see it as an excuse for exploiting women. Robert Ardrey argues that in both man and animals the all-male band is often a stronger natural sub-group than the family, but geared to the hunting or aggressive society.

The desire for self-defence on a co-operative basis is again a fundamental plank in all social structures and is the crux of the development of tribal bravery. We have seen already and will see many more examples of its unfortunate vulnerability to exploitation by leaders bent on personal aggrandisement.

The desire for approval, though it may take the most perverse forms, is nevertheless fundamentally important for moral training. For some people and societies it is the quiet, self-effacing attitude of service to others and performance of duty which makes them happy amongst their peers, for others it may be exhibitionistic self-glorification in the glamour of war or the extremes of asceticism. When the desire for approval is competitive, as Pascal pointed out, then it can be honed to an even sharper point, a concept particularly appreciated by the Jesuits, but made use of to some extent by nearly all societies. And, importantly, the feeling of achieving approval from peers turns into a habit of self-approval or disapproval which is loosely referred to as conscience.

Finally, there is the preference for easy decision making. We have already noted that subjective decision making is hard mental work and breeds doubt and insecurity. Hence there is an observable preference amongst virtually all peoples for a pre-packaged guide to decision making. Most human beings are happy to settle for a communal code which provides them with a set of reflex responses to most situations and casts them in a mould with their peers. Once the conventions which dictate these patterns are seen to be too rigid or to lack credibility there may be a reaction in which members of the group want to rebel or assert their freedom, but they usually just create a new set of adapted conventions to suit their new, younger peer group. The principle remains: there is a demand for packaged codes of moral behaviour.

Traits of character are dispositions to do things of which people approve.

Nowell-Smith

The main components of most moral codes are to do with protection: of life, of the reproductive cycle and of the food supply. All tend to illustrate the essential fragility of human self-discipline, the narrow margin between a convention that is designed to protect and one that causes damage. While most codes protect life, nearly all of them throughout the centuries have also allowed killing. There are a number of specific areas where the standards have varied significantly: killing in war, killing as punishment, killing as sacrifice, killing as population control and killing of self.

War between nations has throughout history been regarded as morally acceptable. Honore Bonet in his *L'arbre des Batailles* (1280) and Grotius in his *War and Peace* (1635) were, like Quakers, ahead of their time in the condemnation of the evils of war, but the history of violence is not a field which indicates any signs of consistent human progress: the ethos which justifies killing in warfare shows only spasmodic signs of decline. In the eighteenth century there was a general expectation that war was on the way out; Louis XIV and his contemporaries encouraged the bloodless surrender of armies as soon as they had been outmanoeuvered by their enemies, and as J.U. Nef put it: 'Wars were costing more money and fewer lives.'

It was the French Revolution that brought the masses back into warfare; the new technology of war enormously increased casualties and involved far more deaths amongst unarmed civilians. As Nef also explains, since the mid-1940s the technology of war has put the range of weapons well beyond the human eye, usually beyond the physical horizon, so dehumanising the act of killing. The Geneva Convention may have outlawed some of the crueller aspects of war, but the essential ethos remains. This hinges on the intellectual fiddlement which still blesses the concept of the fair fight, the defensive war, but blurs the distinction between defence and aggression to the point where both sides may be involved in a war where they regard themselves as defenders. In the fourth century St Athanasius pronounced that it was lawful to kill enemies in war, and when cannons were invented St Barbara's emblem was embossed on them, as she became the patron saint of gunpowder, sanctifying its use. Most religions have had to live with the idea of the justifiable war—Islam relished it. The remaining ethical problem, never really solved, lies in the posturing which is encouraged by almost every military ethos, the fact that most modern wars are caused by having to defend

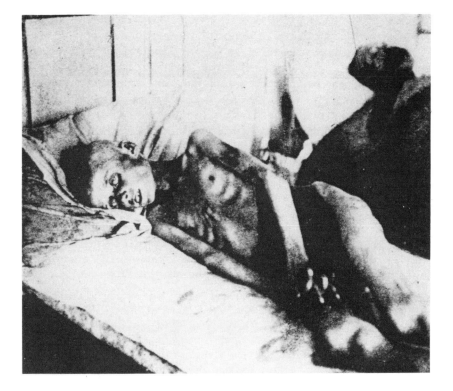

ridiculous postures which should never have been adopted in the first place.

Total abhorrence of killing is found early on in Indian culture but rarely elsewhere until the foundation of the Quaker movement. The Dukhobors, Amish, Quakers and other pacifist sects have tended to be regarded as eccentric.

Attitudes towards the killing of prisoners and non-combatants have varied throughout the ages. The Romans spared their defeated enemies because they soon afterwards recruited them for their armies—the Peruvian Incas did the same. Medieval conquerors spared at least the high ranking captives because they hoped for ransom money, whereas the ancient Egyptians spared their prisoners to become pyramid-builders, the Turks theirs to become galley slaves. Many periods of war have been accompanied by almost unrestricted brutality. The ancient Assyrians, medieval Mongols and modern Japanese are examples of conquerors with a very low estimate of human life who condoned the virtual extermination of those who resisted their will. Numerous other wars have led to more than average brutalisation on both sides—the Thirty Years War (1618–48) or the Russian front of 1943 were examples. Civil wars have often had a tendency to develop along these lines, as with the French religious wars of the 1620s, Cromwell in Ireland

in 1645, the Spanish Civil War in 1936 or the Yugoslav one in the
1990s. Similarly, most acts of genocide have tended to be within the
frontiers of nations or empires, as with the Jews in the Nazi Empire,
the Armenians in Turkey, the Elleuths in China or the Kurds in Iraq.
Like so many acts of both individual and mass brutality they tend to
follow the ethic of the vendetta, the classic justification of homicide on
both a large and small scale. This also applies to the extreme levels of
brutality often committed by frustrated minorities who are too weak to
achieve conventional victories: the Assassins of the twelfth century, the
IRA in Ireland, the PLO in Palestine, the former Mau Mau of Kenya, EOKA
in Cyprus, the Basque ETA, the Baader Meinhof and many others.

Killing as punishment has a long tradition in human history and
has only recently gone into reasonably consistent decline. The cliché
example of men hung for stealing sheep in England was typical of
a long period during which life was taken away, often in a deliberately painful manner, for relatively minor offences. The execution of
runaway slaves in the ancient world, the burning of sodomites in the
Middle Ages, the flaying of disobedient Aztec soldiers or the hanging,
drawing and quartering of English traitors are typical examples. To
this must be added some of the major acts of mass execution which,
at times, have amounted almost to genocide: the mass burning of
Jews and Protestants by the Inquisition; the extermination of the
Albigensian heretics of Languedoc; the multiple witch-burnings of
seventeenth-century Europe; the mass crucifixion of slaves after the
rebellion of Spartacus against the Romans; the crucifixion of Christians
in seventeenth-century Japan; the mass murder of Jews in medieval
and modern Germany; the mass eviction and virtual murder of millions
of kulak peasants in Stalinist Russia—all illustrate the commonplace
nature of mass human cruelty.

Another ongoing example of legalised (and therefore moralised) sadism has been the history of torture. Penal torture, to elicit confessions
or evidence, has been standard procedure for most political regimes
throughout history and has persisted in many regimes right up to the
present day. Rameses II of Egypt tortured prisoners of war. Whipping
was in the moral code of Moses and was equally persistent. The Jews
were unusual in not condoning torture, but the Greeks and Romans
had no hesitation in using it on prisoners and slaves—it was a Roman
who crucified a slave for killing a quail. The rack was also a Roman
invention which was to have a long and unpleasant history.

From the fourth century the Catholic Church began to think in
terms of heresy and therefore of torture (not totally condemned by
St Augustine) as a means of clarifying it. The early Middle Ages was
the period of trial by ordeal, a subtle form of semi-voluntary torture,
the Viking period was the heyday of mutilation, the later Middle
Ages the classic revival of the rack and numerous other variations to

combat the attacks on the Roman Church, with Torquemada as the archetypal organiser and Nicholas Eymericus, author of *Directorium Inquisitoris*, as the acknowledged theorist. The Renaissance brought further refinements—it was Henry VIII of England who introduced boiling to death, with other major practitioners like Frederick II and Ivan the Terrible. The Italians extended the repertoire with variants of the 'strappado' and Paulus Grillandus analysed the five degrees of pain. The seventeenth century was the era of public humiliation, the ducking stool, the stocks and the branding iron, the eighteenth the century of whipping, the nineteenth the century of nasty variants on imprisonment, from transportation, forced labour, treadmills and workhouses to concentration camps. Torture had been made unfashionable by the attacks of Voltaire and Cesare Beccaria, so that most of the enlightened monarchies dispensed with it, but there were numerous revivals. It was always the more paranoid regimes which made use of it, like Naples and Vienna in the 1850s, Stalinist Russia in the 1930s, Nazi Germany and thereafter the new African dictatorships in Kenya and Uganda or many of the less savoury regimes of South and Central America.

Sadistic forms of corporal punishment used for their deterrent value have also regularly been used to maintain discipline—the Russian knout, the English cat-o'-nine-tails and its French counterpart invented by Martinet, Paraguayan water torture. Punishment by maiming has also been prevalent: blinding was a favourite of the Byzantines, ear removal for seventeenth-century Scots, hand amputation for the Arab states, and castration for adulterers a standard medieval response. Multiple castration to create cadres of eunuch servants lasted several thousand years, and genital mutilation amongst African women dates back to ancient Egypt. The administration and execution of much of this corporate sadism has, over the centuries, been conducted by a succession of highly disciplined agencies whose members mostly regarded themselves as operating within both the legal and moral framework of their societies. The Inquisition, the KGB, the Gestapo, Savak and numerous other notorious police forces have demonstrated time and again the uncomfortably close correlation between the imposition of ethical norms on the majority and the resort to unethical methods by the minority. Female foot-binding in China is another long-term example of using mutilation to enforce morality. Corporate bullying in the name of religious, political, moral or economic discipline has caused infinite numbers of cruelties authorised by thousands of respectable regimes.

Killing as sacrifice in the strict sense has, on the whole, been a characteristic of the lower rather than the higher religions; Abraham was willing to sacrifice his son, and Agamemnon his daughter. It was common enough on a relatively small scale in most of the ancient civilisations, particularly the Phoenicians and Carthaginians (who believed in mass burnings when disaster threatened), but was most widespread in South America. There the Aztecs were the most zealous practitioners of it on a large scale with mass human sacrifice as a key component of their total ethical system. In fact, human sacrifice is one of the strangest anomalies of human moral history, such an apparently immoral act for such an apparently moral purpose—religious prostitution is another example—yet perhaps it should not be regarded as so separate from other forms of persecution and mass-execution.

The killing of kings in many societies, as James Frazer showed in *The Golden Bough*, turned into the vilest of sins; in others it became a morally accepted custom. In primitive tribes where the health of kings was associated with the health of crops, it was often customary to kill them if they showed signs of ailing. In Cambodia, the Kings of Fire and Water suffered this fate as did the Chitome of Congo, the King of Meroe in Ethiopia; the kings of Shilluk were stoned to death at Fashoda as soon as they showed signs of impotence and Zulu kings when their hair began to turn grey. In India the Kings of Quil were expected to commit suicide after a fixed reign of twelve years. Sick Dinka rain-makers were buried alive to prevent drought.

Killing consummated by the eating of the victims has only infrequently been blessed by any but the most primitive societies, but on occasions it has been presented as the ultimate test of solidarity. An example was the outbreak in Guangxi during the Cultural Revolution when cannibalism seems briefly to have been part of the extreme Maoist ethic.

Killing as a form of population control also theoretically belongs to the earlier millennia of human history, and to undeveloped communities where the culling of the very old and very young seemed an economic necessity. The Californian Calinomero tribe believed it was a kindly act to kill off their crippled parents, the Hottentots starved their geriatrics to death, reasoning (as did Frazer) 'is it not cruelty to suffer either man or woman to languish under a heavy, motionless old age?' The Greenlanders, Kaffirs and modern Dutch have all accepted a kind of euthanasia in which the seriously ill could be put out of their misery; the practice was strongly condemned by the Catholic Church but championed by men like Sir Thomas More and David Hume.

In many societies infanticide reached huge proportions, and was accepted by the conventional morality. On Sandwich Island, according to Westermarck, two-thirds of all infants were killed at birth; the Line Islanders allowed a maximum family size of four; bastards, twins, female babies, extra children in already large families, plus sick or deformed babies were most vulnerable in all societies. In Russia infanticide was widespread up to the time of Peter the Great, in China female infanticide up to the nineteenth century. In many other societies, particularly deprived ones, it has probably been much more common than the records show. The walling-up of infants in the foundations of new cities goes back to Jericho and supposedly this fear is recalled in the folk song 'London Bridge is falling down, falling down.' The Massacre of the Innocents is a long-term image of the human condition and its reliance on infanticide. Abortion too was widely practised; Aristotle preferred it to infanticide. The Turks resorted to it once they reached their third child and it was practised generally in Moslem areas; it was common in India, the Kariffs allowed it tacit approval. Catholicism and other great religions have found it abhorrent, and Tertullian damned it as murder. In many previous societies it has been tacitly accepted: it is only the more detailed medical knowledge of the present century which has made possible a more precise definition of how, when and why it may be right or wrong. For similar reasons, birth control has been regarded as sinful by the Catholic Church and some other groups.

To the concept of open genocide by sword, bullet or gas chamber should be added the much more common forms of genocide-culling, the getting rid of unwanted races by less direct methods. Racial displacement or mass expulsion may not lead to extermination, but it does make it likely, as for instance with the removal of the Crimean Tatars and various other ethnic groups by Soviet Russia in the 1940s. The mass deportation of Africans by the slavers, the mass forced migrations by the Assyrians, and the frequent forced migrations of the Jews are other examples.

Even more common is the economic culling of unwanted races, usually taking the form of pushing them on to marginal growing lands or into marginal economic activities. This applies to a large proportion of the means by which the North Americans reduced the aboriginal population of their lands, and the South Americans of Spanish and Portuguese origin are still reducing theirs. Such culling by induced malnutrition has happened on the fringes of modern Israel, 1980s Ethiopia and many other ex-colonies where the previous inhabitants or some racial sub-group have simply been unwanted.

While society justified violence by state and Church, it also commonly authorised its use by heads of households. The right of fathers to punish was established in the Old Testament and amongst the Romans this extended to the right to kill. The Elder Cato argued that a man had the right to kill an adulterous wife but there was no reciprocal arrangement. Egnatius Metellus beat his drunken wife to death and was exonerated. The eighteenth-century French argued that a man who was not master of his wife was not worthy of being a man, the Russians condoned wife-beating for centuries, while the English divine Thomas Fuller argued that 'women are of a servile nature such as they may be better beaten'. Typical of many proverbs throughout Europe was the Gloucestershire adage

> a wife, a spaniel, a walnut tree
> the more you beat them the better they be.

To such millennia of domestic injustice must be added the history of the maltreatment of children. 'Spare the rod and spoil the child' is of quite recent vintage, and the long, long history of severe child-beating, both within and outside the family, lacks any form of archaeology, just like the concurrent general topic of child abuse.

Suicide and self-violence have varied considerably in reputation. The Omaha and Dyaks despised suicide. On the other hand, the tribe of Karens in Burma were very prone to suicide, as were the Hos in India, and the Ebos were widely reputed to be the most prone of the African slave tribes to commit mass suicide, partly because they believed that they would meet up again in heaven. The Chinese thought suicide acceptable, and the Jains and Cathari valued the ritual fast to death as used by Gandhi. The Hindus insisted on their own idea of widow suicide, 'suttee', sometimes extended to 'jauhor' (multiple female suicide): but suicide in Moslem countries is extremely low. Semi-ritualised suicide or 'seppuku' held a high place of honour in the Japanese samurai code. Even more extreme was the Japanese tradition of 'Oyaku shinju' or family suicide, in which a parent first murdered his or her children and then committed suicide. The Romans regarded suicide as an honourable way out of failure, an idea copied by many other militaristic societies—doing the decent thing. The early Christians disapproved of suicide, but admired martyrdom intensely and often martyrdom has been a form of suicide. Deliberate self-sacrifice as a form of protest or act of showmanship has persisted because it has been admired: Japanese kamikaze pilots adopted a form of it, students who set fire to themselves in Eastern Europe and the Far East for political protest continued the practice into the twentieth century. Mass suicide by defeated communities has also not been uncommon: the Indians at the time of Alexander the Great, the Jews at Massada when beaten by the Romans, the Taiping after the so-called Opium Wars in China, the self-poisoning citizens of Jonestown in the twentieth century are examples.

Self-injury has had a similarly chequered ethical image; early Christian saints enjoyed self-imposed pain and mortification of the flesh, as did Islamic fakirs. Mutual or self-flagellation was an amazing feature of the crusading and Black Death period in Europe and of the Shiites, amongst others. Self-castration was another facet of the same tendency; it was, for example, practised by the Phrygian worshippers of Attis, by some early Christians and by the Skoptsi in Russia.

Among other forms of self-damage, alcohol abuse has been serious in numerous groups, although Islam has been by far the most successful ethos in suppressing it over a long period (with Buddhism close behind it), whereas early Hinduism was in favour of substantial intakes of intoxicating 'soma'. According to Bosman, the tribes of nineteenth-century Ghana regarded perpetual drunkenness highly, as did the English in the eighteenth century. Tacitus described the first-century Germans as addicted to alcohol and a few centuries later their Anglo-Saxon descendants brought drinking of epidemic proportions to Britain: Theodore, Archbishop of Canterbury, felt moved to launch a major attack on it in the eighth century. The Danes too had a strong reputation for hard drinking as did the Pueblo Indians and (for religious reasons) the Ainu of Japan, devotees of sake. Anti-alcohol movements go back as far as Samson, and during the last two centuries Temperance Societies achieved remarkable (though short-lived) periods of reformation. The later Hindus regarded drunkenness as detestable, Islam condemned it and many quite primitive tribes like the Omaha saw in alcohol a source of social damage and violence.

The relatively recent habit of heavy over-indulgence in hard drugs began in the frustrations of seventeenth-century China, in the wake of tobacco smoking, but spread significantly elsewhere in the nineteenth and twentieth centuries. The cactus drug of South America, peyote, had a long history associated with Aztec and Inca religious ecstasy. The milder drugs like cannabis have an even older history going back to at least 2000 BC in India, where, taken with yoghurt, they were encouraged to help religious lift-off. Islam forbade alcohol but sometimes condoned hashish; for instance, in 1800 Napoleon observed that most of the population of Egypt were addicted to it. The drug known as soma in the Indian Rig Veda was probably the haoma of the ancient Persians, probably the mandrake of the Greeks, probably the magic mushrooms of other Asian and European cults. According to Herodotus, the Scythians were taking cannabis in 430 BC and statues of the sacred mushroom in Guatemala date back to 1000 BC. There are signs that the Greeks took opium. Drug-taking is an escapist vice which, it seems, except among small groups, tends to exhaust itself quite rapidly and past epidemics seem to have always burned themselves out. The new drugs heroin, cocaine and crack belong to the modern era and have proved even more pernicious, but there is nothing new about the concept, only the depth of addiction.

Another area of self-damage against which moral codes have sought to protect mankind is exposure to avoidable diseases, particularly venereal diseases such as syphilis and AIDS, which became part of the argument for chastity. Similarly, the consumption of certain foods has been regarded as damaging: cannibalism was rejected by most societies, the eating of pork or other specific meats by quite a large number, leading into an international patchwork of food taboos.

The second general grouping of ethical ideas surrounds the protection of the reproductive cycle. Few societies have ever chosen to deny or reduce the value of the basic family unit as the nucleus for character and social development—Sparta and some of the modern dictatorships, Germany and Russia, have been amongst them, as to some extent has modern Israel with its Kibbutz ethic. But the definition of those evils which damage the family has varied substantially. Numerous societies have upheld polygamy, whether polygyny or polyandry. Solomon with seven hundred wives and three hundred concubines was the ultimate, but the Jewish Talmud allowed up to four wives, many European Jews keeping up the custom right into the Middle Ages. The Koran, the Rig Veda, the Laws of Manu all allowed polygyny; the Homeric heroes had concubines, as did the Vikings and Merovingian Franks—Christianity was one of the few major codes to condemn it, and then not always. Martin Luther allowed Philip of Hessen to have two wives for reasons of politics. Bigamy was allowed in Germany after the end of the Thirty Years War because of the acute shortage of men in 1648. The general habit, however, even in cultures where the ethic allowed polygyny, was for multiple marriages to be confined to the rich and powerful. The Masai and Kaffirs were relatively unusual in having tribal averages of two to three wives apiece. In Moslem India it is estimated that ninety-five percent of the population were monogamous at the turn of the century. In Iran only about two percent availed themselves of the right to have extra wives. One of the built-in controls on polygyny was the obligation in many such societies for the husband to rotate his wives; a weekly rotation was noted, for example, by Charles Darwin in Chile. The experiment in polygyny in 1534 in Munster rapidly disintegrated, as did that of the Mormons in nineteenth-century Utah.

Turning to polyandry, the much rarer form of polygamy, this has been found amongst the Eskimos, the aboriginals of Lanzarote, the Iroquois and the Hottentots. The tribes of central Ceylon had up to seven husbands per wife until this was outlawed by the British in 1860, but in ancient Britain, according to Julius Caesar, ten husbands per wife was not uncommon. Polyandry has most usually involved a group of brothers sharing a single wife, probably to keep down costs, but in later life more wives have been acquired, thus leading to a kind of group marriage.

Attitudes towards promiscuity vary considerably, but the fashion for it never seems to last particularly long. The demand for pornography or acceptance of it seems to ebb and flow in a similar pattern. The problem of family planning and population control is more recent, but it can be noted that the Bible story of Onan 'spilling the seed' was used to discredit the practice of birth control as early as the ninth century. The Jews, Aztecs and many other societies regarded female adultery as a crime deserving of death. In other societies, such as the

Tantric communities of medieval India, the Anabaptists of Munster or the eighteenth-century European aristocracies, promiscuity has been highly fashionable.

Incest has been almost always a taboo because it was believed to be genetically and emotionally destablilising. Egyptian and Peruvian royalty were notable exceptions, where power was desired to be kept within the family. The Kaniagmut tribe allowed marriage between brothers and sisters or parents and children. The Karens of Tenasserim, some ancient Peruvians, the Mormons (because of a membership shortage) up to 1892, the gypsies (because of a similar reluctance to marry outside the group), the Hindu Sakta sect all at times allowed marriage between brother and sister. In Iran brother-sister marriage was practised to keep land in the family, while the Azande in Africa even allowed father-daughter marriage for high chiefs. Even more acceptable at times has been the marriage of half-brothers and half-sisters—Abraham of Ur was an example. Many societies allowed first cousins to marry, but medieval Christianity was by far the least tolerant ethos, prohibiting even the most remote cousins from marrying each other.

Exogamous monogamy has tended to be the most practically stable moral norm throughout the centuries, but this does not mean that there is necessarily anything universally immoral about other marital codes. Marriage 'till death us do part' has been much romanticised in order to overawe the participants into persisting with what can (at times) be a very trying institution. Marriage has, after all, involved throughout most of history the virtual enslavement of women. Divorce too has been remarkably easy in most periods of history, mainly but not always easier for the husband than the wife. Some Bedouins were known to divorce and remarry up to fifty times and regarded a long marriage as a sign of failure. The Hellenistic Greeks, imperial Romans, the Zoroastrian Persians, the Mongols, the people of Greenland, Tonga, Queensland and Samoa are just a few examples of groups for whom divorce was extremely easy. On the other hand there have been many relatively primitive peoples for whom life-long marriage was the norm: the Maoris, Iroquois, Zulus, Kaffirs, Aztec Mexicans, Karens of Burma, Homeric Greeks and the Solomon Islanders.

Life-long celibacy and oaths of chastity have also had varying reputations. Early Christians, Hindus and Buddhists were great supporters while Luther (who spoke of 'the wicked and impure practice of celibacy') and the Victorian British, amongst others, were fervent critics; but we will often find that admiration for celibacy is simply a rationalisation of necessity—there is an imbalance in the numbers of the sexes or there are economic conditions which make marriage difficult. In 1875, forty-five percent of the Belgian population over the age of fifteen were celibate, well above the European average of thirty-three percent at that time. In 1850 some fifteen percent of the population of Saxony died without ever having been married. Poverty and population differentials made one hundred percent marriage impossible. In polygamous societies there may be an even bigger shortage at the lower end of society.

The image of prostitution has varied considerably over the centuries—it is one of the oldest virtues, as well as the oldest vice of history. Many pre-Christian religions regarded it as a form of divine service, an obligation towards temple fund-raising, to which both respectable females and sometimes males were expected to contribute. Ritual prostitution in Babylon, Heliopolis and Armenia was well known. As a form of temporary or permanent religious service it was common in many parts of India and West Africa. Among the Moslems were the ragged Kedeshim prophets, who were allowed to have their will with otherwise strict matrons. Prostitution was surprisingly blessed by St Augustine and St Aquinas as a means of reducing adultery: it has frequently received state approval. Slave prostitution was blessed in seventeenth-century Spanish America, as a means for the masters to make money. As Leach puts it, from the confusion over the gods' role in sex came 'uncertainty as to whether over-indulgence or under-indulgence in sexual activity is the true mode of holy otherness'. The German Adamites and the English Ranters believed that the Christian God blessed total promiscuity.

Sexual deviation has tended to be seen as conflicting with the family system and therefore declared taboo by most societies. Though it is by no means clear that the Old Testament actually meant that this was the sin of the cities of Sodom and Gomorrah, Moses certainly declared it to be an abomination punishable by death. There are examples of societies where unusual pressures made deviation the norm, just as Desmond Morris created a tank-full of homosexual ten-spined sticklebacks by removing the females. Similarly the European males of Saigon in the nineteenth century were believed to react in the same way because of the shortage of women.

Over the centuries numerous regions have been accused of a homosexual bias, suggested in the saying, 'Even the devil disapproves of unnatural vice except in Alsace.' In places like Tahiti female infanticide often created societies with a sex imbalance which made homosexuality more prevalent. The Moslems, by hiding their women and idolising female chastity, created an atmosphere where homosexuality was more likely in areas such as Morocco, Zanzibar, Afghanistan and India itself. The North American Indians tolerated transvestite 'wives' known as 'berdaches'. Margaret Mead has described the relatively permissive atmosphere of twentieth-century Samoa, where adolescent homosexuality in both sexes and promiscuity were tolerated but seemed in the end to produce a well-adjusted, harmonious society with a relaxed pace of life and a low sense of competition. The Manus in New Guinea, on the other hand, were much more puritanical.

A number of peoples have been far more tolerant of homosexuality than average societies—the Greeks of the classical period, the Vikings, the English Normans, the Prussians, the Masai, the medieval Japanese, the modern Chinese. Lesbianism or women adopting male habits has also been found in a number of societies, notably for instance among the Eskimos, the Hottentots, the peoples of Zanzibar and the harems of Egypt where its development was understandable. The fashion became more open worldwide in the 1960s and was rationalised more effectively than ever before, including the argument that it is justified as a means of population control.

There was a homosexual temple in ancient Jerusalem, but the Jews generally opposed homosexuality, as did the Assyrians, who castrated male practitioners. The Hittites, on the other hand, seemed to have tolerated it, and on the island of Lesbos in the sixth century BC the poetess Sappho waxed lyrical about her female lovers in obviously not too hostile an atmosphere. In fact the Greeks generally seem to have been relaxed about homosexuality, and Epaminondas of Thebes led his famous army of male pairs, who would fight together to the death. Similarly the German Knight Hospitallers in the Holy Land adopted a masculine friendship cult and soldiers of the modern Chinese army were seen walking hand in hand. At times in the twentieth century homosexuality has become literally a fashion, so that in such periods not only is it tolerated, which is always a defensible position, but it is positively encouraged which is (arguably) irresponsible—this assuming a percentage of biologically marginal people who will be influenced by opinion. In the Middle Ages sodomites were buried alive or burned as heretics. Homosexuality was also a regular problem in monastic communities, for instance in the nunnery of St Augustine's sister, and sometimes it was a convenient charge to level at probably innocent celibate communities like the Knights Templar. The original Bulgarian cultists who forbade any further reproduction of the human race, were thus assumed to be homosexual and probably thus gave the word 'bugger' to the English language. From time to time the more decadent imperial courts like Rome, Istanbul and that of William Rufus in England have raised homosexuality to the level of a fashionable diversion, and there have been literary advocates of unrestrained deviation like de Sade, Masoch, and most recently, Michel Foucault. There are also tales of deprived and remote communities where bestiality and other such habits were not uncommon; but the vast majority of societies have tried to restrain the popularity of anything but the unitary family ethic, and most communities have agreed that it is critical to the social fabric and to the emotional stability of each new generation.

Child abuse has been more universally destested but may have been prevalent in ill-housed communities. Pederasty with boys as young as twelve was acceptable in ancient Greece. Forcible marriage of very young girls to old men was a characteristic of India, and certain other societies. Organised paedophilia, often talked about in ancient Greece and Rome, was shown by research in Minneapolis in the 1990s to have a self-perpetuating effect as the victims grew up to become perpetrators. In Morroco it was argued that young boys learned the Koran better if they had been pederasts. Rape has generally been regarded as a vice, but even it has been condoned if not blessed by numerous conquering hordes, and was often regarded as normal in post-conquest situations. A classic recent example has been the mass rape of Bosnian Moslem women by Serbians in the early 1990s. To all this must be added the vast history of private rape—of slaves, servant girls, tenants and wives—to which a blind eye has been turned for millennia.

Moses laid down rules about the undressing of members of the opposite sex in front of each other from which subsequent Christian societies have only slightly deviated. However, attitudes as to what constitutes embarrassing or sinful nakedness have varied substantially throughout the world and the ages. Mohammedan women covered their faces, Chinese women their feet, Sumatrans their knees, Samoans their hands and so on. The Tahitians wore no clothes but felt naked unless tattooed, Alaskan women felt naked without lip plugs. The Victorian British would not bathe together even with concealing costumes on until the late nineteenth century. The Jains of ancient India preached holy nakedness. Japanese of both sexes bathed together naked and ancient Spartans exercised together naked. The colonial Europeans attacked the toplessness of African women in the nineteenth century, and then went to the African beaches topless themselves in the late twentieth, while the local tribes have adopted European prudishness. Plunging female necklines were popular in ancient Crete and imperial Rome, Renaissance Venice, Restoration London, Napoleonic France and many other periods whereas in others they would have caused scandal. There is no universal human law of decent or immoral exposure; naked barbarians were so used to their condition that they would excite themselves greatly by putting on clothes. When the novelty and stimulation of covering the body in different ways have worn off, the fashion changes and to excite attention people start shedding garments again. The one universal rule is that human beings dress with as much or as little as they think will win attention, so the necklines and hemlines keep rising and falling. It is a reasonable generalisation that in Western societies a trend towards greater exposure of the body, or to accentuating the parts which separate the sexes as opposed to obscuring them, tends to accompany increased permissiveness and destabilisation of society. The same would not be true necessarily of societies that have age-old traditions of different styles of so-called decency.

The same tends to be true of other human adornments. Long male hair, for instance, is sometimes associated with effeminacy but Leonidas and his three hundred Spartan heroes had very long hair and so had many other aggressively male communities such as the court of William Rufus in England, while royal Egyptian women had shaven heads. In other communities long hair or baldness can be symbols of holiness. Earrings, girdles, waist compression, bust development, foot compression, tooth clipping—there is no universal rule that any form of beautification belongs to one sex only or is a sign of decadence. The one certainty is that they keep changing.

The other aspect of protection of the family is the instilling of codes of family loyalty. Confucianism, for instance, was particularly strong on this and Victorian Britain was also known for its rigid family ethos. The Romans, on the other hand, put state before family as with the famous model of Brutus executing his own sons for treachery in 510 BC. This can be compared with the teenage Russian hero Pavlic Morozov who in 1932 betrayed his own father for harbouring rebel peasants, was murdered by their neighbours, and later portrayed in numerous statues as the ideal Stalinist 'pioneer'.

The third main segment of ethical modelling surrounds the protection of the food supply, and the two main elements in this have traditionally been property ownership and the work ethic. The property element is less complicated, as theft of property has been deplored and the right to own property has been acknowledged by most codes, except for brief experiments in group ownership or real communism. The Spartans, for instance, discouraged ownership and approved of stealing food, though the objective in both cases was to toughen trainee warriors. For centuries, black slaves *were* property, and had no right to own property for themselves. There have been short-lived regimes in which an attempt was made to abolish private property and this was the aim of theoretical Marxism, but acquisitiveness is a basic human instinct and ownership as close to an original human right as one can get. The additional moral concept which argues that property should be redistributed, if its existing distribution is unfair, also has an ancient history going back at least to Solon in ancient Athens; but it has not come to real prominence until the twentieth century and on a world scale is still a somewhat utopian concept. What we will see are examples of many relatively poor and unsophisticated societies which have been much more sharing in their attitude to property than their supposedly more civilised counterparts.

Acquisition of wealth by force has often been regarded as admirable. The ability to organise successful looting was the basic criterion for a good leader of the Arabs, Huns, Bulgars, Avars, Vikings and many others, with conquest of countries proving the same standard for successful kings for centuries throughout Europe. Similarly piracy has been regarded as a moral and justifiable way of life by the Elizabethan English or the medieval Dalmatians.

One of the most dangerous sub-sections of the property ethic has been the ethic of primogeniture. The paranoidal pressures placed on the recipients and their near-miss next of kin have accounted for many of the most damaging ethical malformations in history—the kings who had to double their kingdoms and the younger sons who had to prove themselves by other means.

The over-developed property ethic also has been seen as a major source of human problems: *radix ominum malorum est cupiditas* or Dante's 'la cieca cupidizia', the basic human urge to own property turned into a blind obsession, what Luke called 'the Mammon of unrighteousness', the urge which has resulted in numerous periods towards gross exploitation of some human beings by others. As de Tocqueville put it, 'materialism is amongst all nations a dangerous desire of the human mind', the ethic of what Marx condemned in modern capitalism or Tawney more mildly as 'the acquisitive society'.

Individual avarice, the elephant-headed god of success, communal avarice known as imperialism, industrial avarice have all had their fashionable moments. The image of usury has undergone frequent changes, condemned by Catholics and Moslems, tolerated by Jews and Protestants, venerated by modern capitalism. Gambling is another associated habit, condemned by St Cyprian, the Talmud, the Puritans and the Koran, tolerated by the Catholics, even the communists. The converse idealisation of poverty has been much lauded by most of the great religions as has the con-committent concept of mendicancy, the best known exponents of both having been Buddha and St Francis.

Avarice also covers the problem of slavery, one of the longest-lasting ill-consequences of rationalised greed in human history. Slavery began as an institution when the Egyptians enslaved vast numbers of their defeated enemies and used them as forced labour on their monuments. This became standard procedure throughout the ancient world and slavery persisted for about forty-eight centuries in most parts of the world. The two greatest victim peoples were the Slavs in the early Middle Ages and the Africans in the fifteenth to eighteenth centuries. In Europe peasant vassaldom virtually replaced slavery for about eight centuries but was only marginally less unpleasant. Specialists types of slavery like galley slavery in the Mediterranean, soldier slaves of Turkey and Egypt, the Janissaries and Mamelukes, or the castrated slaves of the East, the court eunuchs, were further unpleasant variations on an unpleasant theme. In the modern world there have been new, disguised forms of slavery to avoid the international abhorrence: debt bondage in India, chattel slavery in North Africa, sham adoption of children for labour purposes in the Middle East, marriage as a form of enslavement in Islamic countries and new forms of slavery in areas like Afghanistan.

The attitude to work motivation has always varied. In the nineteenth century, middle-class women were expected to swoon, not work. The great preachers of the work ethic have been Hesiod (the Greek poet), St Antony, the Victorian writer Samuel Smiles (author of *Self Help*), and the Russian Stakhanovites who based social prestige on work not wealth. The Hanseatic Germans, Huguenots, Armenians, Jews and modern Japanese have been great practisers of the work ethic. Both Indian and Chinese religions have tended to reduce the status of work, as did the mendicant orders of Catholicism, particularly the Franciscans. In the book of Genesis work was portrayed as a curse inflicted after the Fall. The Protestants are of course very much associated with the modern work ethic of the West, which in the 1930s and 1980s began to see its credibility seriously eroded.

5) EXTREMES AND DEVIATIONS

> Every form of addiction is bad whether the narcotic is alcohol, or morphine or idealism.
>
> Carl Jung

Just as moral codes are the products of their environments, the results of a mixture of economic, psychological and political pressures, so once created they have in turn an influence on the pressures which created them. Sometimes the influence is intensifying, sometimes it is reactive. In the harems of the Ottoman sultan it was regarded as moral for the monarch to father vast numbers of sons, but because of the pressures this induced, it also had to become moral for the eldest son to eliminate all his brothers by execution—so the legitimisation of polygamy led to the legitimisation of fratricide. Several of the great medieval saints were defenders of prostitution because they believed it helped to protect Christian marriage. Las Casas advocated the African slave trade because he wanted to save the aboriginal West Indians from work which he thought was too hard for them.

We can see the causes of the Nazi ethic in the pressurised reaction to humiliating defeat after Versailles, jealousy of apparent Jewish success and a paranoid urge for nationalist revival. But once created, the Nazi ethic grew rapidly more obsessive until it came to condone mass-murder, torture and world conquest, thus leading to the holocaust and self-destructive war. In the same way, fourteenth-century Catholicism produced a morality which encouraged the slow burning

of non-orthodox members of its own faith. The otherwise punctilious Puritans regarded it as moral to drown muddled old women whom they suspected of witchcraft. In the 1990s the married women of Uzbekistan still felt impelled by their society to set themselves on fire if accused of adultery.

Regarding the contortion effect of moral codes on social development, there are four main areas. The first is the development of an acquisitive mentality. The kind of ethic created by a country's need to defend itself becomes one which justifies aggression and conquest. From Nebuchadnezzar to Kaiser Wilhelm II, the cultivation of military patriotism as a male virtue has been one of the most superficially glorious but disastrous perversions of practical ethics. War becomes an enjoyable and stimulating sport, what Ruskin called 'a grand pastime for volunteers'. It produces great deeds of self-sacrifice, avoids social boredom, is dangerously attractive to human vanity, yet seems to have no serious effect on population growth. Mussolini said:

> War alone carries to its highest tension all human energy and sets the seal of nobility on people who have the courage to face it.

But history demonstrates that acquisitive war is a moral trap which usually leads to massive destruction, maiming, painful death and misery. 'Butcher and bolt' was a common British nineteenth-century military motto.

Erasmus could say that 'the one who has conducted himself with the most savagery is the one thought worthy to be captain in the next war'; and the phrase 'Here the conquering hero comes' rings in the ears of the militopath, a beguiling jingle with plumed helmets, jackboots, epaulettes, medals and swooning womenfolk to complete his motivation, white feathers and shame if he fails. This convolution, by which aggressive war becomes morally sanctified, has probably caused more human misery than any other single factor. As Karl Clausewitz pointed out, 'War is an act of force . . . it tends towards the utmost extreme of force. The ruthless user of force who shrinks from no amount of bloodshed must gain an advantage if his opponent does not do the same'.

The second major area of cumulative delusion has been the justification of economic inequality, summarised in the medieval couplet 'The rich man in his castle / The poor man at his gate.' What begins as an ethic which rewards different members of a society at different levels depending on the value of their contribution, thereafter frequently develops into an indefensible justification of permanent inequalities. The prime example of this throughout history has been slavery, where a temporary inequality is turned into a permanent and hereditary subordination of status, part of establishment moral doctrine. Many distinguished philosophers and religious leaders justified it or ignored it, from Aristotle until relatively recent times. In the same way moral sanction for the inferior status of the landless peasant, the working class, on a hereditary or virtually hereditary basis, tended to become part of the establishment ethos in most societies. The persistence of prejudice against the untouchables in India, an act of oppression lasting two millennia, is a remarkable example. Slave-owning was part of the traditional ethos of the American deep South, just as property was a symbol of moral respectability in Victorian Britain. The Calvinists tended to regard wealth as a sign of divine approval, poverty as proof of idleness. The practical self-justifications of one generation become the deep-rooted moral traditions of the next. This parallels the fact that great thinkers like Augustine, Aquinas and Jefferson all accepted prostitution as a necessary part of human existence.

The third main area in which fashions tend to grow into obsessions is appetite control. From time to time, eating, drinking, sex and materialistic self-indulgence grow to a point where they produce a reaction, and abstinence is turned into a virtue. The ancient Greeks did this with their veneration of 'moderation in all things'. Buddha recommended the conquest of cravings and most of the higher religions discourage over-indulgence in all the appetites, particularly if this is at the expense of the poor. But the urge to moderation and self-control in one period becomes extreme asceticism in the next. The relatively mild recommendation of St Paul that priests should be unmarried turned into the obsessive idealisation of celibacy which caused many problems for a large part of the Christian Church over a long period. The scholar Origen castrated himself, the hermit St Antony threw himself into thorn bushes to avoid temptation. Fasting and the self-infliction of pain became means of achieving public admiration and influence, obsessive routes to veneration and even sanctity. St Simeon Stylites perched on his column for twenty years deliberately scratching his open sores, and drew huge crowds; so did the flagellant brethren whipping each other through the streets of Europe, and some of the fakirs and dervishes torturing themselves in the East.

The fourth significant area of moral over-justification is enshrined in what is known as the work ethic. For some individuals, work can become an obsession with a moral authority which makes it the measure of all things. In the nineteenth century, it was given the odour of sanctity by writers like Samuel Smiles, and later by model heroes like the compulsive Russian coalminer, Stakhanov. The problem that it creates is not simply that idleness or unemployment becomes a vice, but that the whole distribution structure of the world is based on a suspect currency. In the words of J.M. Keynes:

> . . . I think with dread of the readjustment in habits and instincts of ordinary man, bred into him for countless generations which he may be asked to discard in a few decades.

In the 1990s, the need for such readjustment was coming closer, accompanied by a massive re-orientation of the work ethic in Eastern Europe after the collapse of European communism.

There have been numerous doctrines which did not prize the work ethic highly; Catholicism, Islam and Buddhism all at times gave moral sanction to begging and alms-giving, the reverse of the wage-work ethic. The ultimate goal of a devout Hindu is to become a non-working mendicant, and the preference for meditation over manual work is a regular theme in Chinese philosophy. The next century may well need to see a revival of these ideas. The gypsies, who have preserved over the centuries a strong moral ethic which nevertheless gave low priority to disciplined work ambitions, may move from being despised ethnic freaks to become admired examples of versatility.

Moral propaganda or training has a tendency to produce élitism, intolerance and reaction, and this is the source of the obsessional twist. The very act of educating people to behave in a certain way requires exaggeration of the ideas that are to be communicated, and some over-motivation of the trained in order to achieve results. The inevitable competition introduces a competitive élitism which has produced many of the odder extremes of moral behaviour in human history. The ethic of the nationalist war-maniac or terrorist is just an exaggeration of normal defensive patriotism; the absurd asceticism of the desert hermit, Trappist monk, or German flagellants, the sustained masochism of the modern Shiite sects, the death and glory missions of the kamikaze, are semi-hysterical extensions of conventional self-denial teachings.

A by-product of moral élitism is intolerance and persecution. There are factors in moral training which tend to suggest that those who follow a code are the elect, the chosen people, the master race, and that all others are deviants. When the moral training is to a high pitch there is a tendency to induce a superiority complex which may be hyper-critical and even violent towards all non-believers. Examples of the results can be observed in the Catholic persecutions of sects like the Waldensians, anti-Semitism throughout the last two thousand years, and Stalin's attack on the kulaks. The burning of witches, McCarthyism, the purging of Trotskyites are all just part of violent intolerance which can arise from a contrived sense of moral superiority.

The third indirect product of intensive moral propaganda is the natural, usually minority, human response of rebellion or reaction. There are always some people whose psychological response to training pressure is to produce their own original twist to the doctrine, or deliberately to adopt a contrary doctrine. It is the behavioural pattern of would-be leaders of society who find themselves out of the driving seat, or of new people who want to achieve more self-prominence than will be possible merely by accepting and practising the code of the main regime. We must therefore distinguish between those deviations which take the form of heresies or splinter groups, which may be sincere, and those of totally contrary reactionaries who are deliberately negative and destructive. The first group includes the great religious and political breakaways: Protestant versus Catholic, Bolshevik versus Menshevik, Shiite versus Sunni and so on; the second group takes in anarchists and nihilists, the original Cynics, de Sade, to some extent Nietzsche and some elements of fascism. Not untypical are two eighteenth-century English phenomena, the gangs of Mohocks and the Bold Bucks. The Mohocks were dedicated to 'doing all possible hurt to our fellow creatures' (according to Macaulay), and the Bold Bucks prided themselves on an even more extreme delight in all forms of violence and rape. Both groups took their recruits from the bored and rebellious sons of the respectable squirearchy, but the illustration is not as narrow as that might suggest.

Throughout history the birth of destructive and violent codes has often been associated with a generation gap, with the frustration of a new generation which feels it has been left nothing to achieve by a previous generation made over-complacent by its own success. The Blues of seventh-century Constantinople, the Hamburg Rockers of the 1970s had as their chief aim the beating-up of helpless old folk. The delinquent youth gangs of Britain in the 1890s, 1930s and 1960s were all similar. The razor-blade carrying Napoo of Manchester cutting off girls' hair, the Bengal Tigers, the Redskins of Glasgow were all, according to Stanley Cohen, 'symbolic folk devils' of society, bored and disillusioned. In the twentieth century these have included Teddy boys, Hell's Angels, beatniks, punks and hysterical football supporters.

Even the most apparently amoral of reactionary groups do tend to develop a code which is often not without signs of sentimental reversion to the homely society out of which it sprang. 'Omerta', the loyalty ethic within the Mafia, the willingness to die rather than betray a colleague, is legendary. In the St Valentine's Day massacre of 1929, Frank Guanberg, who had been shot fourteen times, was asked by the police who shot him and replied, 'Nobody shot me.' 'Honour amongst thieves' is further evidence that every group tends to develop its own moral code for mutual help, even when its central purpose may be anti-social and destructive. 'Thou shalt not grass' is a key ethic amongst criminal groups. Fairness on the draw was part of the cowboy duelling ethic, just as seventeenth-century duellists would allow each other to pick up dropped swords.

One final result of a strong moral prohibition in one era, is its preservation in the next, even when it has lost all validity or reason. In Fernando Po, the King of the Boobies kept a harem of forty but was forbidden to stare at a white man, to look on the sea, or partake of rum, tobacco or salt. The high priest of Rome was not allowed to touch a horse, wear knots or rings, look at the army or eat leavened bread. In Bombay it was a capital offence to paint a moustache on a sleeping woman or otherwise to disguise a sleeper whose soul might thus not be able to find its way back to the right body. In China and elsewhere it was taboo to tread on someone's shadow or let your own shadow fall across a coffin. Amongst the Maoris, and many others, undertakers were treated as polluted outcasts, as often were widows and pregnant women. Similarly, to have a miscarriage was a social crime amongst the Bantu. Taboos before and after battle were common, an embargo on sex being one of the favourites. Frankish kings could not cut their hair, Romans could not cross their legs, Javans could not touch each others' heads. The Phrygian priests of Attis, the Galli, ate no pork, gashed themselves with knives and castrated themselves in a frenzy. The Mikado in Japan could not let his feet touch the ground and no one must eat from his personal crockery. It was a capital offence to see the King of Dahomey eating his meals.

These are just a few examples of customs which were in their time regarded as key parts of ethnic morality, taboos equal to deadly sins. In some cases a residue of logic is fairly visible, in others the taboos were the results of pure imagination, superstition and fear. But it is wrong to imagine that such irrational attitudes do not still exist and in each society groups of such customs, however apparently trivial, help to create the fibre of moral systems, sometimes with beneficial, sometimes with damaging effects.

The moral differences between a Nazi concentration camp com-
mandant and St. Francis of Assisi are not satisfactorily encom-
passed in the statement that the former broke the rules and the
latter kept them. Morality is not just a matter of rules but also of
dispositions or traits.

Derek Wright

Whether one chooses to notice the differences or the similarities
between moral codes of different eras and regions is mainly a question
of emphasis. Nowell-Smith commented that 'The more we study moral
codes the more we find they do not differ on major points.' This is
probably most true for those who have their own fixed idea of virtue
and will not include in their list of moral codes ones which do not
embody their own idea of virtue. For this reason the codes of the
Inquisition or the Nazis are excluded from most people's lists. But if
we include all codes, whether they are good by our standards or not,
then there are still five main characteristics, varying substantially in
intensity and emphasis which are found in them all. These five concepts
are reciprocity, altruism, obedience, absolutes and manners.

The principle of reciprocity is often the justification, motivation and,
in some cases, the essence of a moral code. This is the whole principle
of bartering one favour for another, balancing the scales of justice with
reward and punishment. At its lower level, this is the rule of vendetta,
'an eye for an eye'. Violent behaviour by one group tends to produce
a justification for the morality of violence by any opposing groups.
Thus tsarist oppression in Russia produced Narodnik assassinations:
the White Terror produced the Red Terror. It also produces the theme of
free market valuation of services rendered. At its higher level it becomes
more generous and less mercenary, recognising the superior quality of
the idea as formulated for instance by Lao Tzu in ancient China:

For good return good: for evil return good

Or more recently by Karl Marx:

From each according to his ability; to each according to his need.

The second principle is the concept of altruism, or sacrificing self for
others. Psychologists tend to argue that altruism or unselfishness is
never totally genuine since all self-denial can ultimately be explained
away as some form of twisted self-gratification. It was David Hume
who coined the phrase 'enlightened self-interest'. Even in the crudest
of moral codes it can be shown that soldiers have sacrificed their lives
for their fellows, and ordinary people accept acute suffering in order to

help others, but this can still be explained away as a pre-programmed distortion of self-interest. It is a characteristic of the higher religions and philosophies that they make this concept the most important part of their codes. Moses said, 'Love thy neighbour as thyself'; Confucius said, 'Achieve for others what you want to achieve for yourself'; Buddha said, 'Let a man overcome anger by kindness, evil by good', and there are many more examples. Despite the ease with which it can be presented as hypocritical, the value of conditional altruism in easing the human condition should not be underestimated.

The third major characteristic is the principle of obedience, whether to other people, to the code or to both. Freedom to make decisions can be a burden; it requires tiresome mental effort, whereas unquestioning obedience can be less taxing. The crux of the matter lies in the existence in major codes of some form of objective standard which virtually dictates decisions, as opposed to the subjective view which makes decisions more difficult. As Goethe put it:

> Ages which are regressive and in process of dissolution are always subjective, whereas the trend in a progressive epoch is always objective.

Equally, Robert Nisbet has commented that 'The basis of culture is the presence of values which have external force in the individual's life.' There is comfort in the paths of straightforward duty, where the individual is not required to think too much. In addition to making a virtue out of obedience and duty, this concept also tends to make more of a virtue out of humility.

Lao Tzu's three precious virtues were compassion, economy and humility. The Japanese version was 'Tears flow from a sense of unworthiness and gratitude.' The advantages of what Nietzsche rather contemptuously called 'the slave virtues' were strongly advocated by Roman Catholics and the religions of the Far East. The Greek Stoics preached a similar attitude. In the words of Zeno, 'Happiness lies in accepting the law of the universe', and Epictetus said, 'Do your duty as in the hands of an all-wise providence.' The one problem associated with the idea of obedient humility as a virtue comes later in the life-cycle of a moral code, when the objective authority is beginning for one reason or another to lose credibility, or elements of the code seem outdated and inappropriate.

Fourth, we come to morality's predeliction for absolutes, its preference for blacks and whites as opposed to greys. This springs naturally enough from the need for the greater clarity and simplicity of uncompromising standards. So the numerous 'thou shalt nots' of the ten commandments are the backbone of their simplicity and conviction. Primitive taboos against incest or adultery, the absolute negatives of modern Catholicism against abortion, birth control and euthanasia, the Islamic laws against drinking and gambling—all of these are unequivocal and therefore easy to communicate. Moral codes are designed to produce effective co-operative societies not indecisive, quarrelsome groups.

Finally in this section we come to the characteristic of manners, the tendency which most moral codes have to include a lot of apparently trivial rules of conduct alongside major guidelines for human behaviour. There is the Islamic veto on pork, wine and usury; the Jewish preoccupation with circumcision; the hatred of the Pennsylvanian Amish sect for buttons; St Paul's rule for females to wear veils in church. Moses even gave directions on the digging of latrines and the laundering of bed linen. Confucius provided a complete vocabulary of social attitudes, and detailed rules covering items from the length of male skirts to the proper way to stammer when introduced to a stranger. His view was that etiquette helped to discipline the emotions, ritual was part of the learning process. This all contributes to the cultivation of automatic reflexes which are compatible with the overall moral aim. As Goethe put it, 'There is no outward sign of politeness which has not a profound moral foundation.' Or, as Huizinga commented on the ethics of the Middle Ages, 'All emotions required a rigid system of conventional forms.'

So in many societies manners become the aesthetic extension of a moral standard. The salutations of opposing duellists, the burial rites of the fallen foe, the raising of the hat, the courtly bow, the last cigarette for the condemned man, all are part of the visual display which creates the habit-forming background, the visual focus for a moral code. They are small but significant elements which emphasise the solidarity of the group and the individuality of its code of conduct. Pre-Reformation England was an example of a period when manners were considered more significant than morals. 'It is a wild and rude thing to lean upon your elbows,' wrote Cordericus, and Caxton's *Book of Manners* in 1487 was designed 'to make common people not behave as rude beasts'. Even in twentieth-century Britain odd taboos still survive such as passing on the stairs, killing spiders, or other minor folk customs whose reason has long since been forgotten.

The other facet of manners is that they become emotionally attached to more serious moral attitudes: 'cleanliness is next to godliness'. Physical cleanliness becomes associated with purity, so dirt is evil. Or it may be the other way round. This is part of what anthropologists call the structural aposition of opposites; left and right, evil and good, dirty and clean, woman and man, noisy and quiet, black and white, young and old. Moslems regard their left hand as polluted—Eve came from Adam's left rib. Male long hair is a symbol of permissiveness; female unbound hair a symbol of loss of virginity. The gesture, the symbol, the mannered ritual are all the physical expression of the ethical ideal. A vast mesh of customs memorised in myth and fable, repeated from generation to generation, becomes part of the substructure of the whole moral system and acquires a worth quite unconnected with any rational explanation.

7) MOTIVATIONS AND SANCTIONS

The fact of the instability of evil is the moral order of the world.
Whitehead

Throughout history there have been four main incentives used in different degrees by societies to obtain moral behaviour from their members. The first and most common has been punishment. Large sections of most great moral codes have been enshrined in law and protected by statutory punishments. It is not the purpose of this book to discuss the relative merits of different forms of law or punishment, but it is important to differentiate clearly between the history of law and the history of morality. While in any moral code there are many taboos

which can be enforced by the state using its penal system—protection of life and property, for instance—many of the more positive aspects of the higher moral codes are far too subtle, too omnipresent, too private to be policed by any government. Similarly, there can be numerous offences decreed to exist by a government which have little to do with the accepted moral code of its people. It was a capital offence to eat meat on Fridays in Elizabethan England mainly because of the desire to support the fishing fleet which, in turn, provided the crews for the navy. On that basis Friday fish-eating was part also of the moral and religious ethos of the country over a long period. Law and morality frequently overlap, or may at times be in conflict, depending on whether the particular government is in tune with the majority ethos of its people; but while the law governs numerous areas of life in which anti-social behaviour is subject to a clearcut definition—open to proof, black or white—there remains also a very considerable area of human behaviour, where actions are too minute, too frequent and less open to precise definition, where ethical attitudes ungoverned by the law are far more significant.

The second great moral incentive is the threat of social ostracism. The majority of people throughout history want the companionship, respect, and affection of their fellows, or at least groups of them, what Whyte called 'the quest for normalcy,' one of the great motivators of human behaviour. William Lessa, in a study of behaviour on Ulithi Atoll in the South Pacific in the late 1940s, commented

> Social control is effected through the usual channels of gossip, ridicule and enlightened self-interest, with kinsmen playing a strong role in keeping the individual in line.

For most people in most societies broad moral conformity becomes an imperative. A slight difference has been pointed out between the so-called 'shame cultures' like that of Japan which emphasise public scorn, as opposed to the 'guilt cultures' like Christianity where the emphasis is on inner torment, but the two are essentially similar. Inevitably there is also the minority quest for abnormality, but this is simply the deviant version of the same instinct.

Closely allied to this concept of morality as the key to social harmony is the idea of morality as the key to inner harmony. This involves the traditional idea of conscience, the inner voice which makes a person unhappy if he or she disobeys a given code of conduct. Plato asked, 'What will produce the greater happiness for its possessors, justice or injustice?' The Epicureans and the utilitarians have seen good behaviour as linked to happiness and therefore motivated by the desire for happiness. As Hegel has said, 'the only adequate moral standard is harmony', and a feeling of moral equilibrium which allows the individual to feel at ease remains a powerful underlying incentive which society can use.

The fourth great motivator of the last three thousand years, though now in an apparent state of decline, is the threat of hell or the promise of heaven. Its use has varied a great deal: the ancient Greeks condemned only a very few villains to eternal damnation, while the medieval Christians condemned virtually everyone except their own elect to particularly unpleasant tortures after death.

In Dante's guide to the Inferno, we find that prostitutes and adulterers were condemned to perpetual oscillation in a lightless vortex, frozen heretics to walk on a white-hot desert, bandits to be boiled in a river of blood, homosexuals to be deluged with red-hot rain, and so on. The tortures of the damned were graphically illustrated by Heironymus Bosch, or the devil's cauldron sculpted on the doorway of Bourges Cathedral, just as the magnificence of entry to heaven was painted by El Greco and others. The hell/heaven sanction was, of course, not peculiar to Christianity but present to a greater or lesser degree in all the major religions. The special harshness of the Christian version was its sadistic, eschatological penalties for unorthodoxy from at least the time of St Augustine until after the Reformation. The use of the paradise motivation goes back to the ancient Egyptians and remains strong still in numerous sects throughout the world. Lecky, the great opponent of what he called 'religious terrorism,' drew attention to the way in which the Catholic preoccupation with the hell sanction for religious orthodoxy diverted interest from conventional moral behaviour while on earth and was to justify the most savage persecution of living heretics in the attempt to save their souls.

Parallel to the main motivational tools employed by a society to impose its moral standards are the main sanctions by which it justifies such pressure. We find there are three common themes here which run through history with varying degrees of prominence: the objective sanction, tradition and the social contract.

The concept of an objective sanction has probably been the most common, although it reached a low ebb in the twentieth century. 'Right is right only because God said so' was the opinion of Duns Scotus, while even Voltaire could say that

> All sects differ because they come from men; morality is everywhere the same because it comes from God.

The linking of all moral rules to divine decree, the miraculous carving of laws on tablets of stone, does give them that extra authority and infallibility which reduces the complication of decision making and brooks no argument. Immanuel Kant said:

> Two things fill my mind with ever lasting wonder and awe: the starry heavens above me and the moral law within me.

The second great sanction is tradition or precedent, what the Romans called 'the customs of their ancestors'. The mythology of past perfor-mance is used to sanction the habits of the present. The societies of ancient Rome, China and Japan were particular examples of where a strong conservative strain made for stable, long-term moral codes which emphasised respect for elders.

The social contract, the most recent philosophical concept to have major importance as a moral sanction, derives mainly from the work of Hobbes, Locke and Rousseau, who saw morality as an extension of nature. The needs of man for co-operative self-defence and communal existence required a voluntary surrender of certain absolute freedoms which should be balanced against the retention of certain inalienable rights. This has become the dominating moral sanction of the Western hemisphere in the last two centuries, and protection of natural rights has tended to replace both divine authority and precedent as the driving moral force of the twentieth century. The three are not, of course, mutually exclusive. The great divide in recent history has tended to be in the conflicting emphasis on what tend to be the two most important: freedom and equality. The inability of all modern states to achieve complete fulfilment of both at the same time has been a fundamental source of conflict.

8)   THE SOURCES OF MORAL LEADERSHIP

> Right and wrong is originally a concept connected with power and having to do with the motivation of those who are not bound to obedience.
>
>   Bertrand Russell

There are occasions when dramatic changes in moral direction are achieved by individual leaders—Christ and Mohammed are examples, but the majority of moral concepts are created and imposed by anonymous groups or successions of people working slowly to achieve their ends. These groups fall into seven main categories.

The first group, one of the largest and most significant, includes military oligarchs, dictators, hereditary monarchs and aristocracies. Their vested interest throughout the centuries has tended to lie in the cultivation of a death-or-glory military ethic based on the virtues of obedience and self-sacrificial bravery. The morality projected by Genghis Khan, Queen Elizabeth I, Napoleon and Hitler is not very different in its essentials, although the superficial emphasis may vary. The rewards of ranks and medals have been used to create a crude, glory-hunting ethic, justifying savage violence to fulfil misconceived territorial ambitions.

The second major group are priests and prophets, whose motivations have not been nearly so straightforward. Sometimes they have very much backed up the first group, at other times the monarchy and the clergy have stood apart. In the latter situation, without the requirement to boost the military ethic of lay colleagues, priests and prophets have tended to make a unique contribution to the development of altruistic ethics, to the condemnation of violence and self-indulgence, and to the development of a caring society. We shall see many examples where theological intolerance or worldly corruption have twisted these ideas, but quite a few where they have not.

The third group are the political revolutionaries whose prime interest throughout the ages has ostensibly been the restoration of freedom and the achievement of greater equality. They have often attacked the aristocratic military ethic, only to copy it when they needed it. Otherwise their main moral thrust has tended to be towards the reduction of exploitation. In many cases they have apparently supported an increase in permissiveness and a reduction in authority partly as their reaction against previous regimes, but as idealists they have tended to drift back to traditional ethics once their political ends have been achieved.

Lawyers and professional law-makers are the fourth group. They do make regular contributions to the development of all ethics because they

tend to be operating on the frontier against anti-social behaviour and to become involved in the detail of new patterns of amoral behaviour. Their links with precedent and the sharp end of judicial decision making on new problems force them to arrive at practical solutions to numerous moral dilemmas which are neglected by philosophers. In a detailed and pragmatic way they do therefore tend to add regularly to the body of moral thinking.

The fifth group are the economic communities. Even in quite primitive societies farming priorities tend to create a strong work ethic, submissive tolerance of misfortune, contempt for carelessness. Then there is the factory-owner ethos, again of hard work, pride in skill, profit as the arbiter of behaviour. A factory manager may be good if he is ruthless enough to dismiss idle workers, a sales manager may be good who tells blue jokes and is intemperate. A trade union boss will be good if he opposes technological progress. The cotton trade encouraged a moral code which included slavery, just as the sugar trade developed a convenient myth that black workers ate less than white.

A sixth group is to be found amongst the teachers, social workers and academics, those who are professionally concerned on the fringes of moral training and who, in the twentieth century, tended to take over many of the moral policy-creating roles formerly controlled by priesthoods. The result tends therefore to be a significant contribution to the moulding of the morality of the young without necessarily any genuine analysis of its purpose. The Jesuits, pioneers of the idea of academic competition, had a particular understanding of the ineradicable effects of intensive early training in ideas, as did the Russian communists. In other less committed societies the same power exists but there is often no agreement on what to do with it.

Last we come to the moral creativity of minority pressure groups. Some of these have been religious, such as the Evangelicals and the Quakers in Britain and America, or Soka Gakkai in Japan, all of whom pushed their particular ethical priorities. Then there are political pressure groups, from Sinn Fein to the Campaign for Nuclear Disarmament, again each with its own special moral imperatives. The great humanitarian groups, such as the anti-slavery movement, societies for the protection of children, prisoners, and other disadvantaged groups, all add their pressure towards the formation of the communal ethic in each country. The 'suffragettes', and their successors in the women's rights movements, made major in-roads in traditional ethical ideas in the twentieth century, and there was also the challenge from the issue of homosexuality, once it emerged from the shadow of total illegality. Each racial, sectarian, political or charitable pressure group tends to create its own sub-ethic which, in many instances, influences the main communal ethic of the nation. In due course, many of these pressure ethics become the standard for the whole of a society.

9) MORAL TRAINING—PROPAGANDA

Educate men without religion and you make them clever devils.
The Duke of Wellington

In this study we are not so much concerned with the individual techniques by which parents and others achieve the moral development of children, though that is an important and difficult subject. Our concern is with the broad methods which societies or their leaders use to create new moral attitudes amongst their people and the tools with which they provide their adult members for the moral training of the young.

It was Robert Owen, the industrial welfare pioneer of New Lanark

By the time they reach eighteen,

one of them will have been
subjected to sexual abuse

Z
ZERO TOLERANCE

FROM FLASHING TO RAPE
MALE ABUSE OF POWER IS A CRIME

EDINBURGH DISTRICT COUNCIL WOMEN'S COMMITTEE
WORKING FOR ZERO TOLERANCE OF VIOLENCE AGAINST WOMEN

who remarked that 'Man's character is made for him not by him', and communal moral standards are therefore a facet of mass persuasion.

There have been six main techniques for moral training. One of the oldest, and still perhaps the most important, is the imitation of heroes and heroines. Each society tends to produce its own block of model people, real or fictitious, who become the focus for behavioural mimesis. The Middle Ages, for instance, had its 'neuf pieux' who included Hannibal, Alexander the Great, Charlemagne and, of course, King Arthur. Christ himself, Buddha and Mohammed were and still are of enormous importance as behavioural models, along with numerous others like the Virgin Mary, St Francis, Florence Nightingale, George Washington, Lenin, Mao and so on. For every moral requirement to be taught there tends to appear a heroic model to copy, and to make the image easier to put across there will be pictures, statues, stories and symbolic reminders. Huizinga observed that 'Flamboyance is a necessary part of sanctity'. The saint had to be a showman or image creator, just as the hero had to be larger than life. For the work ethic there was Stakhanov or Andrew Carnegie, for self-sacrifice Nelson or Tom Cornwall, for female goodness Tarquin's Lucretia or Caesar's wife; each society and age had its role model for each virtue.

The second major technique of moral training is the use of ritual. This embraces the pavlovian principle of habit-forming, the palliative lump of sugar at the end of each little altruistic trick that builds up into a permanent armoury of predetermined moral reactions to given situations. Some of these may just be the apparently minor courtesies of everyday behaviour which are in themselves only symbols of moral attitudes rather than the attitudes themselves. Eating with a knife and fork may mean hygiene, giving up a seat on a bus to an old lady respect for the elderly, raising a hat submission and so on. Beyond this there are the more elaborate rituals, adult baptism, the dubbing of knights or the initiation of Freemasons. In eighteenth-century England, school children were made to chant again and again rhymes like

It is a sin
To steal a pin.

These are all part of the process of intensifying the commitment to whatever message is associated with the rituals. And as with Pavlov's rats and dogs most rituals are associated with some form of threat of punishment or promise of reward, the motivational habit-forming so crucial for long-term moral persuasion. One particular form of ritual moral training which has at times been very important is sport. Even Confucius pinpointed archery and athletics as social training in the principles of self-control. Waterloo, as Wellington put it, was won on the playing fields of Eton; cricket was training for fair play in the British Empire and rugby as preparation for trench warfare. Other techniques of active moral training have included the pilgrimage, which reinforces standards in participating groups or the Dominican invention of the rosary, dovetailing verbal repetition with a physical act.

Third, we come to the competitive structure of moral training, the creation of goals and awards, medals and certificates, endless symbols of performance providing fairly petty but effective levels of satisfaction. Virtues can be struck as cheaply as medals, and uniforms can create both saints and sinners, from the monastic habit to Gestapo tunics.

A fourth and very important feature of the training process of the great moral codes has been neat packaging in mnemonic form—the ten commandments, Buddhism's eight ways to heaven and ten depravities, the medieval seven deadly sins, the five values of Sikhism all beginning with K, the five Ms of the Indian Tantra. The reduction of ethical teachings to short, easily remembered formulas is a key component in propaganda and communal moral training. Rhyme has been used in numerous proverbs to reinforce moral points: St Augustine and St Bernard both used rhyme to stress major passages in their sermons. The ancient Frisian moral code was metric and full of alliteration to make it easy to learn and there have been many important poetic presentations of moral codes: the Sanskrit *Panchatansa* of around 200 BC, the *Pricke of Conscience* and many more. This led on into the best-selling moral tracts of the Renaissance, such as *Manners of Children* by Erasmus and *The Courtier* by Castiglione.

Perhaps the greatest tool of didactic morality tends to be the parable, the whole armoury of legendary material in which goods overcome bads and virtues win over evils. Christ was, of course, the great master of the simple parable, but most other great religious leaders have had a quiverful of suitable moral tales. As societies develop, the parable is extended into myths and other art forms in which the same points are made.

Mythology is very relevant to the history of ethics because communal myths are a huge part of the system of behavioural control. Whether in their crude folklore form or worked up into literary or dramatic works of art, each society wanted to put across the faithfulness of loyal warriors, the selflessness of mothers, the vanity of riches, the cruelty of masters, the kindness of peasants, the dangers of offending nature, and so on. Each society creates a great giant-killer or monster-killing hero like Perseus or St George; most have had self-sacrificing saviours. Joseph Campbell described the social function of mythology as that of establishing 'systems of sentiments', behavioural models for all occasions.

Much of the creative effort which produces each generation's new myths is not so much deliberately didactic as it is a sub-conscious desire to rationalise moral attitudes already assumed, and to make them part of the psychological furniture of the creators themselves, their peer groups and, in due course, their offspring. It is partly by this process that moral attitudes which to many societies seem thoroughly inhuman and cruel become rationalised as new traditions. Thus jealous dislike of Jewish small traders was turned into punishment for the crucifixion of Christ, concern for ecclesiastical promotion into competitive hounding of heretics. In the opposite direction, fear of famine was perverted into the need for human sacrifice, fear of a lonely death into the burying alive of widows, fear of future hunger into the need to expose weak babies at birth.

Finally, in the context of ethical training, it is important to look briefly at the role of the arts in moral propaganda. Painting and sculpture have played a significant part in creating ethical models. Numerous painters have been commissioned to idealise the military virtues: Titian's *Charles V at Muhlberg*, Robert Gibbs' *Thin Red Line*, Donatello's *St George*, Kuniyoshi's pictures of the ideal samurai—the list would be considerable. Goya's *Caprichos Firing Squad* and Picasso's *Guernica* are two examples from what would be the rather shorter list of paintings with an anti-military message. Raphael's *Virgin in a Meadow* is just one of a vast number of paintings projecting the ideal of submissive maternal love; the friendly social virtues of Breughel, the permissiveness of Monet's *Olympia*, the marital fidelity of Vermeer's *Betrothal* the dreadful punishments in hell-fire illustrated by Hieronymous Bosch, the noble solidity of Millet's peasants, the self-sacrifice of Messina's *St Sebastian*.

Turning briefly to sculpture, aggressive bravery had been projected by innumerable statues, the bas reliefs of Assyrian warriors, the imperial sculpture factories of Rome, the great equestrian statues like Verrocchio's of Colleoni at Venice, many thousands of 'victory' statues recalling forgotten wars in almost every town and village. Equally the submissive virtues have been well projected by sculptors in many centuries, notably by infinite variations on the theme of the crucifixion and martyrdom, with Michelangelo's *Pieta* as a particularly fine example and by the great Buddhist schools of sculpture with the calm and serenity of their Bodhisattvas.

Architecture has played a lesser but still significant part. Arches of triumph, obelisks, columns and other monuments have been part of the conditioning for a warlike attitude. In only partial contrast the history of churches throughout the world illustrates the use of architectural skills to create a variety of attitudinal tones of humility, awe, loyalty and affection. The huge marble baths of ancient Rome, the palaces of eighteenth-century Europe or the 1920s night-club reflected and encouraged a permissive ethic.

Also, amongst the visual arts, there are a variety of minor applications which cumulatively have contributed to attitudinal training; flags, shields, badges, playing cards, pottery, jewellery, buttons and all kinds of other paraphernalia have been used to carry the symbols of currently fashionable ideas from doves of peace and fasces to playboy 'bunnies'. Young English ladies in the eighteenth century sewed samplers with mottoes like

> Patience is a virtue,
> Virtue is a grace.
> Both put together
> Make a pretty face.

Not only the finished sampler but the corroborative act of sewing it made sure the message went deep.

Moving on to literature, we can touch only briefly on the many areas of ethical didacticism. Poetry, from oral saga to written ode, has been used in most ages to project military loyalty: Homer's *Iliad*, the Hindu *Mahabharata*, the Icelandic sagas, or Mrs Hemans. Almost as effectively, poetry has been a propagandising tool for the submissive virtues: the *Psalms* of David, the *Upanishads*, the works of Dante are just some examples. Poetry has projected marital fidelity, the work ethic, charity and other virtues. With Sappho and Byron it has flouted conventional moralities and tried to create new ones. Numerous unremembered poets have produced mnemonic verses on the evils of drink or dirt, adultery or disobedience. Much poetry important for its moral creativity has been forgotten because it is not of the kind ranked in literary terms: for example, in 1530 Girolamo Francostro wrote his *Syphilis Sive Morbus Gallicus*, inventing a new name for a newish disease in an otherwise forgotten poem.

The novel too has been a potent tool of ethical iconography. Richardson's *Clarissa*, Kingsley's *Water Babies*, Harriet Beecher Stowe's *Uncle Tom's Cabin* are just a few obvious examples from the many (since at least the seventeenth century) where the moral propaganda content has been significant. In this context, pulp fiction is as important as the classics. Shallow story books glorifying war, racism, romantic marriage, violence or permissiveness are often more influential than deeper works of minority interest. Biased biographies of saints or heroes, slanted histories of leaders and races have played a parallel role.

Music, while not articulate in detail, does have the emotional command to fuel a variety of moral attitudes: Wagner's 'Kaisermarsch', the 'Marseillaise', 'All the nice girls love a sailor', 'Goodbye Dolly', 'Horst Wessel', or Verdi's 'Song of the Hebrew Slaves' are examples of the huge repertoire which has fanned the military ethic over the centuries. Drinking songs, love songs, work songs, each type makes its contribution to attitudes. The hymns of Luther or Wesley show that faith is one of the other virtues readily projected by music. According to Plato, F minor was morally debilitating: in the Middle Ages the Ionian was known as the *modus lascivus* whereas the Dorian was supposed to project chastity. Hitler made jazz illegal because of its debilitating effects. Opera and ballet have developed specific themes more extensively, combining the attitude-forming powers of music with the more articulate statements of the theatre. Poulenc's moral opera *The Breast of Tiresias* or Verdi's anti-aristocratic *Rigoletto* are two examples.

Drama, since its earliest days in the hands of the great Athenian tragedians, has been a vehicle for demonstrating moral conflicts. From Aeschylus to Arthur Miller, from Shakespeare to Ionescu, numerous productions have deserved the title 'morality plays'. Cinema, radio and television have extended the arts in the twentieth century and the assessment of influence in the creation of moral attitudes becomes even more complex. There is perpetual controversy as to whether people really learn new attitudes from the mass media, or whether the works they hear and see simply reflect attitudes which are already well-entrenched. From the point of view of a general history of moral attitudes it is sufficient to recognise that the arts and the media are an important on-going sub-section of our study; they do both influence and reflect, but they are not the sole influence nor the sole reflection.

10)   LIFE CYCLES

Permissive legislation is the characteristic of a free people.

Disraeli

History suggests that it is reasonable to make the following generalisation: the vitality and vigour of moral codes tend to reach some kind of peak not long after they have first been promulgated and then gradually to ebb unless revived by fresh ideas or updated to meet contemporary needs. This is true whether the driving force behind the moralities is religious, political or from any other source. There is also a possibly related generalisation that periods of puritanical strictness are usually in the end followed by periods of greater permissiveness which then, in turn, swing back to greater strictness. Inevitably there may be variations in the timing and degree of influence in different strata of society, but at least staggered trends can be observed.

In English history, for example, periods of relative permissiveness are associated with the mid-Norman period, the court of the Tudors (particularly that of Henry VIII), and the reign of James I. A stricter trend becomes obvious under Charles I and Archbishop Laud, peaking with the extreme Puritanism of the Commonwealth period, one of the

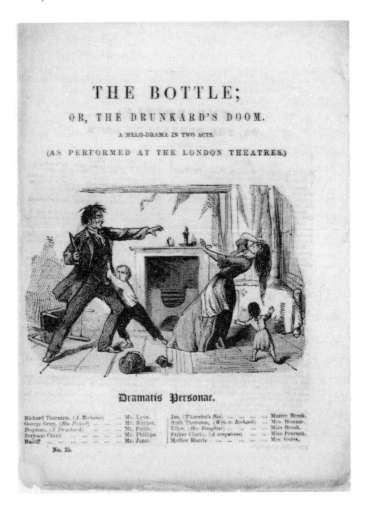

most repressive eras in English history. As the historian Thomas Macaulay, a meticulous observer of this period put it:

> An age of hypocrisy is in the nature of things followed by an age of raffishness.

The swing back from Puritanism to permissiveness at the Restoration was one of the most clear-cut in social history: rakishness was fashionable again. The pendulum swung back again round about 1689 under William III and Queen Anne, to reverse again under the early Georges with the era of cheap gin, *The Rake's Progress* and the romanticisation of highwaymen like Turpin and Shepperd. Mini swings continued, but there was a major swing against permissiveness in the reaction to the French Revolution, and a swing back again with the Regency bucks which was in turn reversed by the evangelical revival and the tide of Victorian respectability. It would be gross oversimplification to classify the whole Victorian period as one of puritanism, though this was an underlying theme which remained dominant until the so-called 'naughty nineties', when, according to the historian E.K. Ensor, 'the revulsion from puritanism to raffishness' inaugurated the era of the music halls, the cult of hedonism. Then, when the Edwardian buck had had his day, there was a brief upright twilight before the First World War, itself followed by the 'gay twenties', then the sobering Depression and war again, the hair shirt until the early 1950s, and then the crashing down of the barriers of censorship in the mid- 1950s ushered in the permissive 'swinging sixties'.

There is of course a danger of over-simplification in discussion of these trends; often they represent the activities of only a fashionable minority and such fashions took time to penetrate to other classes of society and beyond the cities. There were similar overlapping waves of fashion, eddying out from different sources of leadership. There is no question of tidy departmentalisation of each historical pocket; all we want to establish is that there are, in most societies, signs of a semi-regular ebb and flow of moral attitudes.

These changes of fashion in the area of permissiveness do not necessarily keep in step with attitudes towards violence. Some of the puritanical periods, for instance, have also been ages of quite severe cruelty, whereas some permissive periods have been non-violent. What is evident to some extent is that when a society moves into a permissive period then it will most often get even more permissive before there is a back swing to puritanism. When a society becomes violent then it will subsequently become more violent, this trend exacerbated by the mutual brutalisation of competing groups, up to the point when the violence becomes so destructive that there is a reversion to common sense.

It is also true that there have been numerous examples of influential persons and generations who switched from the permissive to the anti-permissive after their own first flush of youth: St Augustine, Louis XIV, Boccaccio, John Donne. So there is a simplistic argument which suggests that when the leaders of a society are older it will be less permissive, but like most generalisations this one is far from universally true. Another common feature is the capacity of even quite strict societies to have brief periods when they cast aside all inhibitions. The Saturnalia and all its descendants are a classic example of this as an annual habit, just as Lent and Ramadan are examples of the reverse.

It is premature to suggest any firm general characteristics of the stages of a moral code's life cycle, but certain tentative suggestions could be borne in mind when looking at social history. A new and virile moral code will show signs of strong leadership, creativity and certainty; it will be visibly contemporary in its approach to life and show concern for its members; it will be very relevant, rely on credible sanctions and use strong, acceptable motivation. At its peak a code may demonstrate signs of intolerance, even violent intolerance. It may become extreme almost to the point of absurdity, its recommendations may have turned into rigid laws, and it may show signs of barely relevant interference in everyday life as its vitality begins to become fixed in stone.

Finally, in the period of decline there will be signs of permissive reaction, of the young no longer accepting the ideas of their elders, a loss of credibility in the sanctions or relevance in the rules, of warmth of spirit and adaptability in the code itself, of corruption in its enforcement. The prime feature of a major change in moral direction is when a younger generation arrives at such a corporate contempt for its elders that they indulge in mass rejection of parental models. Such mass rejection is not rare but is far from universal, and it usually occurs when the elders are still practising a third or fourth-generation ethic accepted by habit rather than choice.

There are plenty of examples of codes in their declining period which have been rejuvenated by a fresh burst of creative energy. This has been true of Christianity and Buddhism in particular, Hinduism and Islam to a slightly lesser extent and of many non-religious ethics. Indeed there is nothing to suggest that a code cannot be perpetually revived. Perhaps there is no better example than the remarkable survival of the Jewish ethos, with persecution seeming almost to reinforce their faith and their cultural identity over a three-thousand year period.

PART TWO

A History of Sin

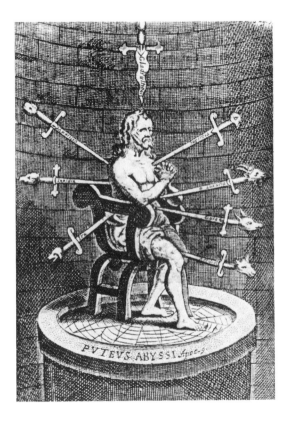

Introduction

Happy the people whose annals are blank in the history books . . .
                                                                    Carlyle

I T IS NOT EASY TO SEE any clear line of progress in human moral history. In social history it is possible to trace a steady improvement in material well-being, in health care, in technology, transport and so on. Even in political history there may be some line of progress in the evolution of democracy and human rights. In moral history, on the other hand, there is first of all the problem that any view of improvement is going to be subjective. Even if a simple definition of a good morality as one in which people are more kind and less cruel to their fellows is accepted, any line of progress which is visible must be seen as very erratic and impermanent, compared with the kind of progress associated with the conquest of the material world.

The narrative which follows is in broadly chronological order, so that comparisons can be drawn between ideas and behaviour in different parts of the world at similar periods. This means that no real attempt can be made to trace the ethical development of individual nations or communities. It also means that different countries will feature prominently in some episodes and not at all in others, depending on the signs of ethical revolution evident in them at that particular time.

If there is no particular pattern of progress, is there any other pattern which we may look for without straining the facts? The one certainty is that moral attitudes keep changing, sometimes quite suddenly, so there are phases and cycles which may resemble some pattern of rise and fall. Young moralities have youthful vigour and later predictably suffer from the weakness or stiffness of old age. Moralities which are strong provoke reactions in the opposite direction; moralities which create one kind of normality create another kind of deviation. One particular pattern of ebb and flow may be of special significance, that is the alternation in some periods between what Nietzsche called the 'slave' or herd virtues and those of the superman, between admiration for the submissive, kindly and self-controlled ethic and admiration for the conquering hero, ruthless, sometimes bloodthirsty, scaling the heights. This oscillation between the ideal of self-denial and the ideal of self-aggrandisement is one of the recurring features of moral history, sometimes even within the lives of particular people.

Another way of looking at the history of morals, which we should bear in mind, is to postulate that human beings have a natural way of behaving which is from time to time overlaid with artificial conventions which change the pattern of nature. For the pessimists this may mean that man is by nature essentially 'bad' and needs the artificial conventions to persuade him to behave better; or, for the optimists, that the human is an essentially decent species who from time to time gets led into bad habits by evil conventions. There is probably some truth in both standpoints. There is continuing evidence of men's better qualities being submerged occasionally by periods of panic, self-pity and cruelty. Equally, in periods of real stress and difficulty, there are innumerable examples of all kinds of people behaving in the most admirable fashion.

Partly because the evidence which survives is most often of the extremes of behaviour, our object is avowedly to concentrate mainly on the famous; because our primary subject is moral leadership, the pathfinders or trendsetters who were followed by the majorities, we look at the models rather than the imitators, although the strength and degree of imitation is also profoundly important. What we are looking for is a tentative history of what Marc Bloch calls 'collective mentalities' or collective errors, and with appropriate attention to successful efforts at achieving long-term communal harmony.

1,500,000 — 3000 BC

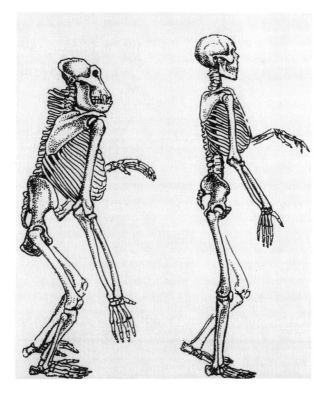

Each pre-civilised society was held together by largely undeclared but continually realised ethical conceptions.

Redfield

*H*OMO ERECTUS, the monkey on two legs with an 800 cc brain, began to share his bananas with others of his species. That sharing of food and work was probably the beginning of human morality. It was this willingness to share, the basis of co-operation, which made man the world's dominant species. This long period of primeval existence saw man make two significant moral advances. The first was the development of family life, which does exist amongst other species, but which was turned into a more advanced unit by humans due to their development of a more extended speech vocabulary than any other animals are known to have. Underlying the family unit was what Clark calls an 'economic partnership of the sexes', a division of labour with a corresponding principle of mutual duty and service, which was not seriously questioned for the next thirty or so millennia. The other moral advance achieved by early man, which was to be a uniquely important human feature was a belief in the importance of proper burial, not just as an act of hygiene but as a duty to the departed which implied a belief in at least some kind of consciousness after death. This was to be the foundation of many ethical ideas for many centuries to follow.

While some recent writers like Fromm have tended to present primitive man as 'the killer ape', the evidence which exists tends to show on the whole that early man was not particularly violent towards his own kind, perhaps partly because he had not yet developed weapons which made organised violence a serious temptation. There are, of course, remains of numerous Stone Age men who met violent deaths; the broken skulls of Peking men from Choukoutien may indicate ritual cannibalism, as may the skull of Verteszollos man (c.350,000 BC) found near Budapest. There was not yet any significant shortage of land or food supplies to cause the pressure which makes violence more likely. Man throughout this period lived only on wild food, animal or vegetable, so life was nomadic, communities small. Occasional violence or cannibalism there may have been, but man-killing must have seemed a low priority.

No special pattern of monogamy or polygamy seems to have been settled, but there is little to suggest that primitive man was markedly less moral in any meaningful sense than modern man. Indeed there were many vices which had yet to be learned. This may not have been an age of primeval innocence, but equally it was a period in which humans had little incentive to be cruel to each other.

While Neanderthal man and his contemporaries (with their 1,500 cc brains) learned the art of language and how to live in communities, they still led a life which, in the words of Hobbes, was 'nasty, brutish and short'. They still had a large single eyebrow ridge, a jutting jaw and apelike posture. The particular feature of their behaviour which was to form the background for a great deal of moral development in this period was care for the dead. Tombs were constructed in the Old Stone Age (from 70,000 BC) which were at least as elaborate as the owner's home whilst alive and in them were placed gifts and utensils for use by the dead person in his after-life. The amount of labour put into this activity and the expenditure of real wealth must have represented a very major sacrifice to the people involved, a sacrifice of immediate benefit on behalf of other people, which is one of the most fundamental features of moral behaviour. For a great deal of this period the dead were sprinkled with ochre dye, probably to reduce their pallor in death. This, plus the burial rites, firmly suggest a belief in life after death which meant a great deal to these people. It also presented their leaders with a major motivational tool for behavioural control.

This obsession with the after-life, as shown in the cairns and chamber tombs of Stone Age man, was to be developed in subsequent genera- tions to become the dominating obsession in many early civilisations, particularly Egypt. And the right to decent burial was to become one of the most deeply rooted and inalienable of the traditional rights of man. In Sophocles' play *Antigone*, reflecting Greek prehistoric mythology, the king refused to allow the burial of some rebellious warriors, thus imposing a dreadful punishment for their insolence; their sister Antigone was willing to die herself for the sake of scattering a little earth over their bodies. The obsession seems in some places to have been connected with human sacrifice and/or ritual cannibalism. The skull drinking cups of Charante date from around 20,000 BC.

The evidence of Stone Age man's other moral habits is slight but there is ough to prove that he hunted the mammoth, a task which involvec :ommunal courage and co-operation, a sharing of danger and disc line. It meant that each member of a mammoth-hunting team mig..t on certain occasions be the one in the circle against whom the mammoth charged, who therefore had to risk his life and depend on the others for help. As Clark says, 'There seems no doubt that man found himself and emerged as a dominant species first and foremost as a hunter'. The communal reward for such demonstrations of courage, the praise and glory on a small scale, were the beginnings of motivation towards the so-called superman virtues. The skeleton of a one-armed, middle-aged cripple found at Shanidar in northern Iran has been cited to show that Neanderthal-type humans were caring and devoted effort to helping the disadvantaged. The need for communal defence against animals, and later against other men, became the basis of tribal patriotism and the military ethic. It also led to the subsidiary role of women. As Margaret Mead put it: 'You don't chase elephants with a baby on your hip.' Man developed his sexual possessiveness, which became the basis for a morality that modern feminists like Marilyn French see as the beginning of a very long period of male domination.

The other great achievement of this period, from 15,000 BC onwards, was the growing of corn, which required one of early man's first great acts of self-restraint: storing seed grain through the winter instead of just eating it. Taming animals instead of eating them instantly involved the same discipline. This early example of controlled abstinence was again to be a foundation for further ethical development and civilisa- tion itself.

It was probably at some time during this period of advance in farming that man made the first mental link between the fertility of the soil and herds and the fertility of his own species. To this period belong the so-called Venus figurines, which are among the earliest religious representations and symbols of respect for a natural force, something beyond comprehension when Cro-Magnon man, the first *homo sapiens sapiens* with a 1,700 cc brain, painted the superb cave paintings. But once the early assessment of fertility had been made, it led to the first great human taboo, the marriage of very close relatives such as brother and sister, father and daughter and so on. Judging by subsequent developments, it is probable that in most communities homosexuality also became a taboo early on. Kohler, however, argued that group marriage was very common in primitive societies.

Just when men first made a regular habit of killing each other, we do not know. Old Stone Age man invented the bow and arrow, described by Gordon Childe as 'the first composite weapon designed by man'; but this was primarily a weapon for hunting animals. It was not until the New Stone Age that the stone battle-axe appeared, the first weapon specifically designed for human combat.

Ardrey argues that it was around 3000 BC that man changed from the defensive to the aggressive, when

> ... organised warfare became a significant human entertainment, perhaps a substitute for the lost hunting way.

Once nature was half-tamed and game-hunting no longer crucial to survival, the skills of the hunt were transferred to human prey. The invention of metallurgy provided the means, the acquisition of settled wealth the provocation.

There follows the question of whether Stone Age men were frequently cannibals and also if they indulged in human sacrifice. Certainly there is some evidence for early cannibalism. Peking man was probably cannibal on occasions and Herodotus, the sixth-century Greek historian, recorded that the Scythian tribe, the Massagetae, ate their dead geriatrics. There is also the doubtful archaelogical evidence of skulls split open for the extraction of brains as a delicacy. Further evidence from traditional mythologies includes the legend of Pelops eating his own children, and Polyphemus, the cannibal giant in Homer's *Odyssey*. Comparison can be drawn also with the primitive tribes in remoter parts of the world, like the Dyaks of Borneo, who preserved a tradition of cannibalism into modern times. Perhaps some cannibalism did exist amongst Stone Age peoples, especially in periods of famine, but it was probably not enormously widespread and rapidly came to be viewed with great horror by most tribes.

On the question of human sacrifice, again there is little firm evidence of it on any major scale in the early period until the rise of the great empires of the Egyptians and Chinese, where slaves were immolated at their masters' funerals. But there is the mystery of Tollund man, the preserved body of an ancient European strangled and left in the Danish marsh. Around 8000 BC we know that the first reindeer hunted down each season in Holstein was sacrificed to the gods. Again the probability is that human sacrifice was a relative rarity until the power of the first empires made it a practicable luxury. The legends of Isaac and Iphigenaia show the developing reaction, but certainly human sacrifice continued to exist into historical times amongst the Celts and Germans. As to infanticide as a means of population control there is no proof either way, but conditions were often so harsh that it must have been temptingly easy.

The special evil which first reared its head in a small way in this period was slavery, introduced when tribes were first large enough to keep prisoners of war alive for their own use and had the organisation to control them but, again, any serious development of this was to wait for the big empires of the next era.

One final comparison is perhaps worthwhile between Stone Age man and the Stone Age tribes who survived into the modern world. Some of these, like the Punans of Borneo, the Arctic Eskimos and the Djahai of Australia never made war, a remarkable achievement in thousands of years and not equalled by many more advanced societies. Other primitive tribes were free from slavery, prostitution, polygamy, cannibalism, infanticide, human sacrifice and many other habits found in civilised societies. This is not to prove that civilisation is inferior to barbarism but is simply a reminder against assumptions of automatic moral progress.

Meanwhile, by the year 7000 BC town life, to many writers the cause of nearly all evils, had begun to develop—the city. Archaeological evidence shows the steady expansion of Jericho from village to fortified town during this period. One great moral principle which evolved from the needs of the new settled communities between 10,000 and 5000 BC was the right to own property, land in particular, and to pass ownership on to the next generation. This was to be the basis for many aspects of protective morality in the subsequent millennia, 'the territorial imperative', source of inequality, criterion for moral laws, acceptable excuse for war. Land-ownership and woman-ownership became the primary inspirations of man-made morals, and a primary justification for violence. One other man-made invention appeared at this time which was probably to be the cause of and certainly to be blamed for many aspects of human misbehaviour—alcohol. There is archaeological evidence for the brewing of strong beer at Catal Huyuk from about 7000 BC, and of huckleberry wine from about 6400 BC.

Overall this was a period in which the development of property ownership, of primitive towns and of offensive weaponry created the basis for many future ethical problems. It was also the period in which humans displayed the first signs of the recurrent neuroses which led them to inflict on each other huge levels of unnecessary pain.

3000 — 2000 BC

The dawn of conscience.

Breasted

I T WAS THE INVENTION OF BRONZE that made possible a new kind of violence, a larger scale of conquest and a bigger area of administration.
This happened first of all in the Middle East, and so it was in that
area that we find the birth of a new kind of morality and immorality.

Egypt was unified by Menes *c.*3100 BC. Perhaps the first conquering
hero known to history (and even he was semi-mythical) was Horus
Ro of Egypt, whose son was known as 'The Scorpion', a prince who
exploited fear on a major scale to impose his will and founded the

I Dynasty c.3000 BC. He made human sacrifice to Ra, the Sun god, for his victories. His heir, Horus, reputedly killed 381 prisoners of war and tore out the tongues of 142. This is the first recorded example of the kind of egocentric sadistic imperialism which has reappeared from time to time in the subsequent 5,000 years.

In the period 3000–2500 BC we see the first main development of Egyptian civilisation bringing both the first mass cruelty and also the first formal concepts of morality. It was what J.H. Breasted called 'the dawn of conscience'. The Nile and its floods offered huge wealth to a ruling class which could control it. The development of an officer ruling class with its code of behaviour in turn made possible the systematic conquest of less efficient neighbours. Pharaoh Seneferu (2613–2590 BC) raided the Sudan and brought back gold, 7,000 slaves and 200,000 cattle and goats. Human sacrifice, particularly the burying alive of red-headed men for the god Set, persisted. Some slaves were buried alive in the tombs of their masters and sometimes infants were buried as a sacrifice in the foundations of new buildings.

By around 2500 BC, and the IV Dynasty, the Egyptian leadership was so powerful that, according to Herodotus, the Pharaoh Khufu (or Cheops) (2598–2568 BC) though not a conqueror himself could force 100,000 slaves to work for twenty years to build his Great Pyramid. Egyptian obsession with death and the paraphernalia of the after-life had reached its climax. On the one hand there was acceptance of the morality of conquest and slavery on a massive scale, shifting nearly 6,000,000 tons of stone for this pyramid alone; on the other was the philosophical view that enjoyment of life after death depended on quality of life in this world as well as standards of burial. In fact, one of Khufu's sons, Habahif, was the world's first recorded philosopher and a few years later we have the earliest evidence of the concept of divine judgement. The pyramid texts composed by the priests of Heliopolis for the tombs of the V Dynasty c.2400 BC show the divine assessment of the dead man's moral behaviour before he is allowed to pass through to the superior kind of after-life. This invention of the hell/heaven sanction by the Egyptians has been of the highest significance in subsequent moral control, and in Egypt, as with most other societies, its function was to support the monarchy.

The Book of the Dead showed the judgement of the god Ra, the guardian of truth and goodness. These qualities were referred to as 'maat', the first known word for virtue. By this time, the average Egyptian officer or civil servant could afford mummification and a reasonably elaborate tomb, but he had also to live the good life to earn full benefits hereafter. Harkuf of Elephantine died c.2400 BC, and in his testament it was recorded that

> A good man is one who gives bread to the hungry, water to the thirsty, raiment to the naked, a boat to one who has none.

This was probably the first recorded definition of virtue. Another burial statement was

> Never have I done any violence to any person. I gave bread to the hungry. I have not oppressed anyone in the possession of his property.

Between 2180 and 2080 BC there was a period of political and moral collapse when, in the words of J. H. Breasted,

> . . . virtuous men threw themselves to the crocodiles in despair. Ah, would that it were the end of men, no conception, no birth.

From around 2000 BC, with the revival under the Middle Kingdom, comes the advice to King Meri Ka Re as he approached the gods for the weighing of his heart in the scales of justice which would qualify him for a good after-life. He had to make statements in reply to forty-two questions, according to Chapter 125 of *The Book of the Dead*, such as

> I have done no violence to a poor man. I have not killed. I have not had sexual relations with a boy. I have not snared the birds of the gods.

Overall, this period of Egyptian history produced a remarkably sophisticated ethical system, gradually more conformist and submissive under the later dynasties. While slavery was a significant part of the system, once the frontiers were established there was relatively little warfare and the accent of society was on constructive humanity rather than destructive over-expansion. There were elements of this ethos passed on in the next period to Moses (a Hebrew slave accidentally brought up as an Egyptian gentleman), and through Moses eventually to the modern world.

Meanwhile, in the area now known as Iraq, there was a parallel, less humane ethical development. There may have been organised warfare in Babylonia as early as the fourth millennium under King Eannata, and the military stele of Susa dates back to *c.*2424 BC, as do the fortifications of cities like Ur. Between the cities of Laggash and Umma there took place *c.*2375 BC one of the earliest recorded wars and shortly afterwards appeared the first successful major warlord, Sargon of Agade (2340–2280 BC), the prototype tyrannical emperor. His son, Rimush, believed in rule by terror, and the wholesale slaughter of prisoners of war known as 'karashum' became a feature of Sumerian kingship. Adding up Rimush's own detailed record of massacres brings a total of 54,000 prisoners killed after battles; in addition, the kings of Ur were accompanied in their tombs by sacrificed human retainers. On the other hand, round about the same time we have an early example of an effort to restrain the exploitation of the Mesopotamian poor by the governor of Urukagima, and note that the people of Laggash had given up the habit of polyandry. King Urnammu (*c.*2200) promoted one of the earliest legal codes including fines for evil-doing. Some time around the end of this millennium prostitution was invented, probably as a form of religious fund-raising: the brothel of Uruk was beside the temple of Anu.

From Babylon *c.*2000 BC came the remarkable *Epic of Gilgamesh*, a poetic tale of the Prince Gilgamesh who began life as a petty tyrant exploiting his subjects, chasing maidens and young boys, desperate for glory, nevertheless gradually emerging as a stable military hero, making the best of his life with little hope or care for the life hereafter but concerned to perform well in this life. This indicates the real difference in ethical motivation between the first two great civilisations; the Mesopotamians did not have a strong hell/heaven sanction, but a tough ethic of civil obedience. Their myth of the flood, a disaster inflicted on man by God for their evil behaviour was the great warning, the first evidence of a collective sense of sin. In both of the two early civilisations of the Middle East, the first semi-formal codes of morality were tools of social control developed by aggressive Bronze Age regimes.

There is less evidence of the earliest stage of Chinese morality, but according to tradition the Hsia dynasty, *c.*2200 BC onwards, did produce a number of mythical law-givers such as Yao and Shun, as well as that great model of the work ethic, the canal-builder, Yu. Oakley cites evidence that in the third millennium the Chinese had already discovered the properties of cannabis, which they referred to as 'the liberation of sin', but no serious consequences are recorded. By about the same time the Greeks had discovered opium.

Generally this had been a millennium notable for the first large-scale wars, the spread of slavery, terrorism and inequality, the first signs of a human sense of guilt. Above all, it had been the era of the first obsessions, with massive empires and massive monuments at whatever cost in terms of human misery.

2000 — 1500 BC

. . . make manifest justice in the land . . .
From Hammurabi's code

I N THIS HALF-MILLENNIUM history again focuses on Egypt and
Mesopotamia, but also brings in Greece, India, China and South
America, producing six centres of ethical development.

In Egypt, these years were roughly equivalent to the Middle Kingdom
which was moving into a more belligerent, materialist era. Just after
this period, Pharaoh Usertsu III (1440–1412 BC) conquered Nubia and
set up a column at Samnal, forbidding blacks to come beyond it. His
hieroglyphs indicated this ethos and that of Egyptians of this era.

My word is the law. I attack my attacker. The man who retreats is a vile
coward. He who is defeated on his own land is no man. Thus is the black.
He falls down at a word of command; when attacked he runs away. The
blacks have no courage, they are weak and timid. I seized their women. I
took their goods. I stopped up their wells. I slew their bulls. I reaped their
crops. I burned their houses. Any son of mine who allows this boundary to
be thrust back is no son of mine and I never begot him. I have set up a statue
of myself not only for your benefit but also that ye should do battle for it.

This is a remarkably early statement of racism, imperialism and militarism, over 3,000 years before Hitler's *Mein Kampf* but very similar
in tone.

Needless to say, the Empire of Usertsu like all others was to be
in due course swamped by outsiders, in this case the war chariots
of the Hyksos. The Middle Kingdom also showed the classic signs
of moral decline—palace intrigue and corruption. Pharaoh Achthoes
was an undoubted sadist. Amenethat II (*c.*1900 BC) was murdered
by his eunuchs, showing the early presence of the vicious practice
of castration on some scale. Ahmes, who reigned from 1580 to 1558
BC, married his own sister, making incest an Egyptian royal tradition
down to the time of the Cleopatras. It was not widespread, but in the
town of Arsinoe it was recorded that two-thirds of all marriages were
technically incestuous. The pharaohs became plundering warmongers,
and instead of passing the test of Osiris for after-life by good behaviour
there was a tendency to buy dispensation with wealth.

Meanwhile, Mesopotamia was reaching its ethical peak. Most of the
legal code imposed by King Hammurabi of Babylon *c.*1800 BC has been
preserved in stone. This code was

> ... to make manifest justice in the land, to destroy the wicked and
> evil-doers and to prevent the strong oppressing the weak.

The ethic of Babylon, if not as permissive as its biblical image, was a
harsh one compared with the Egyptian. Adulterers were to be drowned,
those guilty of incest killed or exiled, homosexuals castrated. Abortion
was a serious offence. Slavery was part of the economic system but was
controlled, and injury to slaves was punishable by a fine. Women had
better rights than in most contemporary societies because in commercial
Babylon they held their own in many craft industries. Both married
and unmarried women had reasonable status. If divorced, a wife could
normally (if not the guilty party) keep her children and share in her
husband's wealth. Men, on the other hand, could also keep concubines
and slave girls. Prostitution centred on the temples where it had both
religious and fund-raising significance, though the euphemistically
named 'women wine-sellers' were regarded as pernicious, the harimate,
the worst whores in Babylon; and at the temple of Ishta there were male

prostitutes as well. Unlike the Egyptians, the Babylonians believed in no after-life; they were a commercially materialistic but practical people. That they perhaps drank a little too much is shown by Hummurabi's specific laws against such over-indulgence.

To the north had emerged the Hittite civilisation, in the area now approximating to Turkey. This society lasted from c.2000–1200 BC. It had a strong military ethic but a more lenient civil code than either Babylon or Egypt. They tolerated homosexuality and their punishments were generally milder. They believed in reparation rather than capital or corporal punishment. The penalty for theft was forced labour rather than death, though slaves had a separate code and one of them who stole or burned property could suffer the death penalty or facial mutilation. However, the stone-carved mythology of King Labarnas of the Hittites (c.1500 BC) was full of moral homilies, including praise for compassion and loyalty.

One other great figure to emerge from the Middle East in this dim dawn of moral history was Abraham (c.1800 BC) the patriarch of Ur. He was a rebellious early pioneer of monotheism and of an ethic which subordinated all human behaviour to obedience to a single god, even to the point of human sacrifice. Some of his story is obviously legend, but there is no need to doubt his existence. His influence as the first philosopher of both Christianity and Islam was immense. The tradition of his stalwart rejection of urban depravity was part of the ethos which explained the destruction of Sodom and Gomorrah as caused by the evil behaviour of their inhabitants. But the fact that he married his own step-sister, a common enough habit in those times would have caused horror to Christian moralists. This early period of Israeli folklore is full enough of the disreputable to make it credible, with Ishmael the typical nomad bandit practising the traditional desert spring raid or 'razzia', Rachel the baby-switcher, Simon and Levi the sadists, Judah the committer of incest, Onan the experimenter in birth control. Though the folklore of Genesis was not set down until some centuries later, its material had for a long time clearly provided a magnificent panorama of the dos and don'ts of a desert nomadic community struggling for divine approval.

In this half-millennium we also have the first real evidence of moral ideas in the Far East. The so-called Shang period began c.1600 BC with an empire based on conquest and slavery, which was also, like the early Egyptians, overlaid with an overwhelming obsession about the after-life and veneration of ancestors. Human sacrifice was normal and complete households of slaves were buried alive in royal tombs such as those of Anyang. As with the Aztecs later, it is possible that conquest was necessary to keep up the supply of prisoner victims for the altar.

Turning briefly to the West we find the first signs of major religious institutions in the Americas with the foundation of the temple in

Kotosh, Peru, some time after 1800 BC. Two pyramids of the same period have been found on the River Seco and there is at least some evidence that these people too were already deeply concerned with the importance of the after-life.

The period 2000–1550 BC is reckoned to cover the so-called Minoan Golden Age of Crete. Despite a wealth of conventional archaeological evidence, little is known of the laws or moral habits of the Cretans who inhabited the remarkable palaces of Knossos and Phaestos. Their cities were unfortified, they had drains, they were great traders, a practical and commercial people with little sign of obsession with the after-life, and much more of the fun-loving ethos, bull-fighting, acrobatics and dancing. While the statuettes of topless snake goddesses might suggest a permissive streak, in fact Sir Arthur Evans drew attention to the genuine absence of permissive material in Minoan art. They did, however, have a tradition of human sacrifice, sometimes by burning.

The Indus Valley also produced its first civilisations during this period, based on the great trading cities of Harappa and Mohenjo-daro. Again we are short on evidence of their ethics, but such as there is suggests efficient, civil-minded commercial communities, successful and materialistic with a liking for gambling and dancing girls, and at least some form of state religion; but since their inscriptions have not been deciphered our knowledge is limited. By the middle of the millennium they were being overwhelmed by new tribes from the north. In terms of the development of both human conscience and human vice, this half-millennium was a significant period. As the ancient civilisations grew more introspective and less busy they found time for new vices : alcoholism, prostitution, human sacrifice, gambling and mass sadism. The human species had seriously begun to lose its way, side-tracked by self-imposed cosmologies and etiolated obsessions.

1500 — 1000 BC

Thou shalt leave alive nothing that breatheth.
Deuteronomy 20

I N THIS PERIOD we will be seeing the last entrance of Egypt as a main
theme, the advent of the Assyrians (with one of the ancient world's
least savoury ethics), brief appearances by India, China and Peru,
and the first appearance of the mainland Greeks.

In Egypt, this was a period of new imperialism. In 1320 BC the
Pharaoh Set I was sacrificing his prisoners of war to the gods. The
three pharaohs Thotmes, particularly Thotmes III (1479/30 BC), were
aggressive conquerors; the last of these decorated the Temple of Karnak

with the list of 500 conquered nations, cut off the hands of his victims and hung a Nubian chief upside down from the prow of his galley. Even the peaceful Tutankhamen (1360–1340 BC) went raiding into Palestine and Syria after the eccentric, sun-worshipping reign of his father-in-law Amenhotep IV and Queen Nefertiti. This Amenhotep changed his name to Akenhaton and briefly introduced some very progressive ideas including the concept of racial equality, truth and family development. Referred to by Breasted as 'the first individual in history', his influence was regrettably short-lived. However, the moral treatise of Ptah Hotep (c.1350 BC) urged restraint and submission, an early example of the humble and meek ethic which was, in this epoch, still very unusual. One sound feature of Egyptian ethics was the generally fair treatment of married women: they had equal rights to property and there were penalties to deter easy divorce. Filial piety was one of the ultimate virtues.

In contrast, the great conqueror Rameses II (1292/25 BC) tortured spies—the first recorded mention of torture in world history—and glorified his war record with new additions to the Karnak decor. The summit of his imperial vanity came with the famous sixty-foot high statues of himself which he had erected at Abu Simbl. He, or one of his dynasty, was responsible for the harsh treatment of the Hebrew slaves and for the systematic infanticide of the male slave population associated with the birth of Moses. On the other hand, Rameses apparently had 160 children of his own, including two daughters whom he himself incestuously married. There are also signs that the Egyptians, particularly in the XVIII Dynasty, were getting fond of alcohol, beer made from bread being part of their staple diet. Heavy drinking among various groups such as the military began to give serious cause for concern.

Without question the greatest ethical thinker of this period was the Hebrew ex-slave, Moses (c.1300–1220 BC), brought up by chance as a member of the Egyptian royal officer class. He murdered a slave overseer in anger and escaped to plan the exodus of his race from Egypt. The fact that he absorbed Egyptian training, but rebelled against parts of it, is a component link in the handing-on of Egyptian behaviour patterns to the later world. Once out of Egypt, Moses removed class distinction amongst the Jews, except between Levites and slaves. Slavery itself was made less harsh, as one would expect from a leader whose career had been inspired by the harsh treatment of slaves. Moses himself suffered from a stammer and found public pronouncements difficult, an area where he was much helped by his brother, the more verbose Aaron, but Moses did have the charismatic sense of occasion:

> Ye heard the voice out of the midst of the darkness for the mountain did burn with fire . . . (Exodus 19)

What Moses produced was not just the ten commandments, the first four of which concentrated on religious loyalty, but a vast number of detailed instructions which form a complete guide for social and national welfare. There is even the item dealing with the camp latrines, important for a nomadic people:

> And thou shalt have a paddle on thy weapon and it shall be when thou wilt ease thyself abroad thou shalt dig therewith and shalt turn back and cover that which cometh from thee. (Leviticus 16)

Then there is all the detail on the stoning to death of those caught in adultery, the punishment for bestiality, the regulations for marriage, polygamy and prostitution, the keeping of lepers outside the camp, the sparing of mother birds (reminiscent of Egypt), the insistence on separate types of clothing for the two sexes. There is the long and detailed instruction in Leviticus on sexual hygiene, with somewhat clinical laundry requirements which do not make for romantic reading. Much more significant were the number of instructions on positive behaviour, the most famous and significant of which—'Love thy neighbour as thyself'—was to become the foundation of the Christian ethic. Homosexuality was declared 'an abomination', there were lengthy rules for avoiding nakedness between unmarried males and females, and a rule against selling daughters into whoredom. The humane part comes through, for instance, in the rule for farmers not to shake their olive trees twice so that there will be a few olives left for the wandering poor. Similarly, they had to leave the gleanings of the corn fields. Without question the worst sin in the decalogue was idolatry, and punishments were severe. When the Midianites were defeated not even the women were spared in the slaughter:

> Thou shalt leave alive nothing that breatheth. (Deuteronomy 20)

But it was a remarkably comprehensive ethical system which more than stands comparison with the code of that other great master of ethical detail, Confucius.

Moses' successor, Joshua (*c.*1250–1200 BC) exterminated the old population of Jerusalem as Jehovah commanded and even organised a miracle so that none of the Canaanite stragglers could escape massacre. He had Ashtar stoned to death in circumstances which suggest it was a human sacrifice. The brutality with which the Jews seem to have eliminated most of the earlier populations of the promised land indicates a very low estimate of human life.

Subsequently, the behaviour of the Jews was mixed. They produced great guerilla leaders such as Gideon, Jeptha and Samson (*c.*1150 BC), but Gideon slaughtered prisoners of war and scourged the elders of Succoth to death with thongs for refusing hospitality, Jeptha sacrificed his own daughter for victory (like Agamemnon and others), and Samson had a weakness for women both professional and otherwise; he was, however, one of the earliest known opponents of alcohol, belonging to the ascetically temperate Nazarite sect. Add the annihilation of Jewish Gibeah, men, women and children, plus incidents like the mass rape of Shiloh, and the models promoted by the Old Testament add up to an often aggressively unattractive message. Many of its heroes were ruthlessly sadistic without any redeeming features, except love of country and loyalty to Jehovah. It was only towards the end of this period that there appeared the first of the great philosophical prophets, the ascetic Samuel (*c.*1080 BC), and even he had Agag hacked to pieces. The other major Jewish ethical thinker is to be found in the immensely complex character of David, the central figure in the series of three very remarkable kings—Saul, David and Solomon—who all showed splendid qualities and were all ultimately corrupted by success.

David (1050–1000 BC), the brilliant guerilla leader whose task for qualifying as Saul's prospective son-in-law was the collection of a hundred Philistine foreskins, was the heir to conflicting standards. As Saul slaughtered the Amalekites, so David killed two out of every three Moabites. He killed the people of Rabbah by putting them under saws, harrows of iron axes and through brick kilns for shaving the beards off his ambassadors. The contrast of his ultimate corruption by Bathsheba, the military murder of Uriah her husband, the effect on him of his large harem, the squabbling and incest of his sons, must be set against the amazing poetry of the psalms, perhaps the supreme example of poetic moral teaching made palatable by the intense fallibility of its patron.

The keeping of concubines was morally acceptable in much of early Israeli history because of the need for male offspring, and celibacy was regarded as a crime. Both alcohol and drugs make early entries in the book of Genesis, the first in connection with over-indulgence by Noah, the second in the alleged use of mandrake by Reuben. Usury, so much associated with later Jewish history, was expressly prohibited at this time.

In Mesopotamia, the old Babylonian civilisation had fallen prey to the hard mountain men of Assyria, the most ruthless people of the ancient world. As Myers put it,

> No ancient nation not even the Romans had practised *realpolitik* with the callous fanaticism, the sheer indifference to human feelings which mark Assyrian warfare, still more Assyrian diplomacy.

They destroyed old Babylon *c.*1275 BC, and the first Assyrian Empire was founded by Tiglath Pilasar I (1150–1100 BC).

The Assyrians, with their bull-headed god Ashur, were noted for their cruelty. They practised the old habit of 'razzia', the nomad's annual raiding expedition, but with a new ruthlessness and ferocity which made their empire large and unpopular. Their sole philosophical motivation was service to their gods whilst on earth and enjoying the resultant glory. Their after-life was a dull hell called 'Kurmigia' with no prospect of redemption or hope, so their harshly ruled subjects did not even have the diversion of a consoling religion. Their private life seems to have been quite strict, with a male-dominant family ethic which allowed for a few concubines but frowned on adultery and homosexuality. Population control was aided by the castration of young boys who became court eunuchs. Their priests practised holy nudity, but for most ranks clothing was reasonably prudish. Both military and civilian punishments were extremely brutal, the ethic destructive and unyielding. Conquered enemies were tortured, flayed, impaled on stakes or mutilated and exposed in cages. If conquered peoples were spared, they were often shifted *en masse* to other parts of the Assyrian Empire. It was probably also the Assyrians who invented the man-propelled warship, the galley, in about 705 BC, a development that was to cause some 2,000 years of misery for innumerable galley-slaves in the Mediterranean.

This period saw the flowering of another ruthless empire, that of the Minoan Cretans of Knossos, and the beginnings of the so-called heroic age of mainland Greece. This was the age of the petty kingdoms of Argos, Mycenae and the Trojan war, the story of which was handed on some six centuries later under the name of the blind poet Homer (*c.*850–800 BC). Possibly the *Iliad* and *Odyssey* are truer of their own time than the time they were meant to portray, but they do largely reflect the typical ethos of a heroic age and they were regarded as something of a moral bible in subsequent years. The heroes of the two great epics stood or fell by their own qualities, strength and courage. They were concerned only with military honour, they had no fear so they told no lies. The three great vices of the Homeric code were cowardice, perjury (Pandarus was the only liar in Homer and he was killed) and treachery towards the helpless, suppliants and the old. It was wrong to gloat over a fallen enemy. Homer described Odysseus as mildly devious, yet also says: 'He had no evil thoughts but was kind as a father to his people'.

The Homeric virtues were those to be expected of a primitive nation preoccupied with war. They also show the superb marriage of Odysseus to the faithful Penelope, model of patience, and the touching farewell of that other delightful couple, Hector and Andromache. 'Aidos' became the Greek concept of conscience, 'nemesis' their sense of guilt. Helen felt it when asked to go with Paris after his poor showing in battle against her husband, Menelaus. The full classical development of the moral tales of the house of Atreus and Agamemnon had to wait several generations, but most basic Greek morality is already clear in Homer.

It is noticeable that various elements of behaviour in the original Homeric stories were censored by later Greeks, such as the torture of Hector before he died, the incest of Alcinous and Acte, the poisoned arrows used by the Greeks, mutilation and stripping of the dead and human sacrifice. The sacrifice by Agamemnon of his daughter,

Iphigenia, was part of Greek folklore, as was the sacrificing of twelve noble Trojans at the pyre of the Greek warrior Patroclus, close friend of the sulky hero, Achilles.

Barely noticeable, but perhaps significant, was the reference in *The Odyssey* to the drug 'nepenthes', which may have been opium. Certainly in classical Greece the god of sleep wore a garland of poppies.

Finally, we turn to the Far East and the West. In India, the early stages of Hinduism were being founded. The first hymns of the Rig Veda (*c.*1000 BC) introduced the caste system, dividing society into four levels. The Upanishads composed throughout this period encouraged a self-realising morality by which followers should rise above the selfish ego, with 'karma', the responsibility to wipe out the effect of bad past deeds by good new ones.

> It is well with him that clings to the good. He who chooses the pleasant misses the end.

The use of the masculine pronoun is typical, since the Upanishads made the role of women strictly secondary. Hindu gods were basically good and truthful, not deceitful: Varunna upheld the moral order of truth, honesty and righteousness, and a good after-life was available to penitents, war heroes and donors of sacrificial gifts.

As is to be expected with a large population over a large area and a long period, Hinduism rapidly became an amalgam of numerous overtaken religions, with fashions changing from adulation of one popular hero-god to another, but the overall ethos marked it out morally as one of the higher religions. In the words of the Gita, sometimes referred to as the Indian New Testament,

> Those who are lowly born, women and slaves, if they take refuge in Krishna, they obtain the highest good.

Also:

> The mother is the highest guru.

Widows, however, were already being pressed to burn themselves on their husbands' pyres, an idea not unconnected with the fact that the presiding Brahmins could inherit a portion of the ladies' wealth.

From relatively early on Hinduism had its ascetic side, the vast carriage of Jaganatha at Puri being towed along by worshippers with hooks in their flesh; yet there was also the permissive streak, with ritual prostitution an obvious sign. In the year 1004 BC, the temple at Tanjore had 400 resident prostitutes. It should be noted also that from a very early period certain sects encouraged the chewing of cannabis as a vehicle for getting closer to God.

In China the Shang dynasty, having exploited its slaves and subject populations for long enough, was overthrown by one of them, the

Chous, *c.*1100 BC. The Chou dynasty, being ex-slaves like the Hebrews, introduced a new ethical philosophy rather like the prophets of Israel, their contemporaries, which was that the king had to be virtuous and disciplined to deserve his crown. He was expected to set an example to achieve moral conformity and if he was evil could be punished by usurpation. The old proverb goes, 'He who succeeds becomes emperor, he who fails a bandit.'

While slavery persisted, at least human sacrifice was probably much curtailed. The climate in China was ripe for the appearance of scholars and philosophers earlier than in most parts of the world.

Evidence for developments in South America at this time is somewhat flimsy, but *c.*1000 BC there appeared a dynamic new religion which spread over large parts of the Andes region, taking its archaeological name from the amazing temple of Chavin de Huantar in Peru, whose gods were cat-like creatures with snake hair. This religion seems to have been spread without need of physical conquest and its artistic styles have even led to a suggestion that it may have had links with the Chou styles of China, but this is far from proven. What is remarkable is that in this early period of history there were so many religions and ethical systems being developed in areas of the world so far apart.

From this period comes the amazing stone fresco of Monte Alban in Mexico, with its 300 mutilated enemy warriors and massacred babies carved into what Joyce Marcus called 'one of the most impressive works of military propaganda in Meso-America', deliberately projecting a sadistic image, as the Assyrians did, to strike fear into the hearts of their enemies and their own peoples. From this one can deduce the typical 'übermensch ethic' which so pleased Nietzsche.

If there is any pattern in this period, it is that morality in most early civilisations meant quality of service to the state, primarily military service, and what the state mainly looked for was bravery, loyalty and self-sacrifice. The code of Moses was different in that it alone developed behavioural patterns which were not purely designed to support an empire. Overall it was a half-millennium of considerable creativity in the development of ethics; having lost its way, the human species was in this era at least making a genuine effort to get back on course.

1000 — 500 BC

Good and bad are one.

Herodotus

THIS HALF-MILLENNIUM was probably the most remarkable of any in the moral development of mankind. It produced some of the greatest propagandising moral teachers of history within a relatively short period: Confucius, Lao Tsu, Buddha, Elijah, Isaac, Zarathustra, Pythagoras, Lycurgus and a number of others, all deserving of discussion.

Egypt, with already more than twenty dynasties behind it, survived as a force but no longer made any novel contribution to the history of virtue or sin. Its influence did, however, continue to be transmitted into the thought of the small kindgom of Israel, which was to become one of the great ethical power houses of the later world. King Solomon (*c.*1015–977 BC) married an Egyptian princess as one of his wives, and in Solomon we have what Milman described as

> The concise definition of all forms of behaviour, in particular the art of being a perfect gentleman . . . the clear-cut practices in Egypt for running a successful court.

There can be no doubt of the importance of this Egyptian background in the formation of the Jewish ethic, first by Moses then by Solomon, which was later so influential on the rest of the world. The code of Solomon, in 1,005 sayings and in his proverbial passion for justice, made him a parallel figure to Hammurabi of Babylon.

It was the increasing prosperity of Israel under kings like Solomon and Ahab which led to increasing materialism in its leading class, to increased exploitation by the wealthy of the poor, and to the sybaritic idolatry which shocked the new breed of prophets. We have a precise record of Jewish commercial complacency in this era being attacked by one great ascetic after another: Elijah (*fl.*875 BC) then Elisha (*fl.*850 BC), Jonah (*fl.*755 BC), Amos (*fl.*750 BC) and finally Isaiah (*fl.*740 BC), with his special emphasis on just behaviour as opposed to mere religious observance. Micah advised, *c.*700 BC: 'Do justly, love mercy and walk humbly with God' (Micah Cap 6.8); and Isaiah was an early pacifist, proclaiming, 'nation shall not raise sword against nation' (Isaiah 2.4).

This group of prophets, who had to assert their unofficial status by using the charisma and eccentricity of their personalities, who risked terrible penalties for poor judgement, made a unique contribution to preserving the qualities of the Jewish soul at a time when neighbouring countries were subsiding into a totally materialistic ethic. Phrygia under the dynasty of Midas, and Lydia under that of Croesus, were both proverbial for their addiction to wealth. The Phoenicians of Tyre and Sidon were renowned as the most ruthlessly materialistic people of the ancient world, and the least popular. It was a Phoenician princess, Jezebel, who married King Ahab of Israel *c.*900 BC and began the persecution of prophets which was the inspiration of Elijah. Jezebel was pilloried as 'the whore of Tyre', but it should not be forgotten that the intolerantly fanatical Elijah was reputed to have ordered the killing of 400 priests of Baal.

The religion of the Phoenicians, the subject of some pretty biased reporting in the Old Testament, did involve human sacrifice on quite a large scale, and also that not uncommon Middle Eastern custom of temple prostitution. A few centuries later, Strabo, the Greek traveller, noted that one town in Cappadocia boasted 6,000 temple prostitutes, while Eusebius even later noted the homosexuals round Astarte's temple at Aphka. Even Israel had its prostitutes, the male ones known as dogs, and the Phoenician habit of human sacrifice to Baal often also spread to the gullible Israelis. King Ahaz in 740 BC had children buried as a sacrifice in the foundations of his new palace.

It was the Phoenicians and their neighbours who provided the Greeks with many of their more permissive gods or heroes: Aphrodite, sometimes called Porne (the Whore), Europa and Hercules. This last had a bisexual, heavy-drinking reputation, as well as being the archetypal superman.

The general reputation of the Phoenicians with the Greeks was permissive, as that of the Greeks, who had learned from them, later seemed to the Romans. Religious prostitution may account for quite a lot of this—in Baalbec, Syria, every maiden had to prostitute herself to a stranger at the temple of Astarte. In Armenia, the noblest girls spent their teenage years as prostitutes in the service of Annitis; in Pontus it was for the goddess Ma, and there were variants of the habit in most Middle-Eastern states.

If the Phoenicians were notorious for commercial greed, it was the new breed of Assyrians who produced the least savoury brand of militarism of the ancient Middle East. Their new empire shot to prominence under Ashur Nasirpah (884–859 BC), who impaled 700 prisoners of war and flayed others alive. Their reign of terror subdued the Middle East: an inscription quoted in Myers says, 'their young men and maidens I burned as a holocaust'. Babylon itself was again destroyed with exaggerated brutality by the Assyrian warlord, Sennacherib (730–681 BC), and he was also responsible for the destruction of the Kingdom of Israel.

It was the conquest of the sister kingdom of Judah by Babylonian warlords in 587 BC which led to the first demonstration of the remarkable resilience of the Jewish ethos. Taken into captivity, languishing on the banks of the rivers of Babylon, a new group of prophets not only enabled the ethos to survive but raised it to new heights. In captivity, the emphasis was changed from this world to the next, the need for a better after-life, and it was Ezekiel (*fl*.590 BC) who gave this shape. Habbakuk railed against the sinful people. It was that resourceful philosopher, Job (*c*.580 BC), the patient sufferer of boils, who tackled the horrendous intellectual problem of reconciling a cruel and miserable life on earth with the existence of any kind of beneficent God. He and Ezekiel, with his brilliant metaphor of the dry bones, created the foundations for Christianity in that their teachings encouraged a submissive attitude in this world aimed at virtue rather than glory. In the vocabulary of Nietzsche, Ezekiel typified the development of the 'slave virtues', as Sennacherib did those of the 'superman' and the master race.

To the north east appeared in this same period another half-legendary prophet in the shape of the Persian Zoroaster, or Zarathustra in its Greek form (*fl.*600 BC), founder of the other major Middle-Eastern religion. This country prophet of the Iranian highlands, first of the Magi, according to Aresta, 'out of love and wisdom and righteousness became a prophet'. His ideas were linked into the wider Indo-European religions spreading through central Asia. His god, Ormazd, personified truth and law which were under continual attack from the greatest evil, falsehood.

Just as the Egyptians had a post-mortem questionnaire from Osiris, so Zoroaster had his heavenly audit of each dying man's good and evil deeds. Depending upon whether the account was in credit or not, a man might proceed to a pleasant after-life. This test, together with the emphasis on the conflict between good and evil and the requirement that each individual make his or her own choice between the two, combined to make Zoroastrianism one of the higher religions, laying greater than usual stress on human behaviour and morality. It spread and developed into a number of popular cults including Mithraism, the cult of the bull, which was a warm, satisfying ethic and later a serious rival to Christianity under the Roman Empire. In fact, it even survived to some extent within Christianity in the Manichaean sect. The vision of Arda Viraf (*c.*AD 300) paints a lurid picture of the Zoroastrian hell, where the adultress had to lick a red-hot stone and the miser on a rack was trampled by demons. Like Judaism, Zoroastrianism laid stress on details of behaviour, on food taboos, circumcision, menstrual purity, even the proper disposal of cut fingernails.

Mainstream Zoroastrianism lasted in Iran till destroyed by Mohammed in AD 638, but lives on in the Bombay area of India amongst the Parsees. The overall emphasis on behaviour rather than ritual is not to be underestimated. Its ethic favoured hard work, obedience, sobriety, honesty, large families, brotherly love and care for the poor; it disapproved strongly of adultery, abortion, usury, pride, gluttony and had a particular abhorrence of homosexuality.

In the sixth century BC, partly inspired by this new ethic, the Persians built up a dynamic new empire, taking over quickly and totally from Assyria. King Cyrus (*c.*580–529 BC) showed his tolerance by releasing the Jews from Babylon and restoring Jerusalem. The Persian Empire, with its highly efficient communications network and bureaucracy of satraps, was initially quite humane and noteable for its multicultural society. King Cambyses (*c.*560–522 BC) was a conqueror, sadist and heavy drinker, who executed his own brother yet installed a temple almoner to care for the poor at Sais in conquered Egypt. His successors, Darius and Xerxes, both invaded Greece and both became obsessed with conquest for its own sake, Xerxes showing distinct signs of brutality and sadism, which he combined with the role of religious reformer and fanatical destroyer of false, primitive gods. Despite the pronouncements of Zoroaster, the Persians also grew dangerously fond of alcohol.

The Greece which rose to withstand the onslaught of these two great kings was now showing the first amazing flowering of philosophical genius, the first great pioneering of rational, agnostic ethics. Lycurgus (*fl*.600 BC) may be partly the creation of Spartan folklore rather than a distinct historical figure like Hammurabi or Moses, but whether he alone or a team of men like him were the authors of the Spartan ethical system or not is immaterial. What was remarkable was the working-out of one of the most completely single-minded ethical systems ever known, an ethic which became proverbial throughout history. The Spartan code was one specially designed for unusual circumstances, the fact that the Spartiates were a small minority ruling caste stamping their authority on a much larger population of peasants or helots, on whose subservience they depended for survival. They therefore had to breed a master race, with compulsory exercises for expectant mothers, free love, postponed marriage, culling of weak babies, and the early application of practical eugenics. It was a crime to be celibate and the display of naked flesh at festivals was expected to reduce this to a minimum, but youthful homosexuality and late male marriage were acceptable. The concept carried over into their educational programme, where child-rearing was removed from the family at the age of seven; there was austere, incessant military training, encouragement to steal food as part of the cultivation of initiative and self-reliance, communal dining and shared property, discouragement of personal wealth by having an unwieldy iron coinage, and above all, immense personal disgrace for military failure or cowardice. The Spartan mother was inured not just to the exposure of sub-normal babies, and to handing her sons over to the state when they were seven, but, in due course, to prefer to get them back lying on their shields dead, rather than having left their shields behind on the battlefield. The Spartiate ethic emphasised light eating and drinking, physical fitness encouraged by communal exercise, naked athletics for both sexes to concentrate all attention on unadorned physical prowess. Courage, obedience and endurance were developed to a level of acute speciality, producing amazing military exploits such as Leonidas and his 300 at Thermopylae; but the very narrowness of the character training ultimately created its vulnerability to the temptations of comfort and wealth which military success inevitably kept bringing. In the words of Tyrtaeus, the lame Spartan poet and songwriter, the psalmist of the code of Lycurgus, and one of the first lyricists to be deliberately harnessed to inspire military morale:

Although he is under the sea he is immortal . . .

They regarded themselves as not belonging to themselves but to their country.

The Spartiate system operated efficiently for at least 300 years, monitored by one of the first secret police forces known to history, and is remarkable as one of the most extreme and complete systems of behavioural control that the world has ever known, one of a line in which the motivating force has been a belief in the real and artificially-enhanced superiority of its own people over all others. While the code of Lycurgus is not remembered as one of the great intellectual philosophies of the Greek mind, it had more practical impact than many of the others.

Not dissimilar from the Spartan ethic was that cultivated not long after Lycurgus, but quite independently, by the early Romans. With the foundation of their Republic in 510 BC, there came to prominence the same sort of belief in the suppression of the individual. Their folklore was of the first Brutus, co-founder of the Republic, who sentenced his own two sons to death for rebellion in 509 BC; or of men like Mucius Scaevola, who thrust his hand into the flames just to prove a point, or Horatius, defender of the Tiber bridge. It all added up to self-effacing, dogged patriotism like that of Sparta. Both had special appeal for the nineteenth-century British and Germans, who much admired this type of attitude with its sanctification of militarism.

In Greece, around the eighth century BC, the Homeric epics took their final form, becoming the panhellenic bible of military and most other forms of human behaviour. Not long afterwards came a further epic poem, the *Works and Days* of Hesiod, which was the first great poetic exposition of the work ethic, the moralistic tale of a brother who lost all his inheritance through extravagance and who was then urged to work his way back to solvency and respectability. Also in Hesiod we find the first spelling-out of the moral justification of the peasant being contented with his submissive, burdensome role in life. The fundamental difference between the ethic of Homer and the ethic of Hesiod was that the one exalted honour, bravery and nomadic pride, the other justice, work and the serenity of settled communities.

Religion on the whole played a less important role in Greek ethics. Pythagoras (*c*.570–515 BC), now mainly remembered as a mathematician, founded at Croton *c*.530 BC an ascetic, semi-monastic community contrasting with the proverbially-wealthy nearby town of Sybaris, which Croton defeated and destroyed. The Pythagoreans, having a mystical belief in the transmigration of dead men's souls into other future men, and in good behaviour as the key to resurrection, were regarded as too subversive and they were persecuted. Thirty-eight were burned to death in a house in Milon, then the rest were hunted down and killed.

This was just one example of the Greek attachment to some of the elements of the Middle-Eastern mystical cults connected with Orpheus of the underworld and Dionysius, the playboy son of Zeus. This involved a mixture of clean living to qualify for a good after-life and occasional indulgence in Dionysiac orgies, or Bacchanalia, in which women particularly reached states of deep hysteria and were rumoured to tear human sacrificial victims to pieces in their frenzy. This was the period of the dramatic reconstruction of the dreadful lives of Oedipus, Agamemnon and Prometheus, a period aware of the chain of unavoidable tragedy which could follow a human error of judgement. In the Dionysiac creeds the Greeks came closest to the idea of original sin. Asia Minor produced a number of cults where frenzied fanatics committed self-castration, at Ephesus for the sake of Artemis, at Heliopolis for Astarte, and in Phrygia for Attis.

Another aspect of popular Greek culture from an early period was the idealisation of athletic prowess embodied in the first Olympic Games of 776 BC. The Greeks were to retain their special reverence for physical as well as mental fitness in the years to follow. On the intellectual front this was the age of the Seven Sages, a group including the philosopher Thales (624–545 BC), whose ethical principles were embodied in the saying, 'We should never do ourselves what we blame in others.'

Another of the sages was Solon (640–560 BC), the great Athenian pioneer of government for the sake of the governed, instead of government for the sake of the state. His predecessor in Athens, Draco (fl.620 BC), had achieved a proverbial reputation for the harshness of his code, said by a contemporary to have been 'written in blood not ink'. Solon's ideal man was healthy and ready to die well. The key to virtuous behaviour was self-control; 'nothing in excess' became the popular Greek maxim and contempt for material wealth was personified by the luckless King Croesus of Lydia. The overall contribution of Solon to the birth of the concept of humane government was immensely important for the development of Athenian democracy in the next century and for the whole evolution of human rights in the European tradition. It was not insignificant that his code tolerated homosexuality as long as it was between members of the same social class, but he encouraged heterosexuality by establishing state brothels at Athens on a non-profit making basis. Contemporary with Solon was the fabulist Aesop (600–501 BC), a most important populariser of many basic ethical concepts.

By contrast, another of the Seven Sages, Periander of Corinth (c.665–585 BC), was a pioneer of the opposite ethic. Historically one of the earliest of the self-made dictators, it was he who gave the famous advice to a fellow tyrant on how to keep his rule secure by 'lopping off the tallest ears of corn', and himself sentenced 300 Corcyran captives to castration.

Lastly, in reviewing the broad spectrum of sixth-century Greek attitudes, there was that short creative and permissive period of élan on the island of Lesbos. The poetry of Alcaeus mirrored the hard-drinking military ethos while that of Sappho, the brilliant Lesbian poet, eponymous patron of a whole movement, gave sparkle to the self-indulgent crushes of the island's playgirls.

The other two great areas of philosophic creativity at this time were India and China. In India, we have already seen that there was a regular flow of new ideas. A century before Buddha, the philosopher Kapila was developing the ideas of Sankya which in due course produced the practice of yoga, a concept of abstention from the appetites and careful observation of certain rituals which led in turn to greater self-realisation. This combination of self-control and mysticism was to become a characteristic Eastern ethos, the use of calm and contemplation to achieve balanced personality.

To some extent the transition from the aggressive ethic of the *Mahabharata* to the new, more submissive ethics reflected the change from a nomadic to a farming way of life. It was the ethos of rice. The emphasis now was on pilgrimage, gifts to Brahmins, washing in the Ganges and productive marriage.

Another important Indian seer, Vardhamana Mahavira (599–527 BC), founded Jainism which also recommended austerity and self-effacement as the route to nirvana. This creed included 'the right path, right knowledge and right conduct', but above all was exceptional in its condemnation of all forms of violence to any living creature. There survives Vardhamana's splendid image of man's knowledge of life being like 'six blind men feeling different parts of an elephant and trying to describe the total'. The Jain respect for living creatures and hatred of violence were so great that they were vegetarians and disliked farming, but by default became very successful traders, a perpetual middle class who thus incurred the jealousy of other sects. The cult was to survive, and had in due course a substantial influence on the ideas of Gandhi, including as it did the idea of ritual suicide by fasting and a preference for minimal clothing, if not nudity. Even married men took oaths of marital chastity and adultery was regarded as a serious sin deserving of amputation.

The Hindus managed to combine the ideal of militant, warlike chivalry as embodied in the *Mahabharata*, India's Homeric epic, with the admirable Indian notion of 'ahimsa' or non-violence. But without question, by far the most influential of all Indian thinkers of this or any other time was Prince Gautama Sidartha or Buddha (c.563–c.480 BC), who rejected his royal inheritance and the material world in one of the most remarkable gestures ever made by a hereditary monarch. His ideas were to prove amongst the most creative of any of the world's great spiritual pioneers and Buddha's influence spread far beyond India.

After his first long period of self-examination and withdrawal, Buddha announced that the root of all evil and suffering in life was desire. This could be extirpated not by extravagant asceticism but just by ordinary self-restraint, love and compassion for all that lives: the middle road. From this emerged the essential doctrine of the middle path between excessive self-indulgence and self-torture. Buddha suggested the middle path to heaven or nirvana based on four accepted truths: pain, craving, the conquest of craving and the eightfold formula of right views, right intention, right action, right livelihood, right effort, right mind, right fitness and right concentration. The end was self-awareness and self-control. The Buddhist testament, the Suttapitaka, advised:

Let a man overcome anger by kindness, evil by good . . .

Even the desire not to crave is desire and therefore leads to unhappiness . . .

The sage governs by ridding the heart of his desires.

The result was a very compassionate creed with a great appeal which brought it numerous converts. Its metaphoric symbol was the wheel, with the rules of conduct as its spokes and truth its axle. Its ethical standards were high but it was theologically tolerant. It was perhaps a little too demanding in its behavioural requirements, which made it something of a professional's ideology, more attuned to the monastic than the ordinary life; this partly accounts for its later decline in India itself and its greater long-term success further East. For the Buddhist monk the path was, 'A razor edge over a sea of flame.' It was difficult for the ordinary observer to practise an ethic in which

Hatred is overcome by refusal to hate and not by hating . . . an enemy is like a treasure in my house since it gives me practice in changing hate to love.

In this exhortation to universal love Buddhism came very close to Christianity and was, like the latter, to win real and lasting dedication from many millions of people over a long period. While it tolerated polygamy, classical Buddhism placed strong emphasis on chastity and admired celibacy. It also forbade alcohol as a deterrent to self-control. One of its great advantages was lack of complex theology; as Buddha was not, in the normal sense, a god, Buddhism could absorb Hindu gods or (as it later proved) those of other countries. Unlike Judaism, it allowed artistic representation and therefore sponsored visual propaganda on a big scale. In India itself there appeared the Aranyakas, the forest ascetics who found their souls in the depths of the jungle and thus won release from the repetitive wheel of life.

China produced in this period two legendary great teachers: Lao Tzu (*c*.600 BC), who may or may not have been a historical personage, and Kung Fu Tzu, or Confucius (*c*.537–*c*.479 BC). Lao Tzu was the pioneer of Chinese humility: 'He who is self-exalting does not stand high.' It was he or one of his followers who reputedly wrote a treatise on the

Tao or 'The Way', which gave its name to his foundation and called on people to renounce the evil world. There were three precious things in life: compassion, economy and humility. Towns he regarded as the root of all evils. Travel was bad and unnecessary, as was technical progress. This creed was both a competitor with Buddhism and like it, in many ways, a forerunner of Christianity in its emphasis on the submissive virtues.

> The soft and the weak overcome the hard and the strong;

> A man of Tao loathes weapons . . . Heroes are to be pitied . . . Glory is built on corpses . . . Generals are murderers.

> I would return good for good. I would also return good for evil.

Taoism, with its connotations of 'turning the other cheek', was to remain a powerful and lasting ethical influence in the East for years to come. It was stoical in tone, wanted to preserve the natural, rustic community as opposed to the city, condemned wealth as a source of evil, government, education, luxury and laws: 'The more laws the more thieves.'

In due course, as it became more often the creed of rebels rather than that of the government, it grew more interested in war and associated itself with skill in the martial arts, ingenious tactics for war and breathing exercises as a method of achieving fitness. So the original loathing of weapons was diminished by circumstances.

Even greater influence was to be achieved by the rather less demanding creed of Kung Fu Tzu, or Confucius in its Latinised form. Confucius found Lao too extreme, and developed for himself guidelines for behaviour based on his experience as a politician and civil servant rather than as a priest, which he was not. As a senior (though none too successful) bureaucrat in Chung-tu, he evolved one of the most influential non-spritual ethics ever to be conceived. It was not a religion but a carefully modulated system of behaviour leading to a virtuous and contented life.

> A gentleman is unselfish, just, noble and considerate.

The five Confucian virtues were benevolence, righteousness, propriety, wisdom and trustworthiness. This was an immensely detailed behavioural control system in which key elements were unconditional obedience to elders and rulers plus a system of collective family responsibility for all actions. Above all, he emphasised the rites of etiquette, a whole vocabulary of social attitudes from the best length for blankets to the correct width of male skirts and the proper way of deliberately stammering when introduced to a stranger. Archery and other sports were used for character-building and training. It was out of this comprehensive pattern for regulation of human behaviour, based on mutual help and respect, that Kung Fu Tzu evolved one of the most complete ethical systems the world has known.

> Achieve for others what you want to achieve for yourself.

This was Confucian 'jen', a concept not all that different from Christian love.

> Among any three men one will be good enough to be a leader . . .

> The virtue of a superior man is like wind and the virtue of the people is like the grass.

Chastity was highly regarded and Confucius discouraged couples from bathing together or even sleeping in the same bed. Food and sex were the two natural human and acceptable desires. Like virtually all major Chinese philosophers, Confucius condemned aggression and despised warfare. Confucianism failed to achieve wide recognition in the teacher's own lifetime, but it was not a revolutionary new religion requiring any overt act of conversion, rather a detailed manual on the conduct of life, and in due course the Chinese politicians were to appreciate its immense value as a tool of social control.

> Lead the people by laws and regulate them by penalties and they will try to keep out of jail, but have no sense of shame. Lead them by rites and restrain them by rules of conduct and they will have a sense of shame and moreover will become good.

The other immensely influential Chinese thinker of the sixth century BC was Mo Tzu who, like Lao and Confucius, was opposed to all forms of warfare except self-defence, but had a greater respect than they did for manual labour. Yu, the great canal-digger, was his heroic model and he advocated a drive towards universal love and welfare based on a work ethic which was almost stakhanovite.

One of the remarkable features of Chinese history is the virtual absence of slavery as an institution. It simply did not suit the paddy-field economy. The political background in China under the eastern Chous was of commercial expansion, population growth and formalised warfare conducted on strict rules of chivalry with minimal casualties.

Finally, we should remember that this was the period of another of the great (though still little understood) early empires of Mexico. The Olmec Empire was based on a dynamic new religion associated with a rain god in the form of a jaguar. It produced massive twenty-ton carvings of idealised heads, beautiful jade statuettes and some of the earliest American pyramid structures. It seems to have been a culture based on trade and religion rather than on war, but as there are no written records our evidence is scant.

Overall, this 500–year period produced in at least three areas—Israel,

China and India—ethical systems which were, by most subsequent standards, of the finest quality; and in two other areas—Greece and Persia—produced ideologies which also were of substantial long-term significance. It could be judged the most creative period in moral evolution in the history of mankind. If the human species could conquer its own neuroses and live with these ideas, then it had excellent prospects for a harmonious future unspoilt by man-made disasters.

500 — 1 BC

The difference between good and evil is the
difference between order and disorder.

Plato

THIS PERIOD COVERS the classical age of Greek moral philosophy, the continued rise and fall of the Roman ethos, the remarkable work of Meng Tzu in China and the extraordinary empire of Asoka in India.

In Athens, the civilisation which produced the Parthenon and the first democracy in the world also bred a new appreciation of rational morality which reached its peak in the dialogues of Socrates, Plato and their pupils. Athens, after its citizen army had successfully withstood the Persian onslaught, was the birthplace of the idea of citizen equality, equality for everyone in the state except slaves, immigrants and, to some extent, women. In the fifty-year period following the Battle of Marathon in 490 BC, the Athenians devoted substantial intellectual energy to major developments in virtually every art form, but particularly (in our context) to the creation of a just form of democratic constitution. Like many democracies, it not only had internal faults but fell into a chauvinist imperial role which led it on into the trap of waging a war it could not win and which therefore brought about its destruction. When the Athenians massacred all the male prisoners of war on Melos in 416 BC, Thucydides thought they had reached their moral nadir.

The product of the intellectual ferment was a remarkable group of men, each pioneering substantial new ideas which are relevant to our theme. The dramatist, Aeschylus (525–456 BC), was obsessed with retribution for evil, the founder of the classic tragedy of conscience and hereditary guilt. His great rival in the Athenian theatre, Sophocles (495–405 BC), produced one of the greatest dramatic presentations of the difference between morality and the law in his *Antigone*, where the law says that traitors should be left unburied, but morality says they should be buried. His *Oedipus* series explored the classical difference between accidental and deliberate immorality, in the story of a man who kills his father without knowing it is his father and marries his mother without knowing it is his mother. The moral problem pin-pointed by Aeschylus, on the other hand, is the dilemma of Orestes and Electra, who plan the murder of their mother but justify it on the grounds of revenge for her murder of their father. In *Choephoroe*, the avenging furies

> ... sue for blood, sue and pursue for it so that at last there is payment ... so shall he pine until the grave receive him and find no grace even in the grave.

The third of the great Athenian playwrights, Euripides (480–406 BC), humanised the theatre with his understanding of the quality of human beings even at their weakest and his understanding of the feelings of both sexes. Medea, for instance, said 'I'd rather fight a battle three times than have a baby once', and in his *Hecuba* he made what was probably the first recorded attack on slavery. The overwhelming feature of Euripides' plays is compassion, sympathy for real human beings who are fine but not perfect, as Euripides (who had had two unsuccessful marriages) knew well enough. His close friend, the sophist Protagoras (480–410 BC), whose works were publicly burned because of his atheism, is said by Plato in *Theaetetus* to have pronounced:

> Man is the measure of all things; of those which are that they are; of those which are not that they are not.

In only partial contrast to the work of the three tragedians was the message of the greatest Athenian comic writer, Aristophanes (444–388 BC), who used a different dramatic technique to make very similar points. His *Lysistrata* is probably now the best known of his plays because it makes a stand for the rights of women, but it is just one example of a number of causes championed by Aristophanes, who also satirised the idea of the man-made morals of Protagoras.

In the mainstream of Greek philosophy, apart from the professional sophists like Protagoras, the most controversial mind was that of Socrates (469–399 BC).

Totally indifferent to wordly success and wealth, but more than willing to do his share as a citizen soldier, Socrates had a probing intellect which ruthlessly exposed and rejected all conventional half-truths. He pursued a clinically analytical dissection of human attitudes to arrive at knowledge which he regarded as the fundamental requirement for virtuous behaviour, but he was condemned (see Plato's *Apology*) by the courts to drink the cup of hemlock

> ... as an evil-doer and a curious person searching into things below the earth and above the heaven and making the worse appear the better cause and teaching all this to others.

Socrates' influence on his followers was to be immense in that he pioneered a rational argument for justice and good behaviour based on pure logic which, in future generations, was to be adapted alongside the spiritual cases for moral behaviour emanating from the great religions. Socrates did, it is true, speak of an inner voice warning him against bad behaviour, but the distinctive feature of his ethic was that it required no hell/heaven sanction, no theological threat, only the aesthetic appeal of a tidy mind in a tidy world, the personal calm achievable by calm treatment of other people.

Generally, virtue in fifth-century Athens meant service to the state and avoidance of all forms of excessive self-indulgence. The ideal Athenian was portrayed by Xenophon (435–354 BC), a pupil of Socrates, whose hero Isomachus was a gentleman of adequate means: he ate little and exercised a great deal, did his duties and looked after his family. Drunkenness was regarded as debasing, and in Sparta it was almost unheard of. Wives on the whole were expected to be quiet and subordinate, except for Socrates' wife who was extremely bossy; but mistresses were allowed to be more extrovert and to keep them at all was blessed by the convenient religious sanction of Aphrodite Pandemos. The upper-class whores or 'hetairai' were an important part of society.

Without question, the vice capital of ancient Greece was Corinth, where (according to Strabo) the temple sheltered 10,000 prostitutes and the tourist trade prospered. Crete and Sparta had conspicuous reputations at that time for homosexuality.

Eros was the god of pederasty, which was encouraged by the atmosphere of the gymnasia and nude wrestling. Rarely was the image of upper-class homosexuality higher, being referred to as 'Doric' with a quasi-military justification. Perhaps not surprisingly, some women found an alternative outlet in Bacchic cults, with their frenzied drug orgies helped by drink, drugs and violent sex. And perhaps the regular practice of infanticide to control the population contributed to low family morale. Deep male friendships were quite common—Alcibiades, the charismatically brilliant but amoral Athenian leader, was a noted bisexual; but it was in Thebes that male friendships were encouraged to the fullest extent as a means of achieving intense military comradeship. Plato eponymously blessed non-physical male crushes, Sophocles went further. Even Zeus was said to have had a homosexual affair with Ganymede to provide a religious sanction for the fashion and there were heroic role models like Harmodius and Cleomachus. King Agesilaus of Sparta was proud of resisting a similar temptation.

Overall, the Greek view of virtue in this period was summed up by the concept of 'kalokagathia'—beautiful and good together—the idea of good behaviour being aesthetically satisfying and bad the reverse. This, as Kenneth Clark demonstrated, was the age of the ideal human statues of Apollo and Venus, physically perfect and beautiful, well-balanced, confident in their nakedness, enjoying life. At the same time, that perceptive contemporary historian, Thucydides, was observing signs of the breakdown of the moral spirit of the Greeks. The story of the collapse of normal values on the island of Corcyra in 427 BC was a particularly bad example of the degeneration of party rivalry into sadistic anarchy. Murder, mutilation, mass suicide, Corcyra was a frightening spectre of the symptoms of 'stasis'. The other worrying example was the Athenians' execution of the prisoners of Melos in 416 BC, a shabby and unnecessary act of revenge which showed the dark side of Athenian imperialism. Similarly, the darker side of Greek behaviour was shown by the tyrants of Sicily, particularly Dionysius, who suppressed rebel towns with huge ferocity and developed the idea of forcible transfer of whole populations as a tool for social control by terror.

There spawned at this time a group of five Greek philosophies which had great, though differing, levels of influence thereafter. Plato (427–347 BC), founder of the Athenian Academy, had a profound intellectual if not practical influence. He was obsessed with improving moral attitudes, 'justice' as he called it, as a means of avoiding class warfare, which he found the most worrying feature of Greek life. To achieve his ends he suggested in the *Republic* an élitist ruling group trained to embody virtue along almost Spartan lines, 'avoiding evil as it if were a disease of the soul', with all-male friendships as a more powerful bond than heterosexual relationships.

Slightly younger than Plato was Diogenes (412–323 BC), the founder of the Cynic school, a name whose meaning has now changed. He was the prototype of those philosophers who insist on getting back to nature and ignoring man-made customs or conventions, despising all desires and ambitions. His tub home, admired (according to legend) by Alexander the Great, was just part of his aim of becoming an extreme ascetic and mendicant, a forerunner of the self-denial ethic practised by the Christian anchorites and mendicants of Islam and Buddhism.

Zeno (342–270 BC), the founder of the Stoics, followed a less extreme but still mildly ascetic path and had substantially longer-term influence. His was the doctrine of self-control and respect for other human beings, which eventually blended very happily with Christianity. He was the first great moralist to denounce slavery in an age when it received virtually universal acceptance. He taught that possessions, wives, children and honours were not the highest priority, only virtue. Life itself was merely a material advantage and his suicide at the age of seventy-two became part of the Stoic ethos. In contrast, Epicurus (341–270 BC), the founder of the rival school which took his name, did not preach quite as much self-indulgence as the name of his school suggests to a modern audience; but he was the first philosopher who said that human happiness could be the end to which all moral effort should aim. This was the source that, in later centuries, grew into the utilitarian view of human endeavour developed by Jeremy Bentham. Though Aristotle tells us of an Epicurean who wanted a throat the length of a crane's so that he could enjoy his food for longer, the real priest of self-indulgent pleasure-seeking was Aristippus, a pupil of Socrates and first of the hedonists, who pronounced that sensations are the only reality, so they ought to be enjoyed. In practice, the greatest scandals related to the worshippers of Bacchus or Dionysius, who primed themselves for their orgies with a mixture perhaps of wine and henbane. Anticyra, near Corinth, was also famous for its drug-induced trances, used amongst other things to try to cure the insane.

Last, we come to the greatest ethical theorist of the Greek world, Aristotle (384–322 BC), the supreme rationalist and founder of the Lyceum School. His *Ethics* were the calm analysis of how best the ordinary good citizen could both rule and be ruled, based not on any religious or political faction but on the traditions of the free city-state. Virtue was 'the golden mean', the half-way house between all the extremes of human reactions to situations, as for instance bravery is the mean between cowardice and foolhardiness. Aristotle's main influence came centuries later when his thought was adapted by Aquinas and the Christian theologians. Significantly, as one brought up in a city which had a slave population, Aristotle believed that slaves were naturally an inferior breed whose status need not seriously be questioned.

Aristotle's most famous pupil, and a rebellious one at that, was without question Alexander the Great (356–323 BC), King of Macedonia, important as the first militopath of the classical world and prototype of the great romantic hero and destructive superman. Model for all the conquering heroes like Napoleon, he was all the more deceptive in this guise because he died while he was still young and successful. He first made practicable the dream of world domination because he was well on the way to it when death cut him short. Admittedly, Alexander has earned some approval by spreading Greek cultural ideas (or Hellenism) through the Middle East and stirring up the ancient world over a huge area from Egypt to India. He was not a sadistic conqueror, but he and his army were prone to heavy drinking and he did destroy both Tyre and Persepolis, murdered his foster brother when he was drunk, created fun and glory for his small team of conquistadores and misery for countless others. His superhuman performance burned up the Greeks as a creative force, and at this point they begin to slide out of our narrative.

The Greek pederastic fashion extended to the whole Middle East: the Apollo statues became more effeminate, poets like Strabo of Sardis and Callimachus of Alexandria extolled permissiveness, Hermaphrodite statues appeared. In the royal house of the Ptolemies brother regularly married sister, and the poet Theocritus produced verse in favour of incest. Significantly, there was also a reaction against the violence caused by war, with Polybius emphasising the stupidity of material destruction and others, like Phylarchus, campaigning for better treatment for prisoners of war. However, on the darker side of Ptolemaic Egypt was the development of anti-Semitism; as early as the second century BC there were murmurings against the Jewish inhabitants of Alexandria, and by AD 138 pogroms had begun.

Before turning to Rome, it is worth considering briefly that remarkable off-shoot of the Phoenicians, the Empire of Carthage. This people, described by Plutarch as 'hard and sinister' do seem to have been tough and ruthlessly ambitious, even more so than those who stayed in the mother country. They worshipped Baal, and at times human sacrifice played an important part in their devotions. In the year 310 BC, at a moment of military crisis, 200 children from the noblest families were burned alive and their parents compelled to rejoice at the spectacle: 6,000 infant bodies have been discovered in sacrificial urns near Tunis. After a victory in Sicily, 3,000 prisoners were also burned alive. Crucifixion and other slow forms of execution were common. Even allowing for the fact that most written accounts came from Rome and were therefore hostile, the Carthaginians do seem to have been particularly materialistic, ruthless and unscrupulous in business, grimly determined in war, ready to sacrifice their own lives but equally happy to resort to the ritual sacrifice of their children as a means of avoiding disaster. In the end, few regretted their defeat by the Romans and the fall of Hannibal (247–182 BC), their greatest leader and an utterly ruthless commander obsessed with the defeat of Rome.

The other enemy of Rome which essentially had an earlier civilisation was the kingdom of the Etruscans, regularly referred to by the Greek and Roman writers as an especially pleasure-loving and promiscuous people. They were rich, enjoyed great luxury, liberal eating and drinking, dancing and theatre. They appear to have been tolerant of both promiscuity and homosexuality and shocked the rest of the ancient world by shaving their bodies and making love with the lights on. Like the Carthaginians, they resorted to human sacrifice when in a panic, using 300 Roman soldiers for the purpose in 356 BC, and burying two couples alive in 216 BC when the war went badly. In their favour, however, it has been pointed out that they gave greater equality to women than most people at that time in the world. In the end their independence was crushed by the more ruthless, ascetic Romans to the south.

The classical Roman ethic was developing a few years behind the Greeks. It was at once more decisive, more definite, less complicated and more politically successful. This was the great period of Republican Rome, culminating in the heroic struggle against Hannibal of Carthage which left Rome as a highly trained superpower. Their ethic was embodied in the concept of 'gravitas' or seriousness, the duty of the Roman officer class to their state, in return for which they shared in a very rewarding career structure, although at least in the Republican period it was unlikely that any one individual could hold power long enough to become a superman. Weak children could be exposed at birth, and strong ones were brought up with extreme discipline. Family life was strong under the firm control of the Roman matron, and there was a deeply ingrained respect for the household gods. The Chief Priest, the Flamen, had to be a married man. Roman women had a higher position than Greek women, with greater respect for the ideal of fidelity as embodied in ladies like Lucretia, who preferred death to dishonour, and the Vestal Virgins who symbolised respect for chastity. Wives were allowed to appear in public with their husbands, unlike Greek wives, and prostitution was discouraged by the compulsory use of hair dyes to brand the prostitutes. Also in contrast to the Greeks, the Republican Romans discouraged nudity and disapproved of homosexuality—two army officers were executed for sodomy in 300 BC.

Roman ethics were based not on any single great epic or philosophic or religious doctrine but on an armoury of folklore packed with legends of self-sacrifice, bravery and modesty. There was Regulus (*fl.*260 BC), the captured general who was returned to Rome on parole, advised against surrender, then, refusing to break his parole oath to the enemy, returned to Carthage to be tortured to death. Then there was Fabius (d.203 BC), another general exemplifying quiet determination, and Cincinnatus (519–438 BC), the successful general who withdrew to his humble farm in an act symbolic of the rejection of personal ambition. Cato the Elder (234–149 BC), the great censor, was the rigid opponent of oriental luxury and upholder of traditional Roman virtues. He urged outlawing of Bacchanalia, which, like other Greek fashions, was edging into Rome, bringing softness of mind and body which he deplored, although (according to Tacitus) he endorsed the existence of native Roman brothels. As often happens after prolonged periods of warfare, the Romans moved into a much more permissive era following the Puric wars.

Equally typical of the old school was his descendant, Cato the Younger (95–46 BC), the last-ditch opponent of Julius Caesar and of the drift towards dictatorship, the idea of one very ambitious man taking to himself the power which should have been shared between selfless equals. Though, as Lecky pointed out, he was a harsh master of his own slaves, Cato chose death after defeat in the civil war rather than live to see Caesar's gaudy success, and committed suicide after an evening spent calmly reading Plato.

It was this remarkable adherence to a solid body of traditions of service and duty, generation after generation, which formed the backbone of the Roman ethic. Even though there were numerous examples of individual corruption in Republican Rome—from Varro, the corrupt governor of Sicily, and Catiline, the playboy revolutionary, to Lucullus, the prototype self-made millionaire who once spent 200,000 sesterces on a single meal—the conformist majority kept the system going. Marcus Antonius was an alcoholic, as was the virtuous Cicero's son, who reputedly drank a gallon and a half of wine at a draft. Marcus Brutus (85–42 BC), the staunch Republican, believed (of course) in tyrannicide but was extortionate in his private business. Rome absorbed Greek luxury and love of art, yet survived. Despite the corruption of a minority of the officer class by wealth and huge power, the basic Roman ethos of military service and obedience lasted the best part of a thousand years, one of the most remarkable examples of basic strength in a system of character that the world has ever known.

The streak of cruelty that was to become an unpleasant feature of Rome under the emperors was already evident at times: the pain threshold was expected to be high. After the defeat of Cannae, four prisoners of war were buried alive in the forum while Spartacus (d.71 BC), the rebel slave leader, was crucified with his comrades by Crassus; Metellus slaughtered the people of Vacca; Sulla's rule of terror in 81 BC included a genocidal slaughter of the Samnites. Julius Caesar (100–44 BC), by his own testimony annihilated two tribes of Germans in a deliberate massacre of what he had earlier estimated at 430,000 people, and when he captured the town of Uxellodunum he cut both the hands off all the garrison. These are just two examples of his ruthlessness in Gaul. Hignett commented in the *Cambridge Ancient History*:

> The total human suffering and misery occasioned by Caesar's Gallic campaigns is terrible to contemplate and it is certain that much of it was unnecessary.

This was not just the sadism of one man, but the culmination of a period in which the Roman ethos generally had become steadily more tolerant of violence. The year 264 BC saw the first recorded organised fight between gladiators at the funeral of another Marcus Brutus, perhaps as a replacement for earlier human sacrifice. Just outside the Roman Empire, in Judaea, the Jewish leader Alexander Jannaeus crucified 800 of his compatriots on a single night, 'slew their wives and enjoyed their concubines'.

Slavery was, of course, regarded as a natural and inevitable part of the Roman way of life, and it is estimated that in the time of Julius Caesar there were two to three million slaves in Italy, about a third of the population. There was a Roman proverb which went, 'every slave is an enemy', and certainly they were not highly regarded; but at the close of the century there was an increasing tendency to free slaves, not so much for moral as for economic reasons, as supply exceeded demand.

The next period of Roman history was to witness examples of sadistic and gross behaviour amongst the emperors, but on the whole the Romans, even as conquerors, were remarkably level-headed and self-controlled, rapidly treating the conquered as equals, which partly accounts for the longevity of their empire. This was all the more remarkable given the lack of a theorist and the lack of any single strong religious theme. Cicero (106–43 BC) was the great articulator of Roman conservatism—*mos maiorum* (the customs of our ancestors)—and wrote a book about *Duty* amongst others. Also remarkable was the poet Lucretius (99–55 BC), who attacked religion as the source of all human misery and preached the calm and tranquil mind as the *summum bonum*, but this extraordinary and magnificent work must be set against the fact that Roman religion, as opposed to Roman ethics, was extremely underdeveloped and transparently lacked credibility.

In northern Europe this was the period of the La Tene Celtic civilisation, of the Druids. These remarkable priests, whose training took twenty years, could recite endless verses by heart and encouraged an ethic of extreme military bravery almost like that of the Spartans. Society was based on constant war, immortality for soldiers, sons brought up communally, torture for thieves and regular human sacrifice, often by burning in wicker cages. When the supply of criminal candidates ran out, ordinary victims were selected. The Celts also had a reputation as heavy drinkers: a contemporary described them as 'a race greedy for wine'. Herodotus also gives us a picture of the Scythians of this period or a little earlier, living in the Ukraine. They were nomads who used up a tenth of their prisoners of war for human sacrifice and blinded many of the others. Their native drink was the mildly alcoholic fermented mares' milk, kumiss, and their top virtue was without question martial bravery; they had a high regard for the concept of blood brothers, male pairs sworn to fight together to the death, even at the expense of other family loyalties. The scalp was the warrior's status symbol, and their indulgence in hemp, described by Herodotus, has been proven by the archaeological evidence of Pazyrgk. The fact that some of their leaders wore make-up and women's clothes led the Greeks to despise them somewhat and refer scathingly to 'the Scythian disease'.

Similarly, the Thracians were heavy drinkers, both men and women; they also used cannabis, particularly as an aid to courage before battle. So low was their view of human life that men played a game which involved hanging with a noose around their necks and trying to escape.

India was, of course, large enough to hold a complete tapestry of ideas and remained constantly creative. Its equivalent to the Roman military ethic was the *Mahabharata*, a Homeric saga which formed the moral framework for the Kshatrujas or knights for nearly a thousand years. The *Mahabharata*, compiled gradually in the period up to 400 BC, put across the same type of knightly ideals of honour and muscular virtue. Its heroes loved feasting, drinking and fighting; the worst sins were inhospitality, disobedience and deceit, the typical ethics of heroic ages everywhere. Duty, love and salvation were the important virtues. Chastity and modesty were highly prized. The people of Marda, accused of incest and sodomy, were described as 'filthy'. The Laws of Manu forbade incest, rape and lesbianism though male homosexuality was not quite so rigidly condemned. Like so many of the early codes, the Laws of Manu went into very great detail on the proper forms of human behaviour, including even dietary rules and domestic detail for the four castes. Overall its ethical standards were high:

> Against an angry man let him not in return show anger.

The Upanishads, other writings which continued into this period, drew attention to the spiritual side of life. Here, sin was seen to give a person the wrong kind of 'karma' so that after death there would come an unpleasant reward, but the reverse was true for a good person, especially one who had led a life of abstinence and contemplation. Certainly the Indian's faith in reincarnation enabled him to take a long view of death. When Alexander captured Agalassi, 20,000 of its inhabitants, both male and female, committed suicide in an act of 'jauhar'. Mass suicide at the mouth of the Ganges, Jain fasting, the voluntary burial alive of lepers, suttee, the masochistic processions of Jaganatha—there were numerous forms of suicide and self-sacrifice.

One of the most interesting of all Indians in moral history appeared in the shape of the Emperor Asoka (274–232 BC). This remarkable empire-builder was a convert to Buddhism who turned in later life into a kind of philosopher-king. In his earlier career as a conqueror he had killed some 100,000 Kaligas but he felt conscience-stricken, according to his autobiography, underwent a sudden conversion and became an ardent advocate of pacifism and non-violence, stating (according to A.K. Sen) that 'The only true conquest is the conquest won by piety.'

It could be argued that, having achieved his empire, Asoka could afford to preach pacifism and use religion for political ends, and this was probably true—but his achievements were genuinely remarkable. He endowed hospitals, dug wells and commissioned numerous public works for the sake of the hereafter. He used religion at two levels: the professional, ascetic level and the simplified level for the ordinary man.

> Even the little man may reap exceeding bliss hereafter by a life of service . . .

> The rite of Dharma is right treatment of slaves, respect to teachers, gentleness to living things, and liberality towards ascetics and Brahmins. Let courtesy to kinfolk prevail; this is the ancient law which leads to strength of days.

Asoka appointed moral censors and missionaries to spread and consolidate the Buddhist ethic in his empire which now covered a massive area of India. Sculpture and architecture reinforced the message. But most distinctive of all was his ethic of non-violence:

> My sons and grandsons should not regard it as their duty to conquer new conquests.

Parallel to Asokan non-violence was the cult of Bodhisattva, the King of the Apes, portrayed in sculpture as a gracious, Apollo-like god, who laid down his life for the sake of his followers and said with his last breath that it was better to save life than to take it: 'It is better to die than to kill'.

The wheel of Dharma was the image of Asokan Buddhism. The mainstream of Mahayana Buddhism now had the maturity to make its appeal to the rest of Asia, to move into Ceylon, Burma and China, later even Japan. Asokan art produced a mass of propagandising material of high calibre, with such universal figures as the Jatakas, found from Turkestan to Java, spreading the concept of Buddhist compassion in the Tipitaka:

> Who so without resentment endures reviling blows and bonds, making patience his stay and support, him I call a Brahmin.

Him I call a Brahmin from whom passion, hate, pride and hyprocisy have dropped off like mustard seed from a needle point.

As a mother protects her only son so let everyone cultivate a boundless compassion towards all that has life.

Finally in this period, we turn back to China. The Chin era (*c.*421 BC) was noted for its cruelty and ruthlessness, with military bravery its greatest virtue. Bonuses were paid to soldiers for the number of heads they cut off. The Chin, 'the ferocious beasts', have been called 'the Assyrians of East Asia'. Willingness to massacre was the sign of a good general. Reputedly 400,000 Chou prisoners of war were massacred in Ch'ang in 200 BC, and massacres by fire were not unknown. Heavy infantry battles with large casualties replaced the light cavalry skirmishes of the Chous. Punishments included amputation and castration as the means of achieving obedience. The Great Wall was erected at enormous human cost. Torture, forced labour, and conscription bolstered the empire and ruthless cruelty was regarded as a sound virtue in a good state official. The court was full of the usual oriental combination of eunuchs and concubines. When the builder of the Wall, Emperor Chin Shi Huang Ti, was buried his household were killed and buried with him and the entire funeral party were executed afterwards for the sake of secrecy. This son of heaven had built numerous palaces which 'block out the sky for three hundred li'.

In this atmosphere of adulation of centralised despotism, 460 philosophers who could not agree with each other were buried alive. Two philosophers of the Chin period did, however, have ideas that had lasting influence. The best known of these was Meng Tzu, or Mencius (372–289 BC), who constructed a highly influential theory of social layers in which the intellectuals ruled and manual work at the lower end was despised. Even more significantly, soldiers, instead of being regarded as an élite, were put below the lowest rung of civilian society. He regarded the cardinal virtues as benevolence, righteousness, moral wisdom and propriety of conduct. His whole ethic was designed for a system of enlightened despotism with a caring government and no room for war. The Book of Meng Tzu says: 'Human nature is neither good nor bad, it depends on the direction in which it is led.'

Hung Ching (298–238 BC) also supported enlightened despotism but did not share Meng Tzu's charitable view of human nature. According to him,

The nature of the man is evil—his goodness is only acquired by training. The original nature of man today is to seek for gain. If this desire is followed strife and rapacity result and courtesy dies. Man originally is envious and naturally hates others . . . hence the civilising influence of teachers and laws, the guidance of rites and justice is absolutely necessary.

China also produced its meditative philosophers like Chuang Tzu (369–286 BC), who wanted to free the individual from the bondage of earthly life—'Life passes by like a galloping horse'—and the cynical hedonist, Yang Chu.

When the Chin era gave way to the Han in 206 BC, the despotism did become more enlightened and from 121 BC Confucianism was adopted as the official state ethic of China, with the political value of well-designed imperial ritual and codes of conduct. The humane Emperor Wen (179–157 BC) abolished mutilation, and slavery declined as free labour was more cost-effective. As the Han lasted some 400 years it inevitably had its ups and downs, and (as ever in China) there tended to be the contrast between middle-class wealth and the enforced asceticism of the majority. According to the historian, Ssuma Chien (145–87 BC):

> Under lax laws the wealthy begin to use their riches for evil purposes of pride and self-aggrandisement and oppression of the weak.

Reaction came from groups like the Taoist 'Red Eyebrow', who insisted on a simple, disciplined life. So far as the role of women was concerned, the Chinese view was put by the female philosopher, Pan Chao: 'Let her love not gossip and silly laughter'.

In this period, Japan was beginning to accept influences from beyond its shores. In 2 BC, when Prince Yamato Hitu was buried a large retinue was buried alongside him. Already the concept of the human pillar, 'hito bashira', the sacrificial victim in the foundations, so common to the ancient world, had arrived here where it was to gather additional importance.

The African continent was not without its own original civilisations in this period. Most noticeable was the Empire of Kush, based at Meroe in the Sudan, which for a 500–year period up to AD 320 preserved a culture that owed something but not everything to its now decadent Egyptian neighbour. We know little of the people so far except that theirs was probably a cavalry ethic and it is recorded that salted meat was made available free in the city to any who needed it. This at least argues for their having an advanced sense of communal welfare.

In reviewing this period, the civilisation of Athens was outstanding for its intellectual probing of the deepest founts of ethical knowledge but in practical terms was much less effective in establishing long-term ethical stability than the simple conservatism of Rome. Asoka was one of the outstanding philosopher-kings of world history, and Meng Tzu one of the major, genuine moral reformers.

The classical age was remarkable in many ways as a period of great self-discipline. There were remarkable achievements, intellectual, artistic and political, based on a very precise definition of what people should expect of life, the balance of self-sacrifice and self-gratification, concentrated effort combined with delegation of menial trivia to the slaves or artisans. Time and again however, even the most talented societies showed that they could throw everything away for the sake of acquisitive obsessions.

AD 1 — 500

*The true joy of man is to be kind to them that
are of the same kind as he is himself.*
Marcus Aurelius

T HE BRIEF LIFE OF JESUS CHRIST (*c*.4 BC-AD 30) presents one of the
most remarkable examples of an ethical revolution in the whole
of human history, and the supreme exposition of the submissive,
compassionate ethic previously observed in Buddha and Lao Tzu.
Christ did not, of course, stand in isolation: he was part of a long
tradition of Jewish prophets and one of several at this time who were
putting forward radical new ideas. Most significant of these was John
the Baptist (*c*.12 BC-AD 27), who seems voluntarily to have allowed his

career to be overshadowed by that of Christ. John was, to some extent, a nationalist, preaching against ill treatment from Roman soldiers and heavy taxes, but he was also very much the champion of old-fashioned values. His most famous attack was on King Herod Antipas (d.c.AD 40) for marrying his own sister-in-law, but John also urged sharing food and clothes, contentment with one's wages and the superiority of abstemious poverty over decadent wealth. In the background too was the Essene sect, described in the Dead Sea scrolls, who swore vows of chastity, poverty, obedience and revenge against all the 'sons of darkness'. This remarkably puritanical sect foreshadowed the monastic communities of Christianity and echoed those of the Buddhists and Hindus. In addition, the Essenes had semi-sacred communal meals and indulged in communal bathing.

Christ's own achievement was the more extraordinary in that his career was so short and his resources so limited. As has frequently been said, there was nothing particularly new or unique about the ethical ideas projected in the Sermon on the Mount. What was so outstanding was the sheer intensity which Christ managed to give to the ethic of caring by the simple strength of his teaching and the barbarous death which he underwent in order to prove his point. No other moral leader in human history has combined such a laser-sharp message with such a demonstration of total commitment; it was this combination which had such amazing influence.

In the words of William Barclay, 'the basis of the Christian ethic is concern'. This was shown in particular in three of the parables; first the story of the sheep and the goats in which, at the final judgement, people are assessed on the level of concern they have shown for those in trouble. Then there was the story of Lazarus and the rich man, where the rich man is shown never even to notice that Lazarus was suffering poverty and distress; such sights meant nothing to him, so he was failing the test of concern. Third is the story of the good Samaritan, demonstrating the simple man caring more about the suffering of fellow creatures than was shown by two professional priests. Christ's exceptional talent for hard-hitting moral cameos and superb visual metaphors, like 'the camel through the eye of the needle' and the 'lilies of the field', made him a superbly effective communicator.

Blessed are the meek for they shall inherit the earth (Matthew 5.3)

was one which was to spread with remarkable rapidity through the subject peoples of the Roman Empire. Yet on occasion he was capable of violent action, such as using the knotted whip against the money-lenders, and this gave added force to his usual pacifism.

It was Paul of Tarsus (c.14–64), a Jew brought up in a Greek-speaking city with Roman citizenship, who, once converted from Phariseeism to

Christianity, was able to translate the new ethos to the wider world beyond Judaea. The message of

> Love your enemies . . . Pray for those that persecute you. (Luke 6.27)

became, in Paul, the concerted missionary effort for the virtues of love, service and forgiveness. In the Letter to the Ephesians 5, he referred to

> . . . the behaviour that belongs to the lower nature: fornication, impurity, indecency, idolatry, sorcery, quarrels, contentious temper, envy, fits of rage, selfish ambition, dissensions, party intrigue and jealousness, drinking bouts and orgies.

He conducted a mopping-up operation, taking in such fringe groups as the sect of John the Baptist's followers in Ephesus. Then, with phenomenal energy and efficiency he conducted a travelling conversion campaign round the eastern Mediterranean. The message was

> Faith, hope and love and the greatest of these is love. (Corinthians 13.1)

Love, or concern, was the element which survived through endless arguments about theology and historical detail. In the words of Bishop Robinson, looking for a way to sum up the Christian ethic in its modern setting,

> Love alone has a built-in moral compass enabling it to home-in intuitively upon the deeper needs of others . . . it is the only ethic which offers a point of constancy in a world of flux and yet remains absolutely free from and free over the changing situation.

This love was the key feature of primitive Christianity which was, in many respects, then at its best. Lecky commented

> There can be little doubt that for two hundred years after its establishment in Europe the Christian community exhibited a moral purity which while it may have been equalled has never for any long period been surpassed.

It still only suffered violence and did not inflict it. It demonstrated charity and philanthropy at their best.

But two great problems dogged the Christian ethic. The first was that it took with it the old Jewish laws, replacing their spirit without replacing them. As soon as followers started asking detailed questions on behaviour which were not answered by the Sermon on the Mount, they found that they were covered by Moses. So there was to come a time when the tail of Mosaic law began to wag the dog of Christianity. Moses had said that witches should be burned, heretics put to death, adulterers stoned, whereas the overall Christian message was much more one of forgiveness. So we find Paul saying that male and female homosexuals are worthy of death, because in an area not dealt with by

Christ he fell back on the law of Moses. During the subsequent history of Christianity there were occasions when it suited to listen to Mosaic harshness rather than Christian forgiveness. The dichotomy remained: the two Testaments survived side by side.

The other problem lay in a series of theological banana skins, the endless theoretical arguments about three Gods or one, the virgin birth, the resurrection. It was all this material for argument (avoided on the whole by Buddhism and Islam) which constantly split Christianity as it simultaneously adopted the Mosaic law of intolerance and savage punishment for all deviations. In 428, Nestor, the monk of Antioch promoted to Patriarch of Constantinople, made disagreement on the date of Easter a capital offence and denied that Mary was the mother of God, creating a new sect ripe for persecution.

The one unifying force was the immensely powerful visual image of the crucifixion. This event was reproduced in innumerable pictures and statues, once the Christians had agreed to allow such representations of the suffering and degradation of their God. The great tragedy of Christianity was that its internal differences were often cruelly allowed to be more important than its similarities.

The other concurrent tragedy was that of the Jews. The Zealots, the murderous Sicarii who dominated Palestinian resistance to Rome in the period 56–70, were possibly high on drugs and led their people to extremes which almost seemed to invite further persecution even by the relatively tolerant Romans, with the bloody seige of Jerusalem and the suicide pact before the fall of Massada.

What was remarkable about the 400–year period of the decline of the Roman Empire was not so much its superficial decadence as the stolid and efficient loyalty of the mass of its population, even of its army. Perhaps one major reason for this was the constant addition of new nations and tribes within the framework of the empire which provided new citizens not yet blasé about the fruits of empire, who appreciated as a novelty the excellent career prospects of the Roman system. On the whole the Romans for practical reasons avoided mass brutality in the treatment of their conquests and favoured absorption rather than genocide. Only a few stubborn subjects like the Jews were treated badly; according to Dio Cassius, some 580,000 Jews were massacred under the Emperor Hadrian in 132, after the rebellion of the new would-be messiah, the fire-breathing Bar Kochva, but this was not typically Roman. The Jews themselves conducted massacres in Alexandria, Cyprus and Palestine, although they were unusual in not practising infanticide.

Even when individual Roman emperors were self-indulgent egomaniacs, which many of them were, they did not destroy the system. Tiberius kept his 'sphinctrian perverts' on Capri and, according to Suetonius, erotic manuals were imported from Elephantis in Egypt, while pornographic pictures were produced by Parrhasius. Caligula (12–41) was sadistic and incestuous, Nero (37–68) effete and incompetent. Galba, Titus, Trajan, Hadrian—a succession of emperors were blatantly homosexual. Commodus (161–192), the first emperor whom Gibbon associates with the decline and fall was 'of a rude and brutish mind', spent his time in a 'seraglio of three hundred women and as many boys', and 'when the arts of seduction proved ineffectual the brutal lover had resource to violence'. Juvenal (55–140), the poetic satirist, condemned the decadence of Rome and the prevalence of unnatural vice, while another poet, Propertius (48–15 BC), indicated a fairly general view when he wrote

> May my enemies fall in love with women and my friends with boys.

Such was the respectability of the pederastic fashion. There was a temple of Isis attended by prostitutes in Roman London up to 350. The Emperor Heliogabalus, an immature sadist of transvestite sympathies, probably marked the all-time low in terms of debaucheries, even selecting his cabinet, as Gibbon delicately puts it, 'magnitudine membrorum'.

The contrast remained. At one end, this society could produce the sadistic and nymphomaniac Empress, Messalina (27–48), and the foppish smut of Ovid (43 BC–AD 17); at the other, the stoical wife who committed suicide to help her husband follow suit, saying 'It doesn't hurt, Paetus'. With unemployment in Rome often as high as thirty percent, the entertainment of the bored and blasé crowds had to become ever more outrageous. The Emperor Probus (240–282) had massacred a thousand ostriches, a thousand stags and a thousand deer: this was not untypical. Eating and drinking among the rich reached new levels of gluttony, as described in the *Trimalchio* of Petronius (32–68), with its stories of emetics to allow people to eat several feasts in succession, rampant alcoholism and orgies of increasing obscenity. Abortion and infanticide became very common to remove the results of promiscuity.

A strain of self-awareness remained in the saying, 'The baths, wine and love corrupt our bodies'; but homosexual cliques wearing green hung around the baths and homosexuals won promotion in the army. The baths became massive marble brothels, with male prostitution a source of official tax revenue until 235. According to Gibbon,

> The vile and wretched populace spent the hours of the night in obscure taverns and brothels in the over-indulgence of gross and vulgar sensuality.

The Hellenistic fashion of pederasty was widespread. The Emperor Hadrian (76–138) erected numerous idealised statues of his effete favourite, Antinous. Just as the Greeks had made Zeus indulge in homosexuality, so some of the fashionable philosophers now preached amorality. In Samaria, Simon Magus (*fl.*AD 37) pronounced that 'promiscuity is perfect love'. The gnostic sect of Nicolaitans 'abandoned themselves to pleasure like goats'.

Most of this depravity, however, remained available only to the relatively rich—the spread of corruption was slow, and there were many unaffected by it. Bribery certainly grew in prevalence as the rewards of top imperial posts became more exciting, but even amongst the Roman plutocracy there were many who maintained the old ideals of imperial service or looked to the newer philosophies. Seneca (5 BC-AD 65), originally tutor and later victim of Nero, was a Roman Stoic with ideas so close to Christianity that a legend grew up about him corresponding with his contemporary St Paul, also a victim of Nero. Seneca preached submission, patience and kindness to others, as did his fellow pagan, Philo (20 BC-AD 60), who condemned slavery more unequivocally than did the Christian Paul. The Emperor Marcus Aurelius (121–180) was one of the most ethically progressive monarchs ever known, very conscious of the Roman imperial duty of pursuing peace, justice and tolerance, although he is suspected of opium addiction. In his *Golden Book of Meditations* his advice was

> Wipe off all idle fancies, and say unto thyself incessantly: now if I will it is in my power to keep out of this my soul all wickedness, all lust and concupiscence, all trouble and confusion . . . The true joy of man is to be kind to them that are of the same kind as he is himself.

The slave-philosopher, Epictetus (50–100), also taught the Stoic virtues of self-renunciation. He advised that one could achieve calm by practising in stages, learning to tolerate first broken cups, then dead dogs, then worse calamities.

While, therefore, Rome appeared superficially all 'bread and circuses', and there was debauchery and cruelty prevalent particularly among the rich, there was also an underlying stability which kept the system going without major human disasters for another 400 years. The rights of Roman citizenship were gradually spread to all parts of the empire regardless of race, colour or creed and there was a steady reduction in slavery as it became economically less important. So far as the persecution of the early Christians was concerned, Nero did, of course, use a few hundred as torches in the arena. Men condemned to the Sardinian lead mines were branded, chained together, had their left eyes put out, a knee tendon cut and, if they were under thirty, were also castrated. The martyr Peter, amongst others under Diocletian, was whipped to the bare bones then slowly burned. The total numbers martyred by the Romans were at most a few thousand, and as Gibbon points out, this was far fewer than were burned by the Inquisition. The later Roman Empire, for all its faults, produced a remarkable number of very able self-made rulers, such as Aurelian (212–275), of whom Gibbon says

His love of justice became a wild and furious passion . . . he was a severe
reformer of a degenerate state.

Another of these was Constantine (274–337), who saw the flaming cross
in 313, made Rome a Christian state and attempted a moral reform,
clamping down on infanticide; sodomy was made illegal again in 324
and divorce was frowned upon.

Over the next few centuries Christianity was perpetually split by
theological controversy, but there were two ethical issues in particular
which taxed it: sex and violence. The sin obsession was perhaps
largely a reaction to Roman decadence. Origen (c.185–254), the great
Alexandrian scholar, was one of the first to turn St Paul's mild request
for priestly celibacy into a chronic obsession. He and the Valesii turned
themselves into eunuchs, finding celibacy 'the first and hardest of the
human virtues'. St Ambrose (339–397), 'the apostle of virginity', wrote
fifty volumes expounding his case. St Hecla was invented as the model
for female chastity.

From the year 402 all priests had to be celibate. The Church began
its attack on marriage between near relations, eventually extending the
prohibition to the unrealistic seven degrees of relationship. In 407
marriage was decreed insoluble and divorce abolished. Lea quotes the
words of Sextus Empiricus (fl.200–250) thus: 'A man who divorces his
wife admits that he is not even able to govern a woman.' The very
sanctification of celibacy as a virtue at all was obscure, but it was
perhaps a reaction against the pervading licentiousness, what Tertullian
called 'the vile ways of the Romans'. It led to the foundation of a host
of celibate institutions with potential for abuse, and to the tortuous
arguments needed to prove that Mary was a virgin mother. It also led
to the immensely influential work of St Augustine of Hippo (354–430),
a self-confessed playboy in his youth:

I wallowed in the streets of Babylon.

He thus had the personal experience to promulgate the theory of
original sin in a way which had a massive influence for centuries to
follow. Having seen the error of his ways, having stolen, drunk and
whored he pronounced:

Man is guilty in the eyes of God and deserving damnation . . . he will be
enslaved by concupiscence until liberated by God . . . desires are sin.

This made the conventionally moral man somewhat inferior, and by
Augustine's doctrine anyone whose faith and observance were not
orthodox was condemned to everlasting torment in hell. Augustine
raised the hell/heaven sanction to new strength and prominence,
making church membership rather than moral performance the criterion. Slavery did not matter to him, it was irrelevant, as was war:

since men must die anyway, these human situations mattered little. All he condemned in warfare was unnecessary cruelty. None of this is particularly surprising when one recalls that Augustine was writing at the time of the total collapse of the Roman Empire which had lasted more than 500 years. The world *did* seem impermanent. In fact, Augustine wrote his *City of God* to explain how it was possible for God to allow the sacking of 'his capital in the west, Rome' by the Goths. For Augustine's last few years his own city of Hippo was under siege by the barbarians.

Augustine understood human appetites well enough, referring to 'lust that excites the indecent parts of the body'; in 423, his sister consulted him about the problem of lesbian relationships in her nunnery and he pronounced that it should be condemned in Mosaic terms. But his sin obsession, together with his attachment of greater importance to orthodoxy than to behaviour, had huge impact on subsequent thinking in the Middle Ages, leading both to further absurdities of asceticism and to the justification of the severest penalties for theological heresy. His essential cynicism is shown by his statement that if prostitution were suppressed 'licence would corrupt society', a view that was shared later by St Thomas Aquinas. He also condemned the new puritan sect of Donatists in North Africa, who (amongst other things) made a virtue out of mass suicide. Donatus (*fl.*312), Bishop of Carthage, regarded wealth and power as sins and accepted violence as a means to achieve his ends.

St Antony of Thebes (251–356) predated Augustine and was the prototype Christian hermit who cut himself off from all forms of society and resisted all temptations, forerunner of a whole group of obsessive self-deniers and desert ascetics. In his *Life*, Athanasius says

> The enemy would suggest filthy thoughts but Antony would dissipate them with his prayers.

He flung himself into thorn bushes to dowse his desires. Antony's countryman, Pachomius (*fl.*318), founded the first monasteries and nunneries; by his death in the middle of the fourth century there were 27,000 nuns in Egypt, a major sacrifice to the ideal of chastity. Possibly the Christian priests' move towards celibacy was in reaction to the Jewish rabbis' insistence on marriage.

Flagellation and abstention from washing also became new virtues, in reaction to Roman softness and bathing. Simeon Stylites (387–454), after years in a monastic cell, emerged to live for twenty years on the top of a column fifty feet high, encouraging his sores to fester so that he would suffer more. He and other fashionably weird anchorites received huge veneration, so that extreme ascetic behaviour and mortification of the flesh became identified with great virtue and holiness. The Jacobite sect of Egypt had five annual lents, during which they gave up meat, eggs, fish, wine and oil—according to Gibbon, 'poverty as well as superstition may inspire their excessive fasts'. St Maron displayed a religious madness that was to live on in Lebanon amongst the Maronites. It was noted that the most vicious and luxurious cities, such as Antioch, produced the most anchorites. It was even regarded as worthy of special reverence for Mutius to drown his own son as an act of asceticism reflecting the virtues of Abraham. In Palestine in 450, anchorites of both sexes bathed together to prove their incorruptibility.

The monastic movement became more formalised when Benedict of Nursia (480–547) left the corruption of Rome to go and found the first Italian monastery at Monte Cassino, the beginning of the mainstream monastic tradition in the West. The sad effect of the ascetic movement was to discredit normal domestic virtues and relegate family love to a poor second place.

The other ethical problem of the early Church was violence. Inevitably, once Christianity became a state religion under Constantine it had to make decisions about war. St Ambrose (339–397) was the greatest Christian patriarch to oppose bloodshed and warfare, even in self-defence. He even condemned and excommunicated the Emperor Theodosius (346–393) for ordering the massacre of 10,000 rebels in Thessalonika in 390—the rebellion had been in support of a popular homosexual charioteer—but he also ordered the burning of synagogues. Similarly, Tertullian (160–220) had said no Christian should serve as a soldier: he also said that it was wicked and unnatural to shave. St Athanasius of Alexandria (296–373), on the other hand, was the first major Christian figure to pronounce that it was justifiable to kill enemies in war. The only significant sect of Christianity to continue non-violence at this time was the Manichaeans, founded to the east by Mani (215–274), a mystic under Zoroastrian influence. In due course the Manichaeans became heretic Christians, attracting even the youthful Augustine before facing a long period of persecution from him and others. The other significant group of Christians to be persecuted out of existence were the Jewish Christians, for whom life was made so difficult by their fellow Christians and others that they either reverted to Judaism or simply died out.

Other general effects of Christianity on the Roman Empire signalled major changes. Abortion and infanticide became less common, gladiatorial shows began to decline—they were condemned in 365, officially abolished in 404. Slavery was moderately affected with further emancipation, but the Christian ethic did not spread instantly and generally things went on much as they had before. The Emperor Constantius (317–361) commented that 'pagans grow worse as Christians', and Valentinian (419–455) still threw offenders to the wild beasts. But on the other hand, Fabiola (d.399) founded a hospital in Rome, St Basil (329–79) provided asylums for lepers and charity increased. There was, as Lecky put it, 'a movement of philanthropy which has never been paralleled'.

Theological controversy once more caused a lot of bitterness and persecution escalated. Hypatia (337–415), the female philosopher of Alexandria, was hacked to death with sea shells by a hysterical Christian mob egged on by the local bishop. In general, however, Christianity coped quite well with its huge additional access to power and massive numbers of new members.

Gibbon's implication that Christianity had contributed directly to the fall of the Roman Empire was a little unkind, but certainly it did not substantially delay the decline. What was more remarkable was its capacity to bridge the fall and project itself to the barbarian hordes who overwhelmed the empire; but it had to relax some of its standards to do so. St John Chrysostom (347–407), great attacker of the vices of the Empress Eudoxia, nevertheless justified lying, the use of pious frauds and fake relics, forged texts and spoof miracles as tools for the conversion of the barbarians. He also pronounced 'I hate the Jews.' The adaptability of the Church, its realisation of the value of music, stagecraft and art, in a recruiting drive where failure meant total extinction, was a stark example of the ends justifying the means, and to the early Christian fathers the act of theological conversion was far more important than earthly ethics. Pope Leo the Great (390–461) commended the use of torture and the execution of heretics.

Outwith the empire, to the north the German tribes had been contrasted by Tacitus with the decadence of his fellow Romans—'no one laughs there yet at vice'. Even Caesar had observed that the Germans had a high standard of pre-marital chastity and married late. They had a particularly broad view of family solidarity with a society based on kinship duties from even distant relations—this pattern was found in societies like the Lombards where German influence was strong. The Germans also had a strong military ethic where the male peer group mattered more than the family. They sometimes indulged in human sacrifice, infanticide and widow suicide. They used trial by ordeal, kept slaves and regarded murder as a relatively minor crime, but they were already developing a distinctive legal system.

The hordes who swept in from the north were not necessarily as resistant to a higher religion or to civilised behaviour, as is sometimes implied. As Gibbon pointed out, the sack of Rome by Alaric and the Goths in 410 was less vicious than the sack of the same city in 1527 by the Christian Emperor Charles V. The Goth Emperor Theoderic had as his most distinguished minister the Roman Christian bureaucrat Boethius (475–524), a fine exponent of Christian duty and an example of those who achieved the transition of Christianity from Rome to the new regimes. The Visigoths under Egida were the first active persecutors of the Jews apart from the Romans; they may have had a substantial admixture of Jewish blood themselves. They were one of the barbarian tribes to make wide use of torture and were less permissive than the Romans; they scourged prostitutes and slit their noses, while the Germans put them on ducking stools or drowned them in the mire. The least responsive tribe amongst barbarians to adopting Roman Christianity was without question the Huns, who, led by Attila 'Scourge of God' (406–443), surged to a short-lived military triumph and achieved a lasting reputation for destructiveness. Gibbon comments:

> Their sole interest was violence, raping . . . Mercy they rarely asked, rarely bestowed.

But there was no theft in their camps. Their moral code was not untypical of aggressive nomad groups who preserve good camping discipline. Of more concern was the blatant terrorism of Gaiseric the Vandal (390–477) who, as a Christian, was a ferocious persecutor of other Christians. His slaughter of orthodox Catholics in Spain amounted almost to genocide.

This was the period of the foundation in Iraq and Iran of the Sassanian Empire of Ardashir I and his feudal knights in 224. This regime was remarkable not just for its military success but for its intensive use of large numbers of prisoners of war to create one of the most complex and massive desert irrigation schemes the world has ever known. This highly industrious empire lasted nearly 400 years, requiring strong, efficient despotism to support the huge labour force needed to keep the canal network operative. By the fifth century, however, alcoholism became a serious problem in this area, and in an effort to curb it, culprits had a string put through their noses and were tied to stakes.

Hindu India seems to have gone through a permissive period at this time. In the third or fourth century, the monkish Mallanaga Vatsayana (*fl.*450) wrote his guide to physical love and sportsmanlike behaviour in the *Kama Sutra*, and Hindu culture, which had already shown signs of erotic obsessions, developed a long tradition of similar works on the more esoteric aspects of sex. Throughout this period Hinduism seems to have been quite tolerant of male homosexuality and the punishment for lesbianism was a mere beating, even if incest was a serious crime. Probably by this time the Thuggee were developing their strange cult of ritual murder as a sacrifice to Kali. They were one of those communities, rare except amongst very primitive peoples, where economic circumstances caused homicide to be accepted as part of normal morality. Because they had no land, they felt it was reasonable to prey on passing travellers who had property.

The Gupta dynasty of India (320–550) provided a remarkably humane regime, absorbing many of the non-violent aspects of both Hinduism and Buddhism, even to the extent of being largely vegetarian. Crime seems to have been almost entirely absent and creativity rich. This was the period of the fleshy sculpture school of Mathura, serving both religions and providing the three-dimensional image of serenity, the relaxed, chubby idols which were a hallmark of the Indian attitude to life for years to come. The one huge anomaly in this calm atmosphere was the continued pressing of suttee by the Brahmins, and the fact that the Gupta had a general veneration for suicide as the climax to noble careers.

For the Buddhists, this was a period of some division, with the development of the three competing 'yanas': Mahayana, Hinayana and Vajrayana. The first preached human self-reliance: life was constantly changing, as symbolised by the flame which goes on burning but is always different. The second yana, more popular in its appeal, concentrated on compassion for weak humans struggling towards nirvana and needing the moral help of selfless saints who had already qualified for entrance but who postponed their own happiness to come back and help lesser mortals; these saints were the Bodhisattvas, warm and friendly figures made real by Mathura sculptures. The third yana concentrated on the female counterpart of Buddha, with the magic formulas of the Tantra and an emphasis on sex in its rituals:

Ah the jewel is indeed the Lotus.

Around the fourth century, the new Tantra sect turned Buddhist carnal asceticism upside down, making sex and the pursuit of pleasure into an integrated part of Buddhism. Ritual wife-swapping was a feature of the Left-hand Tantra. It was as a devotee of Tantra that 800 years later Kublai Khan made Buddhism the state religion of China and himself built 'pleasure domes'. The *Diamond Vehicle* had become the Buddhist equivalent of the *Kama Sutra*, and the tradition of erotically permissive instructional literature (continued up to the Moslem puritan reaction) thereafter reappeared. In the tenth century, Tantra sex rituals were to be found in the monasteries of Java and earlier in those of Pagan, in Burma. In China itself there was a greater than normal tolerance of homosexual behaviour, both by Confucianism and the Tao; men in China held hands in public and lesbianism was also accepted.

The Emperor Wang Mang (*fl.*9–23) was probably the first recorded ruler to abolish the slave trade; his modernistic economic policies failed but his motives were sound.

In the period up to the sixth century, puritan Buddhism (without its Tantra overtones) had begun its rapid spread through China; this was the age of the building of a thousand Buddha grottoes of Tun-huang. Soon there were 40,000 Buddhist temples and vast numbers of monks and nuns. Chinese Buddhism was so full of pomp and ceremony that it was compared to Roman Catholicism in Europe.

The Confucian ethic was going through one of its more effete periods

under the openly homosexual Emperor Wu (140–187), and work-shy
mandarins sported high-heeled shoes, rouged cheeks and immensely
long finger nails as symbols of their remoteness from ordinary toil,
while knightly outlaws roamed 'the Water Margins' providing the
epic raw material for China's equivalents of King Arthur and Robin
Hood. It was probably only the acute demoralisation of the Chinese
in this troubled period which led them to welcome such an ascetic
faith as non-Tantric Buddhism: by 405, around ninety percent of the
northern Chinese were Buddhist. In eastern China, a peasant revolt
inspired by a Taoist magician under the heading *Tai Ping Tao* ('Way
of the Peace', but more popularly known as 'the Yellow Turbans') led
to the final collapse of the Han dynasty in 220, but did not survive
much longer as a movement. The natural anarchy of the Tao had more
appeal now than the ostentatious discipline of current Confucianism.
The *Book of Yang Chu* encouraged a new hedonism. 'The Seven Sages
of the Bamboo Grove' preached the use of alcohol and even nudism,
though their eccentricities were exaggerated by their enemies. Games
were popular but sport frowned upon. Muscles were regarded as ugly
for both sexes, and the anti-military ethic persisted. This did not make
it any easier for them to defend themselves against tribes like the Huns,
who attacked with sadistic ferocity in 221 and in the end only failed to
make a permanent conquest because they quarrelled so much amongst
themselves.

In Japan, the Yamamoto ruling aristocracy were beginning by this
time to develop the ethics of 'Shinto', or the teaching of the gods,
ultimately to become a tool of nationalism and militarism. With characteristic Japanese adaptability, they absorbed from China into native
Shinto the imported Confucian virtues of sincerity, uprightness and filial piety, and later from the same source borrowed Buddhist fatalism.

At this time in South America there emerged at least three new
pyramid-building societies. From around the end of the first century
AD came the great pyramids of Teotihuacan in Mexico and the temples
to fierce merciless gods like Quetzalcoatl, the feathered serpent. There
were large cities with massive labour forces deployed on huge religious
construction projects. Further south *c.*300 came the first Maya pyramids,
part of a bizarre, strongly religious empire but one that was apparently
free from war. Adultery and bigamy were crimes except for nobles and
the Maya were a very appearance-conscious people. They regarded a
squint as a sign of beauty and used balks of wood to encourage it; they
also artificially spread the skull, pierced noses and ears, used body paint
and other beauty aids.

Lastly, at about the same time, we find the Mochica culture in Peru.
Some of their pyramids had as many as 130,000,000 bricks and were the
site of human sacrifices of prisoners of war and young children. This
was an apparently warlike and cruel nation. Criminals had their noses

or upper lips cut off for relatively minor offences, and were flayed or stoned to death for major ones. There are signs that their society was permissive, as shown by the erotic obsessions of their pottery designs, and the indulgent over-dressing of their men.

North America *c.*200 saw the birth of what came to be regarded as a minor human vice, the smoking of tobacco, but its effects on health in that period were probably irrelevant amongst peoples who had a very short life-expectancy anyway.

The birth and expansion of Christianity, and how it survived the shattering collapse of the Roman Empire, was the outstanding event of this period. The Gupta Empire in India, and that of the Maya in South America, provided examples of success without war, whereas Japan and Peru offered two new militaristic ethics. It is easy to see in retrospect that the career of Jesus Christ provided the most exciting shock treatment to the ethical posture of mankind it was ever to receive; yet within a few hundred years, due to the neurotic imbalance of the species, the ill-effects of the treatment were arguably more powerful than the good. The later Roman Empire introduced one other new corporate sin to history—the large-scale destruction of the environment, as vast tracts of North Africa were over-farmed to the point where good land was reduced to desert.

500 — 1000

*These are the loveless days of the
world's last age.*

Alcuin

THIS PERIOD COVERS the Dark Ages of Europe, when Roman
Catholicism survived the death of the Roman Empire to take
over the northern hordes; it covers the remarkable new flowering
of Byzantium, the birth and rapid expansion of Islam and the continued
expansion of Buddhism (including Zen) in the Far East.

Of substantial importance in the history of law, if not morality, was
the career of the Emperor Justinian (482–565), who not only substantially
restored the Roman Empire from his base in Constantinople, but

organised the huge task of codifying all Roman law. There was an element of rational humanity in his code, a reduction in the penal use of mutilation, a temporary amnesty for homosexuals to encourage them to confess, a war on vice and an attempt to curb the use of foul language. The ethic of Byzantium was to last for 1,100 years. Beneath the gloss, however, there remained a sordid streak. The Empress Theodora (500–547), whose career had begun, according to Procopius (499–565), in the most inelegant type of night-club did turn out to have a heart nearly of gold, but women like Antonina, wife of the general Belisarius (505–565), were both promiscuous and sadistic. Constantinople was plagued by the extreme and regular violence of the rival supporters' clubs of the chariot-racing factions, the Blues and the Greens. These gangs of thugs, with their special shirts and unique haircuts, shaven at the front, long at the back, roamed the streets at night looking for victims to rob and murder. It was the classic frustrated youth syndrome in its most extreme form, and Lecky rather unkindly refers to Byzantium as 'the most thoroughly base and despicable civilisation'.

Justinian was also guilty of major persecutions—as Gibbon put it, 'in the creed of Justinian the guilt of murder could not be applied to the slaughter of unbelievers'. Thrace was depopulated, 65,000 exterminated; the genocide of Armenians, probably second only to the Jews as the world's most persecuted nation, was begun, and the Samaritans, another troubled minority nation, were sold as slaves. In Constantinople itself, 35,000 inhabitants were massacred after a period of civil disobedience.

In the West we saw how Boethius was the archetypal Christian servant and teacher of a Gothic ruler. It was appreciation by the new breed of conquerors of the value of Christianity as a unifying and civilising force which greatly helped its adoption during the Dark Age period and then led to its expansion far beyond the frontiers of the old Roman Empire. It was, in fact, the harnessing of barbarian military energy to the cause of the expansion of Christianity.

The barbarian Lombards in northern Italy surprised their subjects with their humanity. They had a gentle and generous disposition—'Their laws', wrote Gibbon, 'have been esteemed the least imperfect of the barbaric codes', and produced 'fair intervals of peace, order and domestic happiness'. Their family ethic exhibited the Germanic view of strong kinship. The reduction of communal objectives put heavy emphasis on the narrow family unit as the basis of society.

The Franks became Christian after their king, Clovis (465–511), married the saintly Clotilde and needed the help of her God in a tough battle against the Germans. Pope Gregory I the Great (560–604) made a unique and massive contribution to the consolidation of Western Catholicism, organising Augustine of Canterbury and the re-conversion of heretical Spain, harnessing music and art to aid the propaganda drive to the illiterate, formalising the ritual and tidying up the structure of the Church. He was also the author of a moral treatise based on the book of Job, and the proponent of more humane treatment of Jews, slaves and heathens. In both religious and humanitarian terms, his was one of the greatest and least tarnished achievements of medieval Christianity.

In Ireland, St Patrick (385–461) had to preach against the ritual infanticide of the pagans, and the Irish St Columba (521–597) may even have allowed St Oran to let himself be buried as a sacrificial victim in the foundations of Iona Abbey. The early Irish had a reputation for promiscuity, with the saucy legends of Queen Medb and the outrageous queen of Ulster who greeted Cuchulain with 610 ladies stripped for action. Ireland in the seventh century exhibited extraordinary spiritual energy.

The English-born St Boniface (680–755) was the pioneering missionary in Germany, where he managed the mass conversion of various tribes, but he suffered from the sad congenital affliction of many dedicated medieval Christians of being more worried by heretical Christian sects than by pagans. He did not hesitate to use force against both, ordering the flogging of a group of out-of-line bishops, and was killed during an armed expedition to convert the Frisians. He attempted the persecution of the humble monk Aldebert, who dared to set himself up as a living saint or messiah who could perform miracles. Similarly, Charlemagne (742–814), the Frankish 'Iron King' and the first Holy Roman Emperor, threatened execution for all Germans, as he conquered them, who would not accept immediate baptism. The thirty-year period of his rule showed the value of Christianity as a unifying tool for an empire. Frankish society, however, demonstrated as well as any the very slow real penetration of Christian ethics amongst peoples who were converted virtually overnight and without consultation by their rulers. The Merovingian Franks had been polygamous, promiscuous and violent. They were guilty of a number of massacres of both Saxons and their own people. Mass deportation was another of their less pleasant tools of social control, in the tradition of the Assyrians. Frankish society went through a self-indulgent and permissive period; their laws, for instance, show that female drunkenness was very common with 'goblets of pure thick wine', homosexuality was not uncommon, adultery and brutality fairly normal. To be a bastard was something of an honour, as shown by Charles Martel, 'the Hammer' (688–741), and the great paladin, Roland. Alcuin (d.778), commented:

> These are the loveless days of the world's last age . . . the land is absolutely submerged under a flood of fornication, adultery and incest.

We hear of 'sexual licence in all ranks of Carolingian society', and Charlemagne initiated laws to clamp down on prostitution. Adult nude baptism was abolished. As a concession to Christian mores he gave up 'raw meat'—prostitutes—for Lent and had them pelted through the streets for entertainment. In 820, Louis the Pious felt obliged to conduct a campaign against vice in Aix. Abortion potions and infanticide were quite common, though birth control was already officially frowned upon by the Church on the strength of texts such as 'Onan was struck down by God for spilling seed' (Genesis 38). New penalties were introduced to discourage abortion and infanticide. The abandonment of babies was common, and in 787 one of the earliest known orphanages was founded in Milan.

The law of marriage was strict, on the German model. Asceticism was becoming more popular. St Giles (d.c.700), the hermit of Arles, was renowned for his holiness. He prayed for his wounds not to heal so that he could demonstrate long-suffering, and recommended having a woman put into one's bed to be left untouched as the real test of chastity. In the ninth century, the historian Agnellus of Ravenna (c.800–850) opposed clerical marriage on the grounds that women were 'like Jezebel in their falseness and like Delilah in their disloyalty'.

Every May was time to start a new season of war, which involved systematic looting, scorched-earth tactics and massacres of the enemy. The Germanic habit of 'faida' or vendetta was strong, and the most important of all virtues in the ninth century was fidelity, the sole bond of the new kingdoms. So Lothair's 'Field of Lies' in 883 symbolised the ultimate evil in breach of trust. Burning and breaking on the wheel were standard instruments of persuasion.

The Church and monastic life were at a lowish ebb, but an interesting new element in the social mix were the Germanic 'geldonias' or guilds, craft associations for self-help and mutual protection which took on a humanitarian role. For instance, in Herstel in 779 guilds formed groups to help the victims of fires and shipwrecks. The guilds were attacked in due course by the Church for encouraging too many drinking bouts and self-indulgent socialising; Bishop Hincmar of Rheims in 858 was one strong critic, but what came to be the Masonic route to welfare economy had begun.

One other virtue of Carolingian society was its understanding and tolerance for the Jews, perhaps, as some have suggested, because of the fraternal, Old Testament quality of Frankish attitudes on most topics.

The Anglo-Saxons were themselves a people with no little measure of moral creativity. The epic poems of Beowulf (c.750) put across a code of honour even to death reminiscent of Homer or some of the other great heroic sagas. Caedmon, the monk of Whitby who died c.680, had been a religious propagandising poet of some merit, and the Abbot Aelfric (995–1020) pronounced his eighty homilies in attractive rhythmic prose. The Saxons' worst vice seems to have been their addiction to alcohol, against which Archbishop Theodore of Canterbury (602–690) raised a campaign in the eighth century. The most serious Saxon sin was disloyalty to king or lord; next came cattle-stealing. Murder had to be paid for in the vendetta, but homicide on behalf of one's master was not a serious offence. In pre-Christian times they had allowed marriage to close relations; men could even marry their stepmothers, so the early bishops fulminated against incest. Divorce was easy in Saxon law and the rights of women remarkably respected. St Hilda (614–680) was the great Saxon protagonist of chastity, peace and charity. King Alfred (849-899) was the detailed legislator who set about tidying up lay society.

Almost as important in shaping the medieval ethos as the slow burgeoning of Christianity amongst its new, northern converts was the switch of emphasis to fighting on horseback. It had been Charlemagne's grandfather, the bastard Charles Martel (688–741) who, in his desperate fight against the Saracens at Poitiers, saw the need for a cavalry élite, a concept which in due course governed the shape of medieval society. The cavalry élite had to be men of leisure, wealth and total loyalty, so from these requirements there grew a complete panoply of feudal oaths, land grants, status and mythology to harness the power for the new states of Europe. Within a few years we hear of the first dubbings of knights, and by the tenth century the ideal of knighthood and the practice of dubbing were universal throughout Western Europe. The ceremony of dubbing, preceded by confession, fasts and vigils became not just a bond of loyalty between knight and overlord, but was sanctified by the blessing of the Church. The ceremony was referred to as an 'ordination', controlled by the Orderie de Chevalerie.

To confirm the code, to control the awesome power in the hands of armed knights, there developed the new folklore which was to change the meaning of chivalry from mere horsemanship to an ideal of knightly behaviour. In due course the tales were to be formalised in great epics like the *Morte d'Arthur* and the *Chanson de Roland*. There were also the tales of the bad knights, like Raoul de Cambrai, described in 943 as a hooligan who murdered nuns, burned churches, killed the old and the sick. In England there was Mandeville of Ely, a Norman knight who used torture, hung peasants by their thumbs or put them in spiked collars. Violence was endemic at all levels, and treatment of serfs was unduly harsh. These were the sort of knights who drank a gallon of wine and ate a haunch of boar at a sitting. The challenge of the Christian states was to convert crude cavalry into less crude chivalry. One major step forward was taken with the Court of Bishops in 981, called to put a limit on violence in war, followed by the Le Puy 'Peace of God'. The Pact of Beauvais of 1023 also restrained violence against churches, peasants and livestock:

To kill a Christian is to spill Christ's blood.

The next stage was to be the harnessing of militarism to the Church, which was achieved after this period by Popes Gregory VII and Urban

II with the concept of the crusades. St George (d.303) became the new, pure hero-figure, the knight in shining armour.

The Dark Ages was also a period in Western Europe during which the law itself was both crude and brutal, the era of trial by ordeal. The Anglo-Saxon law of ordeal was formulated by King Athelstan (895–939). Athelstan's criminal code included stoning for thieving slaves and burning for their female counterparts, a punishment given more propaganda impact by asking eighty other female slaves each to provide one piece of wood for the pyre. Mutilation was recommended as more lenient than death by Archbishop Wulfstan. Queen Emma, mother of Edward the Confessor, was accused by her husband Ethelred the Unready (968–1016) of conducting an illicit affair with a bishop, and was asked to walk over nine red-hot ploughshares to prove her innocence. This she did, and her husband was whipped for his suspicions. Ethelred was also regarded as having made a tactical and ethical blunder with his massacre of defenceless Danes on St Bruce's Day, 1002. When William the Conqueror took over England in 1066, his code of punishment included castration for men caught committing adultery.

Parallel to the slow drive towards crude moral standards amongst the lay population was the problem of slipping standards amongst the clergy. Despite regular papal reform, standards of clerical training were inevitably still low and the monastic movement prone to constant problems of the flesh. Pope Gregory III (680–741) imposed ten-year penances for sodomite priests, and throughout the Dark Ages homosexuality proved worrysome to lay and religious rulers. In the Justinian period an earthquake was blamed on sodomy and burning recommended as the right punishment; the Visigoths believed castration was appropriate. The first major clean-up of clerical chastity and monastic purity began with the new foundation of Cluny in Burgundy in 910, the start of an important new chapter in medieval monasticism. Abbot Odo (d.943), who began Cluny's great expansion, practised 'incessant alms-giving' to the alarm of his colleagues. He believed in the 'scouring of floors and the caring of children'. The great achievement of the Cluniac ethic was not just Church reform but the first real effort to mitigate the hardships caused by uncontrolled warfare, the imposition of 'The Peace of God', and the ruling of a Burgundian court in 959 that 'robbers of the poor' and other despoilers should be excommunicated.

Rome itself set a poor example, many of the popes being corrupt tools of political factions. In 769, Pope Stephen IV used torture and blinding (on the Byzantine model) to impose his will. In 960, Pope John XII turned the Cathedral of St John Lateran into a brothel. In the early tenth century the Theophylactic dynasty of popes, Sergius III, with his sons and grandson, condoned corruption, promiscuity and violence so as to make these regular features of Roman society for several hundred years, except for the brief interludes of strong, reforming popes. In 925, the Council of Spoleto went so far as to prohibit priests from marrying twice, thus tacitly accepting the fact that they were tending to marry at least once.

No sooner was Europe beginning to show signs of having more or less absorbed the Germanic hordes into the Roman-Christian tradition than a new horde appeared. The Vikings of the early eighth century took on the brutal and destructive role associated with the Huns 400 years earlier. They did, of course, have their own native and very strong military ethic based above all on the promise of Valhalla to reward courageous warriors. Bravery, loyalty and honour were the virtues of the sagas. The Vikings were without question ruthlessly violent and killed all in their path. Human victims were used as rollers to launch boats and propitiate the sea gods, while other forms of human sacrifice persisted. Wives were still sometimes buried alive with princes, and, possibly with the help of fly agaric mushrooms, hypnotic trances were induced to create shocktroops immune to pain in the remarkable, drug-induced berserk (bear shirt?) rituals. In an often intensely masculine atmosphere homosexuality was perhaps more lightly regarded than elsewhere. A not untypical Viking was King Knut (994–1035), who cut off the hands, ears and noses of English hostages, a habit of mutilation which was to be preserved by the Viking settlers known as the Normans. In 885, the Normans massacred the peoples of Paris, and (later) William the Conqueror was a regular user of mutilation. Knut's followers hailed his delight that 'the blazing dewellings of men lit thy approach'. He introduced laws against fornication, though adultery had to be condoned because of his own private tastes. Broadly speaking, the Vikings had a quite strong family ethic, which disapproved of adultery apart from provision for a few concubines, but allowed divorce even when it was the woman who took the initiative.

A collection of verse proverbs, the *Havamal*, formed a kind of Norse bible, covering a wide range of moral precepts:

> Glad and blithe should every man be till his death day cometh.

There was also an emphasis on the Norse golden mean:

> No man is so good as to be blameless nor so bad as to be worth nothing.

> The good name never dies of one who has done well.

The Vikings were, to some extent, pioneers of the idea of freedom, being most reluctant to accept central authority and were great asserters of their rights to justice. They did, of course, believe in enjoying themselves, with fighting a favourite sport which dead warriors could look forward to continuing in Valhalla. They were very conscious of their appearance and prided themselves on their well-combed, well-washed shoulder-length hair; they were great feasters and drinkers, immensely energetic explorers. Their ideals were epitomised in the valiant, heavy-drinking Thor, the permissive wind god Vaya, and the virility symbol, Frey. According to the Arab traveller Ibn Faddan, Viking funerals in Russia were preceded by mass rape of a drugged slave girl who was then killed to burn on her master's floating pyre. Human sacrifice and religious prostitution were not uncommon, but the overwhelming impression the Vikings left is one of sheer energy. A great deal of their wealth came from plunder and their very active exploitation of the slave trade.

The Slavs were still in their Dark Age. According to another Arab traveller, Ibrahim Ibn Jakub, in 965 they were 'violent and inclined to aggression'. War for them, as for the Magyars, was a natural way of life; however, they were more generally regarded as non-aggressive and non-military, so that large numbers of them were captured and enslaved, giving the word 'slave' to the world's language system. Though they did not have a high regard for pre-marital chastity, Boniface observed that marriage break-up and adultery were extremely rare among them. Adam of Bremen commented that they were kindly and not malignant or villainous. This rather pleasant people consequently became the chief victim race of the Middle Ages and suffered for centuries. There was estimated to be ninety percent mortality when they were transported to the Mediterranean.

The most violent of the Eastern European peoples at this time were the Magyars or Hungarians: as Gibbon put it, 'both sexes were equally inaccessible to pity' when they pillaged half of northern Europe in 889.

By far the greatest ethical revolution in this period took place in Arabia. When Mohammed (570–632) withdrew from Mecca in 622, it was a reaction against the complacent and commercial materialism of the city created by the wealth of the caravan trade. His doctrine was therefore anti-materialistic and appealed in the first instance, like Christianity, mainly to slaves and the poor. He insisted on submission to the will of God (Islam) and the five daily prayers, fasting during Ramadan, abstinence from wine, gambling and usury. He violently protested against the Arab custom of female infanticide. Mohammed's basic programme of regular prayer, alms-giving and fasting was to bring about a tranquil, happy attitude of mind. The teetotalism provided a permanently sober army. There was little complex theology likely to cause the endless bitter heresies which dogged Christianity, because Mohammed never claimed to be more than the apostle of Allah 'the compassionate and merciful', and there was little of Christianity's obsession with celibacy:

Two prostrations of a married man are worth seventy of a celibate.

It was a strong family faith and had, in the 'umma', the extended family unit. The position of women was, as in most societies of that time, subordinate. The Koran told men 'women are your tillage' and a Moslem was allowed up to four wives so long as he could treat all fairly. He could also beat his wives, divorce them at will and use his female slaves as concubines, but he was not allowed to pander them and prostitution was regarded as despicable. Women were actually regarded as inferior; the familiar parable was the story of Potiphar's wife—'Your guile is great indeed.' But adultery and promiscuity were crimes punishable by stoning to death. Homosexuality was a severe sin, and nudity was not allowed. Islam remained the most prudish of all faiths, though it is one of the few which offers posthumous sex in heaven. Travellers, particularly pilgrims, were allowed some dispensation: even Shiite pilgrims could take a temporary wife in Mecca, while from Turkestan to Morocco it was fairly normal practice for travellers to be offered the hospitality of a night in bed with the wife of the house where they were sheltered. Early Islam was strong on original sin, with an inevitable hell where sinners were fed on boiling water, but Moslem theology fairly soon gave men more responsibility for their own moral behaviour. Mohammed had a basic trust in human conscience—'My community will not agree on what is wrong'—and an allied conservatism which said that even minor regulations should not be changed without a large public majority. He tolerated polygamy, slavery and violence, and at Quraya executed the entire male population of 800 Jews when they refused to be converted. He encouraged the old idea of 'razzia' or plunder, not necessarily accompanied by violence or bloodshed, and pronounced 'Infidelity is more serious than killing', so conversion by force was justified. The Koran teaches that

Paradise is under the shadow of swords.

This meant that his followers could and should attack all non-Moslems, kill, enslave or tax all who refused to be converted. This became the doctrine of 'jihad' or holy war, nearly the sixth pillar of wisdom, and was to be largely responsible for the very rapid spread of Islam:

The sword is the key to heaven and hell.

The Arabs were given remarkable self-confidence and a sense of unified purpose held together partly by the custom of the 'Haj' or pilgrimage to Mecca, like 'Kumah Mela', the great annual Hindu bathe in the Ganges. So the Arab Islamic expansion was more speedy and permanent even than Christianity's—almost the whole of North Africa was wrested from Christianity—and freer from internal persecutions.

Like all religions, there was built into Islam the potential for splinter movements: the Sunni-Shiite divergence started early on. There was the famous massacre of the Shiites by the Sunni in 680, which only the prophet's grandson survived, but the differences were much less damaging than those within Christianity. As the successful Arab despots enjoyed the huge material gains from their conquests, there was inevitably soon a movement amongst the less fortunate to revive the ascetic standards of the original faith and dwell on the fierce punishments which the Koran allotted to those who took too much enjoyment from their lives on this earth. The Shiites, as the non-establishment division of Islam, rejecting the worldly success of the caliphate, chose a somewhat more puritanical path, and with the exception of their great love of Fatima, the prophet's daughter, were particularly hard on the female sex.

At an even more puritanical level, Abu Hashim of Kufa (*c.*720–790) founded a Sufi (hair shirt) monastery in Palestine and preached renunciation of the material life: the Sufi Hallaj was crucified in 922, asking for the forgiveness of his executors as he died. The Sufi virtues were abstinence, poverty, patience and submission, although their imagery was from the world of wine and love. They ignored conventional evil as irrelevant compared with self-realisation, and there developed from this a number of eccentric sub-groups. They produced a long line of female mystics, and the Mawlawis (or dancing dervishes) founded by Jalal ud Din an Rum had to labour without ceasing for a thousand and one days as novitiates—one day's failure meant expulsion. There were also the Rifais (howling dervishes), who ate burning coals or handled red-hot iron, and the Marabout desert dervishes of Algeria. But all of these examples of frontier fanaticism did not weaken the overall impact of Islam, which swept away North-African Christianity almost without trace. More typical of the central core was a man like Caliph Abonbehr who enjoined his subjects to

> Be just. The unjust never prosper; be merciful, valiant, keep your word even to your enemies.

The Ummayad caliphate was kept ethically in line from 690 to 740 by the fanatical sect of the Kharijites. Haroun al Rashid (763–809), hero-patron of *The Arabian Nights*, was beginning to show signs of hedonistic self-indulgence and moody violence as shown by his massacre of the Barmicide clan. The wealth of Baghdad encouraged permissiveness, and the bored eunuchs of the harem did their best to entertain the equally bored concubines. One caliph had 7,000 eunuchs, half of them black, half white. The ethic of razzia unfortunately adapted well to naval piracy and the slave trade, but the overall impetus of Islam remained strong and has remained remarkably virile right up to the present day.

For a long time the neighbouring state which withstood Islam most successfully was the Empire of Byzantium. This state had preserved its slightly oriental version of the Roman-Christian ethic almost intact, as its capital had not been overrun by the northern hordes. The Emperor Justinian had organised the magnificent codification of Roman law and presided over a highly creative twilight of Roman culture. New creative energy and ethical fervour came in the period of the Isaurian dynasty of emperors, the iconoclasts or image-breakers. Unlike Pope Gregory in the West, they believed it was heresy to illustrate Christianity with art, so the Cathedral of Santa Sophia was denuded. Finlay, the great nineteenth-century historian of Byzantium, was deeply impressed by the moral qualities of the Isaurian period (717–820).

> The moral condition of the people of the Byzantine Empire under the iconoclast emperors was superior to that of any equal number of the human race in any preceding period. The superior moral tone of the Byzantine civilisation was one of the causes of its long duration.

The diminution of slavery continued. The abbot Theodore pronounced that 'A monk should not have a slave for a slave is a man made in the image of God,' and society was relatively both peaceful and stable.

The tone changed, however, to one of violence and decadence. In 718, Callinicus invented Greek fire, probably the most vicious weapon of the Middle Ages. The Emperor Michael the Drunkard (839–67) was spoiled by his mother, the regent Theodora, and his reign witnessed a period of debauchery in reaction to the long-strict period of religious controversy between the iconoclasts and the image-worshippers. Finlay was shocked by

> ... the immorality which invaded all ranks of society. The power of conscience became dormant and vice became the fashion of the day.

The alcoholic emperor, a keen charioteer, sang hymns to debauchery. Two senior rebels had their eyes put out and their right hands cut off as punishment, as recorded in the *Life of Belisarius*, and a wrestler, Basil, was promoted to joint-emperor. In 950, when Basil II defeated the Bulgarians he blinded 15,000 prisoners of war. The Paulican Christian heretics were persecuted; 10,000 were executed and many more escaped to the safety of the tolerant caliphate next door. Others in this second great age of Eastern monasticism subjected themselves to the rigid asceticism of the new mountain-top hermitages on Athos—the great Lavra, founded by St Athanasius in 963, held as many as a thousand monks—and the rock-hewn cells in Cappadocia.

In India, where Islam did not really penetrate until after the end of this period, the twin strains of permissiveness and asceticism each strove for prominence in both the Hindu and Buddhist cultures. Shankara (780–820) was the great ascetic thinker and monastic developer of Hinduism, setting up large monasteries devoted to meditation and worship as tranquilising activities in a life which he regarded as a mere illusion. Only the élite who had the capacity to despise and foreswear all earthly happiness could reach to 'jnana', the ultimate wisdom. On the other hand, the Brahmavairasta Puran in the tenth century promoted the erotic cult of Krishna and Radha.

Various cults eventually known as Bhakti emphasised love of God and human inadequacy. A simpler, vernacular form of Hinduism appealed to the artisan classes; they even had a female saint, Amdal. At the upper Aryan end of society, where women were less important, this period saw further early examples of suttee.

Buddhism was beginning to gather the complexities around it which were to lead to its decline in India, but meanwhile both it and Hinduism inspired the decoration of amazing cave temples with didactic sculpture. The humanitarian influence of Buddhism was shown by the development of hospitals and inns for pilgrims.

In China too the dual strain was evident during the unsettled sixth century. Chi-hi (538–597) founded the meditational T'ien-tai movement, and avoided the sordid brutality of everyday life. As one self-made emperor after another struggled for power, Yang Chien invented mass propaganda in 589, when he put out 300,000 leaflets attacking his predecessor. In the seventh century Tsung Hsuan wrote *The Art of Love*, the Chinese equivalent of *Kama Sutra*, and for several centuries the Taoists had sponsored public sex rituals and pornographic ballets. They preached the image of the jade stalk and the cinnabar stone, that celibacy was unhealthy, that the Yin and Yang of the two sexes should be given every reasonable encouragement:

The Yellow Emperor learned the art of the bedchamber from the Dark Girl.

Emperors like Yang Ti (*c*.600) bled the country dry with their huge extravagances and gross abuse of forced labour. Work on the new capital, Logang, involved 2,000,000 slaves, and 5,000,000 were flogged to dig new canals; the rebuilding of the Great Wall alone cost 600,000 lives and 30,000 soldiers were reputedly executed for losing a war against the Koreans. In reaction, the new Tang dynasty was much less harsh. Hilda Hookham tells us that the first emperor, Tang Ta (600–649), announced:

An emperor collecting too heavy taxes is like a man eating his own flesh.

Hsuan Tsung even tried to abolish capital punishment and the Tang produced one of the longest periods of peace in a large area in the whole of history, a period of harmony and content. The permissive streak also continued under the Tang, however, and the delightful lyric poetry of the period was full of wine and love. Li Po (701–62) was a popular but alcoholic poet, one of a series of hedonist writers at the time of the permissive Empress Wu. Female necklines plunged and homosexuality seems to have been condoned. On the other hand, this was a period of Confucian discipline combined with Buddhist expansion and creativity in China, a period of exquisite pagoda-building. One of the earliest examples of printing was the ninth-century *Diamond Sutra*. Buddhism was persecuted by the Tang in its declining period, with the destruction in 845 of 4,500 Buddhist temples by Wu Tsung, and 250,000 Buddhist monks were expelled.

In 520, an Indian Buddhist philosopher, Bodhidharma, had introduced to China a new sect. Hui Nang (660–713) developed this new puritan movement, called Chan in China or Zen in Japan, which rejected theories and sermons, preferring to suggest tough self-contemplation as the route to holiness and enlightenment. They laid a special emphasis on hard manual work on behalf of ordinary people:

> No work, no food.

The typical Zen kindness is in the greeting, 'have a cup of tea'; and their self-effacement in the saying,

> If a man seeks the Buddha, he loses the Buddha ... his head is covered with ashes, his face is smeared with mud.

In China, Zen was to die out under the Mings in the fourteenth century, but taken to Japan it lived on. In that country, meanwhile, appeared the scholar-king Shotoku Taish (594–622), known for the serious introduction of basic Buddhism from Korea, which was to be developed with the special Japanese admixture of fatalism and honour. Lin Chi (c.800–867) founded the Rinzai school of Japanese Zen, which used the technique of angry, violent outbursts to achieve its effect.

Also arriving in Japan from China at this time was the new Taoist reverence for sex. The detailed anatomical concern with the subject, and the desire to develop rather than smother it, was by now a characteristic of much of the Eastern hemisphere, quite the opposite of the direction in which it was moving in the West. Alcohol, on the other hand, was considered a serious impediment to national success, so the Yamamuro attempted a period of prohibition during the period 646–777.

Overall, the second half of the first millennium after Christ was a period of massive energy, of long-distance migrations and conquest, of experimenting with new moral ideas. This was accompanied by great ruthlessness and cruelty, as well as a dominantly permissive theme. It was becoming increasingly evident that while the human species was perfectly capable of managing its own affairs with kindness and dignity, it was nevertheless too prone to illogical obsessions to maintain any such sensible regimen for more than a few generations.

1000 — 1400

You who long for the knightly order.

Deschamps

THIS WAS THE GREAT PERIOD of the growth of the christian kingdoms and a major peak of Christian self-confidence; it also saw the advent of Islam into India and the advance of Zen in Japan, the destructive mass conquests of the Mongols and, in South America, the peak of Mayan human sacrifice.

This central part of the European Middle Ages was essentially the period of duties and rights, the reciprocal principle of the feudal concept, however unfair the barter might be. As the proverb had it:

God hath shapen lives three,
Poor and knight and priest they be.

Here was acceptance of the inevitability of the separate levels of the three estates. Attention in this period was turned towards confirmation of Roman Catholicism, the attack on Islam and the power of the new nation states.

At the beginning of the eleventh century there was little sense of direction, with widespread permissiveness both lay and clerical. The court of William Rufus (*c*.1056–1100) in England had a particularly unsavoury reputation. Dim lighting at night was fashionable; the court drank and diced all night, slept all day, and homosexuality appeared to be on the increase. According to the historian Ordericus Vitalis (1075–1143):

> Effeminates set the fashion in many parts of the world . . . catamites doomed to eternal fire . . . parted hair from crown to forehead, grew long locks like women . . . wore overtight shirts and trousers.

The new fashion for shoes with curling toes (*poulaines*) was particularly prevalent and there developed a mincing walk to go with them. Peter Damian (1007–72), in his *Liber Gomorrheanus*, claimed that sodomy was rife amongst the clergy, although it also rebuked a bishop for playing chess.

Maheu, Bishop of Tour, whose favourite concubine was one of his own illegitimate daughters, was deposed in 1212 but still managed to organise the murder of his successor. Cardinal Pier Leone had children by his own sister. Women still had a very poor image characteristic of the early Middle Ages, with Jezebel and Delilah regarded as the typical models of their sex, not yet the Virgin Mary.

There was also throughout Europe a kind of depression. The year 1000 had been expected to see the world disappear in fire and brimstone, and expectations of imminent doom not only persisted for several centuries as a real prospect but also deflected interest away from earthly ambitions and behaviour. There was, as a result, a quite genuine and intense interest in pilgrimage to the holy places. This began to focus Europe's disgust and resentment on the presence of Moslem invaders in Spain, Sicily, Bulgaria and, of course, Palestine. It was the Tuscan carpenter's son Hildebrand (1020–85), later Pope Gregory VII, who personified and crystallised the self-disgust of his century, the contempt for all earthly ambition and the need for a unifying Christian cause. He combined a remarkably courageous willingness to impose his personality on all the crowned heads of Europe with a self-deprecating, monkish humility. He wrote:

> I behold myself so sunk in iniquity that prayer from my lips is of no avail. My life indeed is blameless but my actions are of this world; therefore I do beseech the devout to pray for me.

Though Gregory died before the first crusade was launched, it was without question his inspiration, as was the spiritual change which swept through Europe. In considering the cruelty and violence that accompanied the crusades we should bear in mind that this was not simply a question of religious enthusiasm out of control, though that it was. There was also a sincere belief in the irrelevance of death, a minor event in the panoptic holocaust of the crusader's imagination. In particular, the killing of Jews, the nation of Judas, was certainly not seen as inhumane. The Jews in Gaul had been persecuted as early as 558, and around 1010 occurred the earliest of a series of local massacres. In 1063, Christian knights on their way to Jerusalem slaughtered a group of Jews and there were to be outbreaks of violent anti-Semitism throughout the crusading period. In 1095, the unruly amateur crusade led by Peter the Hermit (*c.*1050–1115) massacred the Jews of Treves and began a whole series of massacres of Jews in Rhineland towns, with 'Hep, (later Hip Hip) Hierosolymna est perdita' (Jerusalem is lost) as their motto. In 1108, massacres of Jews at Worms were followed by mass suicides to avoid forcible baptism, and in 1146 the monk Roger de Haveden was regularly pulling large crowds to his bitterly anti-Semitic sermons in the area around Mainz, material not unworthy of Goebbels. There was a Jewish massacre in England at the time of the third crusade, and later Edward I expelled 3,000 Jews. In Palestine itself, when Godfrey captured Jerusalem from the infidel, the Jews were burned alive in their synagogues. Anti-Semitism was at least partly encouraged by the Church, not least by Pope Innocent III (1160–1216), and in 1267 the Council of Vienna decreed complete segregation, with Jews excluded from Christian baths, shops and homes, from marriage with Christians and even domestic service with them. Apart from lepers and paupers, Jews were the only people not allowed into most medieval brothels. Innocent argued that every cleric must obey the Pope, even if what he commanded was evil.

The Jews were not the only people to suffer from the violence of the crusades. There was much gratuitous killing of Moslems also: in the siege of Nicaea in 1097, human heads were used for catapult ammunition; and Richard I (1157–99), Coeur de Lion and a man of limited moral imagination, slaughtered 2,700 prisoners of war at Acre when their ransom was delayed. He was also the first ruler to make general use of the new 'immoral weapon' of its time, the crossbow, which was condemned as such by the Lateran Council of 1397 and barred for use against other Christians. Ironically, Richard died a lingering death from a crossbow wound.

In due course the crusaders began to attack their fellow Christians, sacking the Christian city of Constantinople to please the Venetian capitalists. In 1396, crusaders massacred 3,000 Turco-Bulgar prisoners after the battle of Vidim, only to suffer the same fate themselves soon afterwards. There were also large numbers of deaths due to sheer irresponsibility. Of the 350,000 who followed the call of Peter the Hermit, at least eighty percent were sold by Christian merchants as slaves to the infidel. It is estimated that some 9,000,000 people died as a result of crusading activity between 1091 and 1291, of whom approximately half were Christians.

The crusades made violence more respectable than it had been: the battlefield was the clear path to heaven, the duty of war was preached from every pulpit. While the indulgences from sin given to many crusaders were grossly abused, there were also many heroic feats of endurance and courage. The romance of distant battles in an idealistic cause did much to lift the image of medieval knighthood and pave the way for the new concept of chivalry. The Saracens, by coincidence, were at a similar stage in the growth cycle of a chivalrous ethic. The autobiography of Usamah gives a vivid picture of the Saracens' gentlemanly code, an Islamic version of Christian chivalry.

The ideal of knightly celibacy was harder to maintain, particularly when faced with the temptations of the East. It seems likely that amongst the many other ideas and inventions to which the eyes of the crusaders were opened by their travels was the survival of the old Roman tradition of using bath-houses as brothels. In 1160, we hear first of the 'stews' or bath and bawdy houses of London about which Henry II (1133–89) later had to legislate. The prostitutes of the Southwark stews were known as 'Winchester Geese' because the Bishop of Winchester was their landlord. There was, according to Otis, a 'grete multiplicacyon of orrible synn amongst syngle women'. Three hundred French prostitutes accompanied the third crusade, and there 'they dedicated as a holy offering what they kept between their thighs'.

William IX of Aquitaine was typical of the crusader who achieved extended gratification of his physical needs and Henry II of England was 'given to fleshly lust beyond measure'. The Abbot of Nogent complained in 1100,

> Alas how maidenly modesty and honour have fallen off and the mother's care decayed . . . wanton gait and most ridiculous manners . . . the widening of sleeves and the tightening of bodices . . . we may see how shame is cast aside.

Prostitution grew to substantial proportions throughout Europe. When that ideal crusader-saint, King Louis of France (1215–70), tried to tackle the problem there were an estimated 12,000 prostitutes in Paris out of a total population of 150,000. In 1309, Bishop Johann of Strasbourg built a new brothel as a commercial investment for his see, and at some periods the Vatican also held the leases of similar properties in Rome. Even St Thomas Aquinas (1225–74), having conceded that sex was a sin 'only if it submerged the reason', admitted that prostitution in his era was a necessary evil. Significantly, St Louis decreed the penalty of death by fire for men who kept Jewish mistresses, that being a heresy rather than just a sin.

The less seamy side of the liberal or permissive mood which caught Europe after the crusades was the new concept of courtly love, the part of knightly behaviour associated with the mannered sparring of flirtation and fidelity. The concept may well have been adopted from the Moors, whose books like *The Dove's Neck Ring* of 1027 put across a new and gentler idea of love. One example of a trendsetter in this field was the far-travelled, twice-married Eleanor of Aquitaine (1122–1204), wife of Henry II of England. This flamboyant ex-Queen of France and rebellious Queen of England boasted of her extra-marital adventures, and through her two sets of children encouraged courts full of troubadours. The pleasures of wine and women were sung in the goliards, by the feckless singing scholars, later collected as the *Carmina Burana*. Guillaume de Lorris's *Roman de la Rose* in 1240 was the outstanding saga of the period, combining the undercurrent of an earthly love story with the elaborate rituals of courtly love—'an honest woman is as rare as a black swan'. Lovers could only enter the garden of happiness if free from hatred, felony, villainy, avarice, envy, sadness, hypocrisy and poverty. This involved a remarkable duality — on the one hand, the ideal of rarely requited love; on the other, the crude jokes and smut surrounding the public bedding of newly marrieds. As Huizinga, the historian of late medieval manners, put it:

> Civilisation needed to wrap up the idea of love in veils of fancy, to exalt and refine it and thereby forget the cruel reality.

The principles of courtly love were set out by Andreas Capellanus in his *Art of Courtly Love* (1184). The emphasis was on courtesy rather than morality, but the image of romantic chivalry, later to be mocked in the form of Don Quixote, was becoming at least a partial reality. The ritual trappings of dubbing, the mythology of the *Chanson de Roland* (the epic poem preaching loyalty), the model of Lancelot, Hannibal and the rest of 'les neuf pieux' formed the ideal which inspired men like St Louis and Charles the Bold of Burgundy. Wolfram von Eschenbach's *Parzifal* was the perfect knight with three virtues: courage, compassion and loyalty. The *Niebelungenlied* projected a frenzy of Germanic heroism, while *Tristan and Isolde* placed duty ahead of love. The religious epic *St Alexis* projected faith, justice and love. The French poet Chretien de Troyes (d.1183) pronounced that it was the usage of the time that if a knight found a damsel alone he would sooner cut his throat than offer her dishonour, but if she had a man with her could happily kill him and insist on her favours.

The great medieval cathedrals of the thirteenth century were decorated with personifications of good and evil: Folly, Humility and

Pride were carved as stone figures with many others on the porches of Chartres Cathedral. The Virtues appeared as warrior maidens at Amiens and 'Decadent Luxury' was one of the rose windows at Notre Dame in Paris.

As Georges Duby has shown, the Church had generally been working away diligently to clean up lay marriage, in particular cracking down on incest, which came to mean marriage with almost any relation however distant. Sex, even within marriage, was severely castigated. In his collection of sentences, Peter Lombard (c.1100–1064) said that 'for a man to love his wife was worse than adultery' and the 'chemise cagoule' (a long, thick nightgown) was invented to take the pleasure out of it. Marital sex was pronounced a sin on Sundays, Wednesdays, Fridays, Easter and Christmas.

There is no doubt that during the crusading period the person most responsible for the drive to purify the Church, and to constrain lay knighthood to Christian objectives, was the Burgundian monk, Bernard of Clairvaux (1090–1153), a fervent and eloquent ascetic. This son of a wealthy family was the founder of the revived Cistercian monastic order which led to the founding of seventy new monasteries throughout Europe, with a new, puritan vision of their role. He was not only a major instigator of the crusades, he was also the person responsible for the ultimate Christian sanction of aggressive war: 'Let them kill the enemies or die', and he referred to the killing of non-Christians as 'malicide not homicide'. In addition he was a harsh opponent of the new philosophies of men like Peter Abelard (1079–1142) whose punishment by castration for clerical inchastity he wrathfully endorsed.

A great surge of asceticism swept across Europe during the eleventh century. Lawrence tells us the Benedictines held the view that

Poverty is the virtue from which all others stem.

St Margaret (1045–93), Queen of Scots, ostentatiously gave breakfast to two dozen beggars every day and tried to suppress slavery in Scotland. Her daughter, Queen Matilda of England, washed the feet of lepers and founded the hospital of St Giles. Stephen of Murat commented, 'poverty is the secret ladder to heaven'.

The even more ascetic Carthusian Order developed from 1084 under the influence of St Bruno, and the Austin Canons had been reformed in 1060. Spain produced models like St Isadore, the peasant patron of the work ethic, while in the Balkans, St Sava, the patron saint of Serbia, was opening new monasteries on the cliffs of Mount Athos from 1196. The numbers of monks and nuns increased substantially. Bernard was massively energetic and inspired others with at least some of his own fervour:

Rouse yourself, gird your loins . . . put aside idleness, grasp the nettle.

The monastic movement created a substantial advance in the provision of humanitarian services, in care for the poor, sick and pilgrims as well as education.

Bernard was not tolerant of the less committed, referring to the Bishop of Winchester for instance as an 'old whore'. He had a pioneering influence on the cult of the Virgin Mary, which itself contributed so much to the medieval reverence for chastity and female tenderness. In 1128, Bernard was involved in the formal establishment of the Order of Knights Templar, the first main group of military monks who were to set a new trend for the image of Christian knighthood. The parallel Hospital of Jerusalem, founded in 1113 by Gerard and formalised in John of Ibelin's *Assizes of Jerusalem*, had as its priorities:

> The sick give orders, the brothers obey.

After a heroic struggle in Palestine this remarkably long-lived order defended Rhodes for over 200 years, and thereafter Malta for even longer. A third great order, the Teutonic Knights, took on the forcible conversion to Christianity of eastern Prussia, Poland and Lithuania, with a mixture again of amazing bravery and sanctified violence. The massacres of the Wendish Slavs by the Germans were typical, yet the German hospitallers also acquired for themselves a reputation (perhaps just the usual medieval slander) for condoning homosexuality.

The knightly tradition was later developed by writers like Ramon Lull (1232–1315) in his *Order of Chivalry* (1310), translated into English by Caxton:

> To a knight apperteyneth that he be a lover of the common weel. For the comynalte of the people was the chevalrye founded.

Or, as Huizinga quotes Eustache Deschamps (*c.*1345–1406):

> You who long for the knightly order,
> It is fitting you should lead a new life
> Devoutly keeping watch in prayer
> Fleeing from sin, pride and villainy.

The troubadour, Bertrand de Born (1140–1215), boasted:

> I adore battle . . . to see peasants scatter, the breaking of heads and arms.

It was a breach of the knightly code, an affair with a vassal's wife, that first led to the downfall of King John of England (1167–1216). Because of it, he had to fight the Battle of Bouvines, which he lost and subsequently had to submit to that remarkable statement of chivalrous rights, Magna Carta, a description (in a way) of the moral standards expected of a king as head of a knightly order.

At home, knighthood frequently fell short of its ideals, and inevitably there were numerous examples of exploitation and cruelty. In England, Thomas Lord Berkeley (1245–1321) bought and sold wardships on a commercial basis to sustain his patrimony, and there are numerous tales of abuse of wives such as that of the Knight de la Tour (d.1372) who tells in Philip Mason's *The English Gentleman* of a wife given a good beating and getting a broken nose 'for her ill language'.

There were further signs of increasingly ruthless violence off the battlefield as well as on. Henry I of England (1068–1165) had ordered the castration of money-lenders. In 1189, Henry II authorised torture of the London Knights Templar to help extract confessions of homosexuality so that he could strip them of their wealth. Not surprisingly, he succeeded. From 1307, Philip IV of France (1268–1314) used the same preliminaries before having most of the French Templars burned at the stake, again for the sake of the cash gathered by their banking activities. Philip, a dedicated moralist who tolerated no promiscuity at court, was also a notable persecutor of the Jews. He employed the devious lawyer William of Nogaret (d.1313), one of whose preparatory techniques was to coat witnesses in honey and expose them to swarms of bees. It was he who concocted a sodomy charge against Pope Boniface VIII. Philip even humiliated his own sons, proclaiming their cuckoldry by imprisoning their wives for adultery and torturing their wives' lovers to death. Equally, Boniface had (for political reasons) organised the massacre of the townspeople of Palestrina, which led Dante to consign him to the eighth layer of hell.

Even more ruthless was Frederick II (1194–1250), Emperor of Germany and known as 'Stupor Mundi', the self-styled new tyrant of Sicily who modelled himself on Alexander the Great as an imperialist. His technique included the encasing of rebels in lead for slow roasting, and the mutilation and slaughter of hostages to turn people into 'multitudes destitute of will'. He referred to 'the sword of vengeance against abhorred freedom', and used blinding, castration and torture as tools of terror. His local henchman, Ezzelino de Romana (1196–1257), savagely executed some 50,000 Paduans, more Sicilians; he was a forerunner of the totally amoral 'condottieri' or mercenary generals of Renaissance Italy. Frederick II was a man of remarkable intellect, a great encourager of the arts and sciences; his one untypical moral quality was his defence of the Jews. His court at Palermo included his personal harem and a group of refugee troubadours. It sported more than a hint of oriental luxury, yet for political reasons he was an avid supporter of the mendicant Franciscan monks whom he used as his opposition to the papal hierarchy. In the period of violence and confusion that followed, Dante Alighieri (1265–1321), the supreme poet of medieval Italy, was to preach obedience to royal authority as the greatest Christian virtue and treachery against one's rightful king as the greatest sin. Significantly, Judas, the betrayer of his leader, and Brutus, the murderer of his, were both pictured in Dante's *Inferno* as suffering the appalling torment of the very lowest circle of hell.

In 1195, Alain de Lille produced his thesis on the Waldensian doctrine of non-violence. The ethos of the creed was ascetic, puritan and vegetarian, and had a mystical quality which spread rapidly in southern France and Italy. Yet judged by the record of the Pyrenean village of Montaillon in 1300, sexual standards were fairly relaxed, with ten percent of couples co-habiting and no strong prejudice against bastardy.

A marriage of convenience between Church and state now began to assert the right to do violence against all who rejected their orthodoxy. Henry V (c.1080–1135), an earlier German emperor, issued a statute for the burning of heretics; in 1197, King Peter of Aragon burned his first heretic. The Inquisition itself was founded in 1208 by Pope Innocent III (1160–1216) and was followed by the systematic massacre of the Albigensian or Waldensian heretics in the south of France. The crusader Simon de Montfort (1160–1218), the main villain of this episode, employed torture and was known to gouge out the eyes and slit the noses of his victims. Many more Albigensians were burned on the orders of Pope Gregory IX in 1231. The massacre at Beziers claimed 20,000, for which the royal saint King Louis has to share some of the blame. It is estimated that up to 1,000,000 Albigensians were killed in the effort to stamp out this relatively harmless heresy which had developed a few years before in the area south of Turin. Its doctrines were as innocuous as total objection to violence, both warfare and corporal punishment, plus regarding humility as their most prized virtue. Like the Jains of India, they had an admiration for ritual suicide, usually by starvation, and their martyrs showed remarkable stoicism when they faced the stake.

Robert le Bougre (*fl.*1239) was the pioneer inquisitor in northern France, Peter de Verona (d.1252) in Italy, Conrad of Narburg (*fl.*1250) in the Rhineland. A bull of Pope Innocent IV (d.1254) allowed the use of torture and burning, while in 1256 Pope Alexander IV gave inquisitors the right to absolve each other for inflicting torture. Ordeal by water, 'strappado' (the pulley torture), the wheel, the rack, 'stivaletto' (the boot torture)—all were given papal blessing in one of the most gruesome periods of institutionalised sadism known to history.

The Venetian Inquisition began its work in 1249. Both the Dominican and Franciscan orders provided numerous dedicated inquisitors, particularly in the extirpation of the Cathars, the Italian arm of the Albigensians. In 1266, eight wagonloads of them were burned at Piacenza. Then in 1323, a breakaway sect of the Franciscans were themselves condemned as heretics and it is estimated that around 15,000 of these 'Fraticelli' (or 'little brothers') were executed. Similarly, the new female ascetic movement of the Beguines was too advanced for the hierarchy and they too were persecuted heavily in the fourteenth century, though the beguinages were to expand steadily in northern Europe, just as the original Beghards, the 'voluntary poor', thronged the streets asserting their superiority to the official priesthood. Meanwhile, discipline amongst the more traditional orders often collapsed: Johan Galer of Strasbourg said that his sister would be safer in a brothel than a nunnery, and in Friesia the nunneries and monasteries joined forces to expand their social lives.

This was also a period when homosexuals and witches, as well as heretics, were burned at the stake. In 1285, Edward I issued a law for the burning of those guilty of sodomy and bestiality. Ironically, his own son Edward II was to be accused of a self-indulgent infatuation with Piers Gaveston which did not end until 1312, while his wife Isabella was entertained by Mortimer, Earl of March. By the *Customs of Argue* in 1231, a thieving concubine could be buried alive.

Traitors were hung, drawn and quartered, a punishment inflicted on the Scottish national leader, William Wallace (1274–1305), for alleged war crimes in that he had killed some civilians during his rebellion. Numerous other Scots suffered the same fate or even crucifixion at the hands of Edward's armies. Even lepers were regarded as proven sinners suffering divine punishment; in 1316 a group of them were burned in France, and Philip V made leprosy a capital offence. In 1390, 4,000 Spanish Jews were massacred in Seville with encouragement from the preaching of Hernando Martines; and St Vincent Ferrer (1350–1419), who attracted vast crowds to his sermons, was another prominent originator of anti-Semitism. The general sadistic trait of the thirteenth century is illustrated by the numerous paintings of saints in torment, Catherine wheels, St Lawrence's gridirons and St Sebastian pierced with arrows.

A small band of Manichaean heretics in Bulgaria, who found the world so dreadful that they refused to reproduce their own species, were branded as homosexuals and probably thus gave a new word—'buggers'—to the English language. Though the Middle Ages often showed great sympathy for the poor and weak, it also had its streak of cruelty towards the abnormal. There are stories of the baiting of blind beggars in the Low Countries and, as later recorded by the painter Velasquez, dwarfs were exploited to amuse the Spanish Court.

The cruelty of medieval *realpolitik* is well illustrated by the careers of Edward III (1312–77) and his son, the Black Prince (1330–76), both of whom adopted a policy of total war and mass destruction as a means of achieving results. In 1369, Edward massacred 3,000 French people at Limoges in his part of the Hundred Years War. This king, who introduced the first orders of the chivalry in England, was also well known for his intended brutality after the siege of Calais. The gaols of England had been emptied to help recruitment to the army. The Black Prince has been referred to by G.H. Perris as 'a freebooter adept at foul butchery', although he has also been idealised as a British military hero, the victor of Poitiers. This very period saw the introduction of what has for the last six centuries been the world's most destructive weapon, gunpowder; the first cannons, sanctified with the emblem of their patron St Barbara, appeared in 1329. It also saw the first attempt to produce laws for the humane conduct of war in Honore Bonet's remarkable *L'Arbre des Battailles*, the application of the rules of chivalry to the cruel practice of war. It is nevertheless significant that even Bonet thought it legitimate to kill prisoners of war.

While St Thomas Aquinas was the great theoretical moralist of this period, the most influential moral revolutionary was without question Francis of Assisi (1181–1216). He revived the ideas of monkish poverty and care for all living creatures, even lepers and plague victims, although as a loyal papal supporter he did not oppose the Albigensian purges in France.

The role of the preaching Franciscan friars, the new propaganda force of Catholicism, raised mendicancy to new heights and was also later caught up in the hysteria which swept through Europe in the wake of the bubonic plague or Black Death. This created a deep sense of impending doom, was believed to be divine punishment and greeted with guilt-ridden panic. Enthused groups of friars and millennialists wandered through the towns of Europe, whipping each other until their flesh was raw. The Brethren of the Cross used bells, psalms and scourging to induce crowd hysteria leading to mass confession of sins. Frenzied dancing became a regular feature, with uncontrolled mobs dancing till they dropped. Flagellomania, which originated in northern Italy, spread in epidemics in 1259, 1262, 1296, 1334 and 1348, invented by a hermit of Perugia. It was part of a trend of deliberate masochism which was welcomed throughout Europe as an antidote to the impending doom of the world and the pains of hell-fire. Flagellants dressed in crusader uniforms scourged themselves three times daily with hooked thongs, causing themselves severe bleeding and drawing huge crowds bent on penitence. Numbers were substantial: in two months 5,300 flagellants arived at Tournai and 3,000 camped outside Erfurt. Such outbreaks were accompanied by robbers giving back their loot, money-lenders their interest, by waves of public penance and a making-up of quarrels. In Germany, the flagellant leaders produced a marble tablet shining with supernatural light and preached specifically against the vices of the wealthy, namely, ostentation, pride, adultery and usury.

The image of St Francis was given artistic brilliance by the hagio-graphic paintings of Giotto (1267–1337) and poetic vision by the didactic poet Jacopone da Todi (1230–1306). Similarly, the black friars founded by Dominic de Guana (1170–1221) concentrated on preaching and teaching, though they were also to become heavily embroiled in persecution. Also part of this reaction against clerical complacency were John Wycliff (1329–84), the English ex-government pamphleteer, and John Huss (1369–1415), the Bohemian martyr—the two pioneers of de-Latinisation of the Catholic faith. This movement was to form the basis of the great revival in individual conscience, and shifted the emphasis of human behaviour from theology to morality.

St Catherine of Siena (1347–80), patroness of the Dominican friars, led an attack on the debauches and carousing of the priests. St Bridget of Sweden (1302–73), a mother of eight children, founded a new order which eventually had seventy-four houses in different parts of Europe. In Florence in 1233, the Seven Servites reacted against prevalent immorality to found a mendicant order; Zitta, the servant girl of Lucca, became a model for exalted servitude in 1278; Margaret of Cortona founded the Poverelle hospitals for the poor in 1286, and Raymond Nonnatus the Order of Mercadarians in 1280 to rescue Christian prisoners from the Moors. The pursuit of anorectic chastity was an élitist fashion. This was the period of the spread of the beguinages, semi-official monastic communities who organised plans for the redemption of prostitutes, the ransoming of prisoners of war, and help for lepers and the blind. In 1160, Guy de Montpellier had founded the Order of the Holy Spirit to rescue abandoned babies. The large number of beguinages in German towns—there were a hundred in Cologne alone, keeping between them at least a thousand sisters—reflected the excess of females over males at this time: they outnumbered men by around twenty percent, sometimes more, so up to a third of women might never marry, thus the demographic trend may have contributed to the exaggerated admiration for female celibacy.

A heightening of moral conscience in England in the fourteenth century is shown by the flowering of moral literature and the increased interest in the miracle plays from 1311 onwards. *The Golden Legend*, a compendium of saints' lives, remained an extremely popular book. The English educationist William of Wykeham (1324–1404), founder of Winchester School reputedly pronounced that 'manners makyth man'.

In 1395, that remarkable English group, the Lollards, condemned all war and raised the first significant voice against violence in the West in the Middle Ages, apart from the Albigensians. They were also ahead of their time in claiming an element of equality for women, but were persecuted by monarchs such as Henry V. St Bernardino of Siena (1380–1444), a popular preacher, encouraged a more sympathetic attitude towards women as admirable mother figures rather than causes of sin. Origo's biography tells us that Bernardino encouraged men to 'Mark well thy wife how she travails in childbirth'.

Meanwhile, at the upper end of European society there seems to have been a quite sudden swing towards promiscuity after the 1350s. Otis observes that men switched from long cloaks to short tunics 'with scandalous immodesty', and female necklines plunged. Queen Joanna of Naples founded the Avignon state brothel in 1347, and Duke Albert IV of Austria ran one in Vienna forty years later. Prostitutes in European cities tended to wear recognisable uniforms, like those of Leipzig who had yellow cloaks with blue trimming.

In Cologne, the Beghard mystic Heinrich Suso (1295–1366) decided, after a vision, to give up flagellation and self-torment for ever, regarding himself as reborn in a state with no sin, so that he could now eat, drink and be promiscuous. His popular book, *Das Buchlein der ewigen Weisheit* (1328), pronounced:

> The Brethren regard women for the use of men just as cattle are for the use of humans.

Sex required religious sanction and adultery was an act of liberation.

France had introduced laws to curb extravagant expenditure on clothes under Philip IV; England did the same under Edward III. In self-made Venice, the wealthy merchants continued to wear sober black for another century but elsewhere the upturn in trade after the Black Death, the growth in credit and banking, created a new enthusiasm for luxury while promiscuity was supposed conveniently to be an antidote to the plague. The plague itself had created a further hysteria involving Jew-baiting and flagellant masochism. In 1348, the usual well-poisoning story reached Strasbourg and 2,000 Jews were said to have been burned. The confinement of Jews in ghettos began.

The mystery plays started their transition from Church propaganda to anti-clerical protest, and the survivors of the plague faced the future with a new and earthly confidence. In the fairs, the bank lottery was all the rage and the gaming houses of Leipzig did excellent business as gambling fever spread.

Parallel to St Francis, the great ascetic of the West, there appeared also an Islamic opposite number in the shape of Shuhammad al Ghaza (1058–1111). He was the reviver of Sunni Islam during the period of crisis after the first crusade, an academic who gave up a promising career, wealth and family to search for truth. In 1160, Abdul al Qadir al Jilar founded a philanthropic dervish order in Baghdad caring for the poor and sick. In Moslem India, mendicant Sufi monks helped spread the word; in Cairo in 1009, Druzism was founded, a small but remarkably resilient puritan sect which began round the martyred Caliph Al Hakim, who had tried to reunite the whole of Islam. The sect survived, albeit mainly in the Lebanon, with a strong moral code and remarkable long-term immunity from outside influences.

The Moslems did not have the Christian problem of a celibate clergy with high ideals periodically succumbing to temptations of wealth and flesh, because Islam had no property-owning priesthood. Also, since Islam's ritual was simpler and its theology much less complex, with no miracles and no obsession with chastity, it was more tolerant of deviations and therefore less inclined to persecute heretics. There were, of course, eccentric sects, not least in this period the one led by Hassan i Suffah, the original 'old man of the mountain,' whose followers from about 1090 onwards pursued an ethic encouraging political murders against the Seljuks and Christians alike. Known as the Assassins, possibly because they were hashish-takers, they were not stamped out until 1256. Certainly hashish, reputedly the discovery of a previously ascetic monk called Haldir, was becoming the standard intoxicant of the teetotal Moslem world, and there was some concern in the twelfth century that it was reaching epidemic proportions. Oakley refers to opium or hashish as 'the primary social drug of Islam'.

There were, however, increasing signs of intolerance and persecution in Islam too. The Sufi were frequently persecuted and there were outbreaks of anti-Semitism in Iran. In 1024 the great Hindu temple of Somnath was sacked by the Moslems, Mahmud of Ghazni creating a tradition of Islamic intolerance and ferocity amongst the Hindus. The conflict between the two religions was to erupt regularly during the next thousand years.

Further East, this period saw the efforts of two of the most destructive and sadistic warlords of all human history up to the twentieth century. Genghis Khan (1162–1227), the Mongol emperor, was superficially a firm upholder of the typical nomad warrior ethic, with a conscience totally impervious to worries about normal human suffering. As he exterminated the Hsia in 1224 he was, according to Kei Kwei Sun, 'savouring his enemies' despair, outraging their wives and daughters'. The Mongols, a people toughened by the desert, internal strife and self-culling, conquered the Chinese who outnumbered them a hundred to one; but, as the explorer Marco Polo (1254–1324) in his *Travels* observed, the Chinese had remained anti-military so they perhaps paid the penalty, if it was a penalty, of absorbing more conquerors. There was a saying in the Sung period:

Nails are not made out of good iron
Nor soldiers out of good men.

Genghis Khan, on the other hand, was totally ruthless and told his followers: 'The hay is cut, now feed your horses.' The Mongols despised the work ethic but placed loyalty as the highest virtue. Heavy drinking and indulgence in cannabis were acceptable. Genghis Khan was famed for his devotion and obedience to his mother: in war, he was merciless. His massacre at Samarkand was horrendous and this was followed by his revenge on the city of Herat, which had rebelled, and where he was reputed to have killed over 1,000,000 people. Even allowing for exaggeration, the total cost in human lives of his empire was enormous. Captives were used as expendable human shields during sieges. Estimates suggest that 18,000,000 may have died during the conquests. Decapitation, skull-piling and even disembowelling often followed massacres.

His grandson, Kublah Khan (1214–94), the first non-Chinese Emperor of China, made Buddhism the Mongol religion, but his was the hedonistic Tantra version suited to a builder of pleasure domes, rather than the ascetic Buddhism of Asoka. The Mongols were described by a contemporary as being 'dirty, drunk and cruel', as well as greedy and corrupt. They did provoke the easy-going Chinese eventually into forming a secret society, the White Lotus, which provided mutual aid and care for welfare resembling the European Masonic movement some four centuries later. Meanwhile, they enjoyed their new home—Marco Polo described the 20,000 exotic prostitutes of Hangchow.

The other particularly destructive warlord was Timur the Lame, or Tamerlane (1336–1405), Tartar Mongol chief of Samarkand and conqueror of vast tracts of central Asia, a Moslem who defeated nearly all the other Islamic kingdoms with spectacular sadism. He made his famous tower of 70,000 human skulls at Ispahan, massacred 20,000 people at his capture of Baghdad and 100,000 at Delhi. He sometimes buried prisoners of war alive. On one occasion he buried alive 400, walled up 2,000 and impaled 5,000. This Mongol Empire was even more short-lived than that of Genghis Khan, but the main Mongol dynasties lasted seven centuries—a remarkable tribute to the well-cultivated ethic of total obedience, 'batu'.

The China conquered by the Mongols was that of the southern Sung dynasty, in a period noted for urban materialism and an emphasis on the more self-indulgent aspects of the Tao. Infanticide to get rid of unwanted children, corruption in government and heavy drinking marked the regime of Hangzhou, which reputedly boasted a number of restaurants specialising in dishes of human flesh. The plight of the have-nots in this society did, however, inspire a number of movements of private philanthropy, showing the same spirit which created the White Lotus.

The rest of China had seen a revival of Confucianism in the period up to the Mongol conquest. Apart from the vulnerabilty arising from a perhaps too-great disgust with self-defence, the Chinese maintained a remarkably sane moral consensus. They retained their passion for education and exams, for the three or four-generation extended family unit living under one roof and exercising great moral authority, with the parental bond stronger than the marital. The subordinate status of women was emphasised round about the eleventh century by developing the custom of foot-binding, which was to half-immobilise Chinese women for nearly 900 years: and the revealing fashions of the T'ang were replaced by the high collars of the Sung. Chu Hsi (1130–1200), the Chinese Aquinas, preached a puritan version of Confucianism which recommended that widows should die soon after their husbands. Chu Hsi became the popular philosopher of the Ming because of his doctrine of service and encouragement to suppress the 'jen' or weaker side of human nature. The evils of alcohol caused serious concern, and for a period the Chinese attempted to enforce prohibition. The other remarkable feature of Chinese philosophies and religions was their amazing tolerance of each other, with virtually no religious persecution or strife.

In India, this was the period of the rise of the Brahmins as feudal landlords with a strong feudal ethic and a liking for the erotic romanticisation of Krishna; the carvings on the Black Pagoda of Konarak even blessed bestiality. Some of the Tantric sects indulged in strange rites involving sacrifice and sexual orgies, dissident groups using extreme non-conformity as a protest against the rigid laws of the Brahmins. The Rajput feudal barons were so obsessed with their image as good warriors that they would seek any excuse for prolonging or re-starting wars, following the ethos of the mandala which makes each person's neighbours his natural rivals and enemies. The heroic virtues were induced from birth, and the greatest possible glory was to die in battle.

Mainstream Buddhism had fallen into decay. Moslem conquerors had slaughtered many Buddhist monks and were imposing their religion alongside Hinduism, but beyond India the strength of Buddhism survived. In Tibet, this was the time of the great Buddhist saint Mila-ras-pa (1040–1123), and Tibet was becoming one of the most intensely Buddhist countries in the East, with a large monastic population and a deep interest also in the magical qualities of the Tantra sect, with its sexual overtones.

Meanwhile, Zen Buddhism began its deeper infiltration of Japan. The collection of *A Hundred Riddles*, the typical Zen text, appeared in 1125, and Eisai (1141–1215) was a major exponent:

Pass over the bridge:

Lo the water floweth not, but the bridge doth flow.

Minamoto Yoritomo (1147–99) was the main pioneer of the ethic which was to make Japan such a dedicated military state for many centuries, ready to erupt to full destructiveness when given the technology to achieve it. This leader of the Kamakura Shogun was an extremely devious operator who eliminated his own chief helpers, including one Benkii who committed 'hara kiri' and became a mythical prototype of suicidal loyalty. Yoritomo first gave real status to the samurai, the feudal knights of Japan with an ethos which included loyalty to death. The concept of 'bushido', of blind, fatalistic obedience, had smatterings of both Zen Buddhism and Confucianism, both borrowed from the Chinese, and it included the ritual drinking of tea as an aid to meditation.

The link between artistic endeavour and manners was an essential ingredient in the control of behaviour. The elaborate and masochistic ritual of 'seppuku' or hara kiri was simply an extension of bushido; in 1156, a warrior called Tametomo killed himself after a defeat and provided a new role model. This extraordinary habit, which was to resurrect itself in the ideal of the kamikaze, also went back to the old Shinto idea of the human pillar, living people buried in the foundations of important buildings as a deliberate sacrifice. The *Tale of Genji*, written c.1000 by the Lady Murasaka, showed the development of the folk ethic, and Zen preached by Honen (1123–1212) emphasised the fatalistic ebb and flow of human fortunes, the transitory nature of earthly glory and surrender to one's karma, which was also the theme of the other great Japanese folk epic, *The Tale of the Taira*.

The true Japanese warrior, said the proverb, regarded life as 'no more worth than a feather'. He should ignore all worldly attachments and, if necessary, ride over the corpses of brothers, sons or fathers into battle. Unlike the European knight, the samurai had no romantic devotion to the lady of his choice, though there were many tales of devotion and sacrifice by women. Alongside Zen was Shingon, the Japanese version of the Tantric sects with its mystical mandala, pillow books, magic and slight permissive streak. The Tachikawa sect, founded by Nin Kan, had a strong sex obsession and lasted some 300 years. Also, as with so many military societies, the samurai had a high tolerance of homosexuality, although this may have been exaggerated by the Jesuit missionaries in order to discredit Buddhism.

Turning West, the new Mayan Empire in Central America was significant. This was the Toltec age of human sacrifice to the messenger god Chac Mool, in the Temple of a Thousand Columns at Chichen Itza. This was a ruthlessly militaristic regime based on conquest, slavery and trade in cocoa; it also had a mercilessly demanding religion. The ethos of this empire (which collapsed about 1224) was to be passed on to the Aztecs. The Mayans encouraged a high birth-rate by compulsory early marriage and, apart from their empire's obvious unpopularity, there is a hint that drug-taking was becoming a problem, as measures were taken to restrict it. These features may have contributed to the empire's collapse.

In North America, the fourteenth century saw the migration south of the Navajo tribe, who had evolved a harmonious balance of goods and evils reminiscent of the Zoroastrians. Their code involved achieving equilibrium by avoiding excess, not breaking taboos, respecting nature and thriving on warfare.

Meanwhile, the Byzantine Empire was not only shrinking physically after its buffeting by both Turks and crusaders, it was also sliding into

another moral decline. According to Finlay, the reign of the Emperor
Constantine IX (1042/54)

> ... typified the moral degradation into which the Byzantine society had
> fallen, for his vices were tolerated if not approved by a large portion of his
> subjects.

This third husband of the redoubtable Empress Zoe (980–1050) kept
a mistress, Skleraina, and a court of uncontrolled extravagance. The
Emperor Michael Palaeologus (1234–82) used torture and blinding to
achieve his rule of terror, as did the sadistic Empress Irene. In 1183,
vast numbers of Latins in Constantinople were slaughtered and 4,000
survivors sold to the Turks as slaves; Gibbon tells us that 'priests
and monks were loudest and most active in the destruction', and the
Emperor Isaac Angelus had a domestic staff at this time of 20,000, many
of whom were eunuchs. The decline and fall of the Byzantine Empire
meant the end of one of the longest-surviving consensus moralities in
human history.

Finally in this period there is the ethical history, albeit hardly
recorded, of the continent of Africa. The fourteenth century witnessed
the peak of the empire of Mali in western Africa, under Kankan Musa.
Africa, in the period just before it was contaminated by the European
slave-traders, seems to have had a number of quite successful and not
necessarily unhappy empires. The traveller Ibn Battuta (1304–68), who
visited western Africa, commented on the fact that his journeys were
free from fear of robbery.

> Among the admirable qualities of the blacks there is the small number of acts
> of injustice that you find there, for of all peoples the blacks are those who
> most hate injustice and their emperor pardons nobody who is guilty of it.

This had been a period of huge energy and extravagance in which
individual pain was considered of minor importance beside the grand
gesture. The most significant trends, towards religious fanaticism and
mindless empire-building, were set against a shortish life-span into
which humans tried to cram as much as possible. Despite having
worked out sound philosophies on a worldwide scale, the human species, instead of following tenets for a pleasant, peaceful life, opted rather
to admire the self-destructive obsessions of its most neurotic heroes.

1400 — 1600

Nothing is cheaper than life.

Pontavio

N OW WAS THE AGE of increasing self-confidence, even arrogance, when the strong believed so much in their own stars that they were totally ruthless in pursuit, and the rebels had the confidence to assert their differences whatever the cost. Since it was also a period of massive exploration and expansion, the spread of Renaissance ruthlessness was almost worldwide.

King Henry V of England (1387–1414) was the first in a series of militaristic supermen; his melodramatic and unprovoked conquest of France has been described by Perris as a 'wanton and barbarous adventure', although his military panache and charismatic leadership excited the appropriate hero worship. The spectacular nature of his victories tended to cloud the motives for the war and his harsh treatment of the conquered included killing prisoners of war after Agincourt. He was also a rigid persecutor of the Lollards. Nevertheless, in medieval terms, he fulfilled the requirements of honour admirably. His character was what Huizinga called 'a strange mixture of conscience and egotism compatible with many vices and susceptible to extravagant delusions'.

This was the period when the admiration of the superheroes of Greece and Rome, first revived by the Italian poet Petrarch (1304–74), advanced spectacularly. The pictures by the Renaissance artists changed from self-effacing, physically unattractive saints to the proud, boastful Venus-figures of Donatello and Michelangelo. What Kenneth Clark called 'the appetite for provocative nudity' had returned to sweep away the two-dimensional icons of pre-Renaissance painting. The codpiece became an unusually brazen fashion for men. The new painting was the expression of new confidence in the body and mind, the new humanism. Of the Florentine humanists, Chartier quotes Cardinal Dominici of Padua as saying:

> They were the instrument used to corrupt politics, religion, the family and education.

This new, human self-confidence, combined with thirst for glory and the determination to win it at all costs, reduced moral considerations to a lower level. The cruelty of the new breed of Italian 'condottieri' and the German and Swiss 'landsknechte' became a by-word.

In this mould was Cesare Borgia (1476–1507), son of one of the most corrupt of the popes, Alexander VI (1431–1503). This would-be builder of an Italian papal state was a model of sadism and political manipulation, admired in his own time by Niccolo Macchiavelli (1469-1527), the distinguished Florentine theoriser of *realpolitik*, and later by Nietzsche as the prototype Renaissance superman. Borgia was a murderer, torturer, cheat and power maniac, as were a number of the other early condottieri like Galeazzo Sforza (1444–76), the debauched and prodigal Duke of Milan, and Sigismondo Malatesta (1417–68), the sadistic soldier of fortune of Rimini. Significantly, it was in Italy in 1476 that Bartolomeo Colleoni (glorified in a magnificent equestrian statue by Verrocchio) conducted the first recorded serious deployment of artillery in the history of warfare, marking the commencement of a long period of destruction. In 1479, gratuitous violence was rare enough for that of Niccolo Vitelli's brutal campaign to excite comment—thereafter it became commonplace. In 1480, there was a total breakdown of law and order in the city of Parma, with robbers ruling the streets by day and night.

Courtly ruthlessness was evident on a much grander scale in the career of the Emperor Charles V (1500–55) of Austria and Spain, who sacked Rome in 1527 more violently than Alaric the Goth. Charles was renowned for his cruel treatment of Hesse and Saxony in 1548, and condemned the entire population of the Netherlands to death for insurrection, actually executing some 50,000. His pursuit of personal glory in facile competition with Francis I of France cost the best part of thirty years of warfare, yet his image was given Alexandrine charisma by the art of the great Venetian painter Titian (1490–1576), who painted a succession of portraits culminating in the majestic, equestrian *Charles V at the Battle of Muhlberg*. Two years after this painting of himself as a knight in shining armour, he had his court issue a 'Criminal Code' which Lecky describes as 'a pornographic treatise of mutilations, burnings, blindings and torture with red-hot pincers'. Adultery was forbidden on pain of death, mothers guilty of infanticide were to be impaled and buried alive.

Charles did, of course, have heroic qualities but exemplified above all the subjection of all other sanctions to the Renaissance thirst for glory inspired by their new reading of the mythology of Greece and Rome. The ruthlessness was given philosophical backing by Macchiavelli and the veneer of elegant chivalry was given full expression by Castiglione (1478–1529), the Italian professional diplomat described by Charles V as 'the greatest gentleman in the world'. His treatise *The Courtier* became the model for aristocratic manners throughout Western Europe. This was also, particularly in Italy, the period of the hired assassin, the agents of the Borgias, Charles V and others proving Pontavio's comment, 'nothing is cheaper than life'.

One special example of Renaissance egotism was the career of King Henry VIII (1491–1547). In his less permissive early years he introduced face-branding for the army's female camp-followers and made 'buggerie' a hanging offence. The use of torture had already begun to revive in England: John, Earl of Worcester (1427–70), known as the 'Butcher of England', was a cultivated and inventive Renaissance sadist working in royal employ before the Tudors, and Richard III (1452–85) had been a model Macchiavellian ruler. The rack was introduced to the Tower of London by the Duke of Exeter, and in 1542 boiling to death was still a recognised punishment. Sir Leonard Skevington brought in 'The Scavenger's Daughter' which crushed its victims and was in regular use under Henry VIII and Elizabeth I. Other instruments included the pilboes, which crushed ankles, the pilliwinks for fingers and the brakes for teeth, the last being particularly used to extract the confessions of the friends of Queen Katherine Howard before her and their executions. Holinshed estimated that there were 72,000 executions under Henry VIII and torture became a semi-official part of political persuasion. 'Peine forte et dure' was in legal use in England until about 1726.

In Russia, Ivan the Terrible (1530–84) pursued his own version of the European fashion, hurling his subjects to the bears so that he could observe their reactions and torturing, it was said, some 64,000 people to death in Novgorod. He devastated Livonia, laid huge tracts of his own country waste and had Jews drowned in considerable numbers. To assist his finances, he nationalised all public inns and encouraged heavy alcohol consumption to improve his revenues.

Ivan was led on into ever more eccentric sadism by the strange German, Dr Elijah Bomel (fl.1570). Five hundred monks were cudgelled to make them give up their treasure while several of the clergy of Pskov were burned at the stake. The diplomat Ivan Viskovetski was whipped before having his ears, nose, hands and feet removed. All this violence at the center was mirrored by an unusually high level of domestic violence. Wife-beating was standard—the Russian proverb said:

> Beat your shuba [fur coat] and she will be warmer, your wife and she will be sweeter.

This was accompanied by a reputation for widespread alcoholism, even in the period before vodka (a derivative of the Renaissance medicine, 'aquavit') had become popular. Fondness for alcohol, it was believed, had saved Russia from the northward spread of Islam. And the reputation for deviation also persisted; as one contemporary, Fennel, put it:

> The people live, flow and wallowe in the verie hight of their lust and wickedness of the crienge Sodomitical sines.

Ivan found it easy enough to dethrone the Archbishop of Novgorod on a charge of sodomy before having him sewn up in bearskins and mauled to death by dogs.

Another pillar of Renaissance chivalry who had his share of sadistic tendencies was the gallantly impetuous Charles the Bold (1433–77) of Burgundy, a great admirer of 'les neuf pieux' who showed his savagery at Granson in Switzerland and at Liege. While not exactly a puritan in his private life he was rebuked, by Huizinga and others, for 'continence unbecoming a prince', and for not enjoying himself enough in 'the stews'.

In 1444, an unruly group of unemployed mercenaries who became known as 'the Ecorcheurs' were led on an expedition by Louis XI of France in which they raped, pillaged, and hung their victims by the ankles or nailed them to doors. The English mercenary John Hawkwood (d.1394) and his White Company were infamous for their unbridled violence in Italy, and the new breed of Swiss mercenaries won fame for needless brutality, for instance after the Battle of Novara in 1513. Such was the era of insensitivity to human suffering created by new knowledge and the wealth and hunger for glory of the Renaissance.

Nor was violence confined to the professionals; in 1488, for example, the citizens of Bruges so much enjoyed the spectacle of public torture of some of their magistrates that they asked for more and halted the executioner from administering the *coup de grace* to a man who had already endured torture. Punishment was to remain a source of public entertainment for years to come. The citizens of Mons actually bought a spare criminal from a neighbouring town so that they could enjoy seeing him drawn and quartered.

The effort to retain at least a veneer of chivalry persisted, but with more of a classical strain. In 1430, Ghillebert of Lannoy produced his *Enseignements Paternels* using Roman models to train Burgundian heroes. The lives of Caesar and Alexander, the classic supermen, became ever more popular; the *Tratie de Noblesse* by Diego de Valera in 1454 followed the same pattern. This was also the popular period of the image of princes as romantic figures wandering the streets in disguise, like James V of Scotland, 'the King and the Cobbler'. In 1470, Malory's *Morte d'Arthur* showed Lancelot as 'the kindest man that ever struck with the sword, the meakest man that ever ate in the hall with ladies'.

Another feature of Renaissance regression was the revival of the European slave trade. As early as 1300 the Venetians were using black slaves on their sugar plantations in Cyprus, and between 1414 and 1423, for example, 10,000 slaves were bought and sold by Venetians. When the Portuguese admiral Alfonso d'Albuquerque (1453–1515) seized Goa, the Moslem inhabitants were massacred and all the Mediterranean states aped the Turkish interest in the African slave trade. A Portugese raid on the coast of Senegal in 1441 was the first to return with black slaves.

Turning to religious intolerance, we find there the same tendencies which characterised political life. In 1401 came the Inquisition bull *De haereticis comburendo*, and the rule of the zealous Dominican monk, Bernard Guy, as Chief Inquisitor. He looked back to their patron saint, Peter Martyr, the pioneering inquisitor of Como who had been murdered because of his urgent hunting of heretics. In 1481, Tomas de Torquemada (1420–98), the torture specialist, was making the Spanish Inquisition a by-word for cruelty, not just for burning Christian heretics but also for persecuting the large minority of Jews and Moors, over 1,000,000 of whom were driven out of Spain and Portugal during this period, many of the Jews seeking refuge in Eastern Europe. In 1391, 4,000 of them had been massacred and the rest had to wear a yellow badge on their chests. In 1481, 298 Jews were burned in Spain, the beginning of *auto-da-fé*. In 1506, 2,000 Jews were executed in Portugal. King Ferdinand of Spain (1452–1516) introduced condemnation to the galleys as a punishment for heretics.

The last of the Spanish Jews were to suffer the anger of King Philip II (1527–98) who gave them the blame for the defeat of the Armada. This fanatical monarch attempted to exterminate whole rebel towns in the Netherlands, was a substantial user of the Inquisition, yet meanwhile amused himself commissioning exotic nudes from Titian, such as the voluptuous *Danae* and the *Venus-Adonis*, compositions which he could secretly admire in his palace. In both 1578 and 1596 he demanded public investigations into the prevalence of sin, dismissing courtiers who were having affairs and calling for a moral purge. Between 1515 and 1610 the statistics show that thirty-two percent of all prisoners of the Spanish Inquisition were tortured. In addition to his wrath against Jews and Protestants, Philip was also an avid witch-burner, introducing the habit to Flanders.

In 1529, Marsilius of Bologna invented the idea of torture by sleeplessness, and in 1539 a book called *Scaligerama* explained techniques for the slow burning of heretics in Guienne using damp wood. Total burnings by the Spanish Inquisition alone were declared to be 31,000. As the victims were led to the flames they wore a special uniform depicting the torments of hell which they had to look forward to at the end of their earthly ordeal. In Holland, the Duke of Alva (1508–82) claimed to have executed 18,000 Protestants in five years, many of them by burning. Henry III of France (1557–89) executed 30,000, mostly Protestants. Francis I got his family to join him in physically setting light to French heretics, and the massacre of St Bartholomew's Day just rounded off the trend. Burnings in England under Queen Mary, in the Netherlands and many other European countries must have been well in excess of 100,000. In addition, many others were tortured. In England, for instance, a Protestant called Ann Askew was permanently crippled by the rack in the reign of Henry VIII, and later the Jesuit Edward Campion was tortured nearly to death in 1581 under Queen Elizabeth.

The other general victim of the Inquisition was the witch. In 1486 appeared the *Malleus Maleficarum* by Heinrich Kramer and Jacob Sprenger, an extremely sadistic guide to the disposal of witches, sponsored by the anti-Semitic Pope Innocent VIII (1438–98) and creating a whole new mythology of witch behaviour, developing on the earlier folk myths of John Nider's *Formicarius*. St Peter Canisius (1521–97) was the Jesuit witch-hunting patron, but the persecution was conducted by Protestant and Catholic alike. In all, Norman Cohn has calculated that over 200,000 so-called witches were executed in Europe in the sixteenth and seventeenth centuries, possibly many more, constituting one of the worst legal crimes in history. The new French inquisitor, Nicolas Remy, burned 800 women in one day.

Spain, as we have already seen in the reign of Charles V and will shortly see at work in the New World, was acquiring perhaps the greatest of all reputations for violence in the sixteenth century. Buckle comments on the extraordinary level of loyalty demanded and given to the Spanish kings: all courtiers spoke to Philip only from their knees, a loyalty fostered by epics such as *El Cid*, the supreme example of putting patriotism before other virtues. The next two Philips were to retain power despite devoting themselves to 'the lowest and most sordid pleasures'.

Two other individuals stand out in this period as examples of abnormal sadism, in an atmosphere which perhaps condoned at least minor cruelty. Giles de Retz, Sieur de Laval (1404–40), later nicknamed 'Bluebeard', was accused of bathing in the blood of infants until he was burned at the stake as a heretic in 1440. The charges may, however, have been trumped-up because he was an associate of Joan of Arc who died accused of witchcraft only nine years earlier. Count Vlad the Impaler of Wallachia, model for Dracula and nationalist leader against the Turks, was reputed to have executed some 40,000 peasants and enemies in his own unique way during his six years of office which came to an end in 1462.

Probably the most remarkable and successful opponent of male egotism in the Renaissance was the amazing Joan of Arc (1412–31), a model both of female chastity and of knightly valour in the service of a new kind of popular nationalism. In due course, she became the martyred champion of the small, feminist movement which responded to Renaissance man's generally low view of women. The later parts of *Roman de la Rose* had been particularly misogynist and Christine de Pisan's response, *Le dit de la Rose* (c.1400), was followed by a number of works which used Joan as their example. Pictures of her by Rubens and others developed the image of the maid in armour. *Le Champion des Dames* (1530) was just one of a series of feminist treatises in this period. The fact that the Inquisition accused Joan of witchcraft was another foretaste of the way in which the institutionalised sadism of this organisation now switched from Jews and heretics to eccentric women in its search for victims.

The double standards of Renaissance life, both lay and clerical, were not simply confined to the field of violence. A cult of the permissive had begun to be evident in the late fourteenth century; Boccaccio (1313–75) as a youth made fun of promiscuity in his hilarious *Decameron*, and his English imitator Chaucer (1345–1400), though many of his pilgrims' tales were highly moral, also had a good ear for salacious gossip and was clearly not unsympathetic towards his lusty young student and apprentice heroes. 'Alas, alas that ever love was sinne', said the Wife of Bath. The daughters of the Spanish nobility thought it an honour to be paraded naked before Charles V, who, ultimately satiated by this and constant warfare, was to retire to a monastery.

The Chevalier de la Tour Landry wrote his comprehensive guide to the obscurer forms of love, *'pour mes filles aprandre à romancier'*. Pope Pius II (1405–64) had himself written a daringly salacious novel before his promotion, and John Burchard, the slightly biased servant and biographer of the Borgias, described the orgies in which, for instance, at a papal feast fifty naked prostitutes crawled round the floor for chestnuts. Both Alexander Borgia (1431–1503) and Sigismondo Malatesta (1417–68) were openly accused of incest. In 1514, under Pope Leo X, Rome boasted 7,000 official prostitutes for a total population of 50,000, while the Pope indulged in lavish banquets of sixty-five different courses. Imperia Cognata, the famous Roman whore, was the model for Raphael's (1483–1520) *Parnassus*, and the Florentines invented the chastity belt, the use of which spread through Europe for the next two centuries and Spain for the next three. Fallopio invented his primitive protective device to reduce the spread of the new venereal diseases, because in 1494 (as if by divine ordinance) a new one, syphilis, appeared from nowhere to attack the promiscuous. In 1431, Henry VI of England was greeted in a French town by a tableau of three naked mermaids. In 1442, Agnes Sorel, the mistress of Charles VII, brazenly flaunted her body at court and even Louis XI was greeted with a topless charade in 1461. In the court of Francis 1, any man without a mistress as well as a wife was referred to as a 'nincompoop'.

In the German towns, necklines were so low that the burghers' wives were said by du Boulay to have 'opened the shutters'. Renaissance men attached prestige to successful promiscuity, and fifteenth-century mystery plays now echoed the trend with very explicit Garden of Eden scenes and the advent of 'indecent dances'. In 1476, the middle-class housewives of Lubeck took up prostitution in the evenings to ease their boredom. A Spanish nobleman who visited Bruges in 1438 was scandalised by the immodesty and promiscuity of the public baths, which Andrew McCall says 'the inhabitants considered as honest as our own going to church'.

The murdered Bishop Henry III of Liege had sixty-five bastard children; the priests of France had been forbidden to stay with their mothers and sisters because of the rise in incest. Masson has noted that when ex-pirate Balthasar Cossa (1362–1415) had been elected Pope John XXIII after the great Western schism, 'two hundred maids, matrons and widows, including a few nuns, fell victims to his lust'. There were 1,500 prostitutes on duty at the ecclesiastical Council of Constance in 1414, one of them earning 900 duckats a night. During the siege of Neuss, Charles the Bold of Burgundy provided one whore for every four men in his army. At one time after 1348 there was a belief that venereal disease was an antidote for the plague, and a major outbreak of promiscuity followed the myth. Francois Villon (1431–70) was the great Parisian poet of the low-life, serving himself as an attendant at Fat Margot's Brothel, one of thirty in Paris, while the great sculptor and silversmith Benvenuto Cellini (1500–71) showed in his diaries the violent amorality of Florentine life. As Jacob Burckhardt put it:

By the side profound corruption appeared personalities of the noblest harmony and artistic splendour.

Venice, thanks to the writings of Aretino and the copper plates of Giulio Romano in 1524, became the centre of a thriving trade in pornography. Female necklines were extravagantly low and even pack mules were doused with perfume. An attempt to expel the prostitutes from Venice had failed abysmally. In Italy, so Burckhardt observed,

Marriage and its rights were more deeply and deliberately trampled underfoot than anywhere else.

Masson quotes Bardello, who argued that women had an equal right to promiscuity:

Women continue to follow their passions careless of their honour and their lives.

Blonde hair and low necklines were the fashion. According to Giordanio, of 10,000 going to the altar not one was a virgin.

Florence, at its artistic peak, seems to have been a city on the edge of overliving, a city Chartier describes as full of 'gluttons, frequenters of taverns, whoremongers and other thieving scum'. The traditional Italian vendetta was enjoyed to the full; boxing, falconry and to-the-death tournaments provided good sport. Homosexuality seems to have become more prevalent, perhaps as the senses were over-indulged, perhaps in the wake of a permissive atmosphere. San Bernardino of Siena attacked fifteenth-century permissiveness, including 'boys who paint their cheeks and practise sodomy for gain'. In Germany at this time, homosexuals were known as 'Florenzin'. According to the Count of Brandome, lesbianism was spreading from Italy to France. In Paris, the last of the Valois kings was a homosexual who indulged in transvestite orgies and flagellation, surrounded by his 'mignons'. The Florentines imposed the penalty of castration for sodomites, flogging for their young male friends, and the burning of their homes for parents who sent their children to such trade. Male pimps suffered hand amputation and Florence at last deployed a new vice squad to police its own evils.

In Spain, the puritan interlude of Ferdinand and Isabella was followed by a period of relaxation. The Inquisition was more interested in doctrine than morality. Prostitution was regarded as a healthy protection for wedlock, and the increasing number of bordellos was justified by the belief that payment for extra-marital sex somehow purged the sin. Homosexuality was regarded as detestable, but there were organised rackets amongst the still significant minority of slaves and moriscoes who otherwise found economic survival difficult.

Medieval Russian life had been relatively strict: dancing, games, theatre and public mixing of the sexes (except in bath-houses) were forbidden. A wife who injured her husband could be buried alive, and the entire ethos was one of unquestioning obedience to tsar and Church. But, according to Olearius (*fl.*1630), the period after Ivan the Terrible saw a swing to greater permissiveness—'They are addicts to vile depravities, not only with boys but with men and horses.' Homosexuality was no longer severely punished and heavy drinking became common.

However, as so often in history, the puritan reaction was building up. In 1435, the *Book of Horns* by Catherine of Cleves pronounced 'The Seven Deadly Sins'. In 1470, the English homilist, Thomas Malory, finished his *Morte d'Arthur*, a moral epic poem. *The Castle of Perseverance*, the first morality play but really a dramatised sermon, appeared in 1401 and grew in popularity as did the play *Everyman*, which originated in Holland; that other entertainment with a message, 'the dance of death', first appeared in Bezançon in 1420. In 1400, there was a drive against homosexuals in Venice, followed in 1450 by a campaign against pre-marital sex. William Caxton (*c.*1422–1491), the pioneering English printer, regarded himself primarily as a moral propagandist, producing titles such as *The Game of Chess Moralised*, *The Order of Chivalry*, *The Book of Good Manners* and many others.

In 1489, the Florentine monk Girolamo Savonarola (1452–98) delivered his famous sermon on sin and announced his new Christian commonwealth. A couple of years later he lit his 'bonfire of vanities' onto which the ladies of Florence were invited to throw all their jewellery, and he attacked the great artists of his city for 'tricking out the Mother of God in the frippery of a courtesan'. His radicalism was, however, in advance of his time and after his brief hegemony he was himself burned as a heretic. Very similar was the career of Hans Böhm (d.1474), the Drummer of Niklashausen, who preached repentance, the evils of jewellery and extravagant clothing (such as pointed shoes for men); he established himself as a prophet and was burned in Wurzburg in 1474.

At about the same time began the outstanding teaching career of the incisive Dutch ex-monk Erasmus (1466–1536), who was influenced by the ascetic beguinages of the Low Countries and who established a European reputation for removing layers of medieval humbug from the traditional Church.

In Bohemia, John Ziska (*c.*1370–1424) had carried on the Hussite tradition and founded the remarkable community of Tabor where his followers were bound together in brotherly love, where ownership of property was a mortal sin, and where there briefly existed a remarkably futuristic communal ethic. The free spirits of Tabor, the original 'Bohemians', established an advanced commune at Usti in 1419 which survived temporarily by raiding its neighbours. These people had given away all their personal property, often burning

down their own homes to create a community without personal property:

> As mine and thine do not exist at Tabor, whoever owns private property
> commits a sin.

Sadly, this led to a neglect of the work ethic and a resultant shortage of
food, so that robbery and violence had to be the next stage. Both the
Taborites and their German enemies were guilty of appalling atrocities
when they met in battle.

In 1509, Erasmus castigated the Carnival of Siena as unchristian and
grossly over-indulgent. In England, the Maypole was attacked for its
blatant frivolity. Philip Stubbes, in his *Anatomy of Abuses*, went on
about 'the horrible vice of pestiferous dancing' leading to 'filthy
groping'. Football was nearly as bad—'a murthering play'—and in
Languedoc there was a drive against the leaping dances in which skirts
flew indecorously high. In Zwickau after 1540, bridal couples were no
longer allowed to bathe in public as part of the wedding ceremony.
Nudity once more became an all-round source of embarassment. In
1530, Erasmus produced his best-selling *Manners of Children*, a treatise
on ethical training which went to eighty editions and was translated
into fourteen languages. Francis I abolished the French 'stews' in 1530,
as did Henry VIII the English in 1546, possibly in both cases because
of the dangers of syphilis.

Without question the greatest step in the ethical revolution was taken
by Martin Luther (1483–1540), who masterminded the biggest shift in
European ethical emphasis since St Augustine. This shift was in the
value attached to behaviour as opposed to theology in the estimation
of post-mortem rewards and punishments. It was Luther who gave
respectability to the idea of conscience and of ordinary work. The
first glimmerings of the so-called 'Protestant work ethic' came simply
from the greater importance attached to worldly success. The medieval
sin of usury, which had led to the branding of the Jews as almost
the only money-lenders, gradually vanished so that capitalism could
become more respectable. With the reduced role of the meditative
priest there was less question of blind obedience to doctrine, and
more consideration given to the rational appraisal of one's behaviour:
the conscience achieved new stature.

Not that Luther, an immensely devout man who could spend six
hours confessing his sins, was himself immune from a temptation
to persecute. He made his famous recommendation that rebellious
peasants should be 'killed like mad dogs' and, in 1543, that synagogues
be burned—Jews were 'poisonous bitter worms'. The Jews had been
blamed by the Germans for a number of major fires in 1542. Similarly,
the Bohemian Protestants also turned on the Jews and expelled them
from Prague—perhaps as usurers they were no longer needed. Indeed

most of the new sects were as intolerant as the old ones: Anabaptists were drowned in Protestant Switzerland; Quakers were persecuted even in the American Puritan colonies.

Moral thinking in England in the sixteenth century was evolutionary rather than revolutionary. Sir Thomas More (1478–1535) was to die defending the old religion, but his moral puritanism was evident in his *Utopia* where 'decency and integrity prevailed' and the family was the most important human institution.

In the *Boke of the Governour* (1531), Sir Thomas Elyot defined the virtues required of princes and ordinary individuals. Edmund Spenser (1552–99) wrote *The Faerie Queen,* a magnificent didactic poem based on Castiglione's *The Courtier,* 'to fashion a gentleman or noble person in vertuous or gentle discipline'. He was a close friend of Sir Philip Sidney (1554–80) 'the president of the noblesse and chevalrie' who was the moral hero of the Elizabethan era, with his legendary dying act of quixotry on the battlefield of Zutphen, refusing a drink as he lay wounded and directing it towards another wounded soldier, saying 'his need is greater than mine'.

Many writers took very seriously the role of poetry as a teacher of morality. William Webbe, commenting on *The Odyssey,* said its readers could

> ... learne many noble vertues and also learne to escape and avoyde the subtyll practices and perillous entrappings of naughty persons.

The work of the Italian, Ariosto (1474–1533), was now dismissed as obscene and trivial, as was the *Morte d'Arthur* as a glorification of 'manslaughter and bold bawdry'.

England in the early years of Elizabeth I (1533–1603) was to see a reversion to stricter sexual ethics compared with the permissive atmosphere of the second half of Henry VIII's reign. There was a trend towards later marriage, and norms of conduct were maintained by the Church with fines and penances: the Archdeacon's court was known as 'the Bawdy Court' because of the amount of time given to these matters. Bastardy was very much frowned on, as moralists became aware of the expensive growth of population, a burden on the well-off. Female fashions changed to figure-hiding garments while male clothes grew dandyish and almost effeminate. The Virgin Queen set the tone with her emphasis on the state rather than the family. Laurence Stone comments on what he calls 'the massive propaganda campaign for loyalty by the English monarchy in the sixteenth century'.

It is easy to take for granted the very large ethical content in the works of William Shakespeare (1562–1616). In the early part of his career the erotic poetry of *Venus and Adonis* was dedicated to that ideal Renaissance man, the Earl of Southampton; but once he had got over 'the dark lady', Shakespeare began to bring to the Elizabethan stage a complete re-working of all the classical moral themes with a style and vigour hardly matched before or since. Plays like *King Lear* gave a new dimension to the portrayal of the struggle between good and evil, and the full range of moral conflict was explored in the other great tragedies. *The Tempest* had some of the overtones of the previous century's morality plays, with the victory of virtue.

More revolutionary than the Lutheran tradition was that of Jean Calvin (1509–64), founder in Geneva of one of the most morally strict regimes in the whole of human history and pioneer of what became the Puritan movement. His ban on dancing, public drinking and cards, let alone adultery and conventional vices, was so severe that there was a year-long rebellion against it by the libertines in 1538, and it was some time before Calvin's supremacy in Geneva was complete. Unlike Luther, Calvin essentially reduced the importance of moral decision making by his emphasis on church membership as the sole criterion for entry to heaven, his predestinarian dogmatism being spiritually closer to Augustine. Calvin did insist, however, on very strict moral standards for church membership: adultery, blasphemy and heresy were all punishable by death, and the Spanish Unitarian, Servetus (1513–53), was burned at the stake in Geneva having escaped the clutches of the Spanish Inquisition. Some twenty-five homosexuals were executed in Calvinist Geneva and others severely punished. Despite or because of this intolerance, Calvinism was (according to Hunt) 'one of the most successful systems the world has ever seen' and was to spread into France, Holland, Britain and America. In France, the Calvinist Huguenots set themselves apart by adopting a new appearance; the short-haired 'razats' were a precursor of the English 'roundheads'.

Most extreme of all the new sects were the Anabaptists, northern Germans who (in general) were anti-permissive, repudiated luxury, forbade games like dice and cards, and dismissed long hair and fashionable clothing as arrogant vanity. They believed strongly in pacifism, brotherly love and charitable giving, sometimes in shared property: as such, their influence was to survive in a number of Christian sects.

The Anabaptists of Munster, however, went through a more extravagant phase. First, a wandering visionary, Melchior Hoffmann, in 1533 preached the Second Coming with such fervour that the populace became gripped by a mass obsession. Then came the Anabaptist conversion of Dutch preacher, Jan Mattys, followed by the even more fanatical John (Bockelson) of Leyden (1500–35), who took over the city and defended it against the armies of the neighbouring city states. The regime began as a quasi-communist one, with money and private property abolished, yet the death penalty and torture were required to maintain discipline during the long and difficult siege. Initially the attitude towards sex was very puritan, but as the siege continued many men escaped and the remainder found they were outnumbered three to one. John of Leyden introduced compulsory polygamy, setting an example himself by taking fifteen new wives, including the widow of his predecessor. Any wives of exiles who refused to accept compulsory new husbands, or quarrelled with other members of the harem, could be executed: divorce was made easier and rapidly the situation degenerated into promiscuity. Thus the switch from extreme puritanism to total permissiveness happened within a single year, paralleled by a similar cycle from extreme democracy to absolute despotism, as John Bockelson made himself King John of Leyden in the same period. The fear that this strange episode in ethical history generated amongst neighbouring countries was such that when the siege was ended the inhabitants of Munster were all exterminated, either by the sword or by deliberate, slow starvation.

The Anabaptists were given further notoriety by other small offshoots, like the Blood Friends founded in 1557 by Claus Ludwig of Tungeda, who abandoned conventional marriage and created the image of the Adamite orgies. The original Adamites regarded property and exclusive marriage as sins, and declared that the chaste were unworthy to enter the messianic kingdom; so they were given to naked ritual dances and hymn-singing round the fire. Based on an island on the River Nezarka in Bohemia, they waged a holy war against the rest of the world which they wanted to convert to their own version of Eden. They were exterminated in 1421 by John Ziska's Taborite army. Anabaptism was to be revived by Menno Simon (1496–1561), with his remarkable repudiation of violence, and later by Jacob Hutter in Moravia; 200 years later, the pacifist Moravians refused to join in the defence of American Georgia when it was attacked by the Spaniards.

Protestantism has, of course, been connected with a revival of the work ethic as well as supporting the moralisation of money-lending, which fostered the growth of capitalism. Certainly Tudor England was already conducting an attack on the work-shy. In 1531, idle vagabonds were to be whipped publicly and in the rest of that decade the established Church preached continuously on the wickedness of feckless unemployment. Throughout Europe a social norm of late marriage was established, as in peasant families the sons did not inherit the plot until they were in their late twenties; and in towns artisans did not marry until they became master-craftsmen at about twenty-eight. As the upper end of those two groups prospered they produced the new puritan ethos of patiently waiting for a sober, successful family life in early middle-age. It was what Lawrence Stone called 'a remarkably chaste society managing to avoid both illegitimacy and repression by the carefully policed concept of intimate courting'. It was an era of immaculate white collars, demonstrating the cleanliness and self-control of the wearer. Yet it was a period in which the Puritans were constantly worried by the probable revival of lax ways. Philip Stubbes wrote in 1580:

> Was there ever seen less obedience in youth of all sorts towards their superiors, parents, masters and governors?

The Catholic response to the desertion of so many of its former adherents to both Lutheranism and Calvinism was a dramatic shake-up of its own moral attitudes and performance. The change was embodied particularly in the career of Ignatius Loyola (1491–1556), a dynamic new force in the old tradition both of monastic revival and of militant Christianity. An extreme ascetic, he not only swore the customary oath of chastity and poverty but mortified the flesh with fasting and daily scourging. He had a remarkable understanding of the techniques of brain-washing as he built up his network. His example inspired a major revival in Roman Catholicism and the appearance of a new kind of pope, such as the barefoot ascetic Pius V (1504–72) who outlawed prostitution in Rome in 1566, an amazing turnaround from the Borgia era. Not only was the new Catholicism purer, it was also more severe and competitive, justifying violence and even tyrannicide in the pursuit of Catholic objectives. The new confidence was symbolised by the first baroque church (also the first Jesuit church) built in Rome, and the new Catholic puritanism by the fig leaves attached to the Michelangelo masterpieces in the Vatican. The revulsion against the Renaissance classical nudes of the great masters was total, and they were formally condemned by the Council of Trent. In France, one of Louis XII's ministers had a major Michelangelo masterpiece burned as a dirty picture. In Rome, Cardinal Carafa (1476–1559) became pope and revived the Roman Inquisition with an attempt at a moral dictatorship in the city almost like Calvin's in Geneva. Again Puritanism was half-associated with violence; and in Spain, John of the Cross (1542–91) and Teresa of Avila (1515–82) together reformed the barefoot Carmelite orders, where there was no such association.

In 1565, the confessional box was invented by the Council of Valencia to help purge Europe of its sins. At the same time Catholicism condoned numerous acts of violence, not least Catherine de Medici's Massacre of St Bartholomew's Day in 1572, in which as many as 30,000 Huguenots were murdered. Prostitution in France had been made illegal in 1560; at Toulouse, prostitutes were branded and ducked in the river three times.

A new wave of masochism characterised some of the saints. St Mary Magdalene dei Pazzi in 1585 rolled on thorns, whipped herself, had hot wax poured over her, had herself tied to a post and made a novice stand on her mouth. St Margaret Marie Alacoque ate rotten fruit, drank dirty laundry water and licked the vomit of her patients as a penance.

Despite his condemnation by the Jesuits, the work of Cornelius Jansen of Utrecht (1585–1638) was essentially also towards a more puritan version of Catholicism, as was the movement of the Pietists in Germany. Overall this period saw a quite remarkable revival in the moral standards of the Catholic Church, reflected in the amazing missionary achievements of the Jesuits in China, Japan and South America. There was, of course, still a streak of violence in the treatment of heretics; but as we have seen, the Protestants were (for a period) also still guilty of the same tendency.

The other particular feature of the Jesuit moral drive was the encouragement of the cult of the Virgin Mary. The raising of attitudes towards women through the creation of a female saint and heroine, venerated particularly for her combination of chastity and motherhood, was a significant Jesuit contribution, although there was the danger that ordinary women would be seen as unchaste and therefore contemptible. The cult of Mary was spread over South America and the Far East but, despite stereotypes like the Virgin of Guadeloupe, the Spanish and Portugese males believed 'Fornicar no es pecada'—for men to fornicate is not sin, for women different.

If religious persecution and political amorality were the first two great crimes of the sixteenth century, the third and worst was the escalation of slavery which followed the discovery of the New World. It began when Henry the Navigator opened up the new routes to western Africa in 1442. Christopher Columbus (1451–1506), who hunted the natives of Hispaniola with dogs, sent back 500 Indian slaves to Queen Isabella of Spain after his first transatlantic landing in 1492, but she released them and sent them back. Nevertheless, within a few years the disastrous transportation of labour from western Africa to the West Indies had begun. John Hawkins (1532–95) in 1562 conducted the pioneering slave expedition which developed into a business. By 1786 this had extracted some eleven or twelve million Africans from their homelands and shipped them westwards, a cruelly high percentage of them dying in great misery en route. It must rank as one of the most callous periods of exploitation and partial genocide in civilised history. It resulted also in the Spanish Caribbean becoming what Perris referred to as 'a happy hunting ground for British hooligans'. It involved the systematic degradation of slaves by branding, stripping of clothes and 'close packing' in boats. The trade was always vicious but became more so as the slavers grew hardened by habit and by pressure for profit.

Christian justification for the new outbreak of slavery came first of all from the monks of St Jerome in the West Indies in 1509, but much more far-reaching were the arguments put forward by the great Spanish bishop Las Casas (1474–1566), the Apostle of the Indies. His motive for condoning the importation of tough African labour was his desire to protect the (as he judged it) less fit aboriginal population of the

Caribbean who were succumbing to the harsh Spanish discipline in the sugar plantations. He was simply choosing what appeared to be the lesser of two evils but he took as biblical backing the legend of Ham, the first negro in the Old Testament, who had been offensive to his drunken father. The Spaniards had justified their Caribbean genocide on the grounds that the 'Caribees' were cannibals, an unfair assertion. What can be said in defence of Spanish slave-ownership, as opposed to British, was that the Spaniards did not break up families deliberately as the British did, and they encouraged slave baptism whereas the British did not. But in Surinam the use of slave labour was so wasteful that 50,000 slaves became extinct every twenty years and had to be replaced with fresh imports. The problems caused by the transportation were to fester for many years and were only partially resolved by the American Civil War some 300 years after Hawkins. After 400 years the struggle for civil rights was still continuing, and the bitterness engendered by the cruel uprooting lingers on.

Meanwhile the Portuguese also developed the use of slavery in their sugar plantations on the Congo from the 1550s, and with massive expansion in Brazil, where their regime was noted for a toughness and tolerance of multi-racial promiscuity which produced an unusual depth of racial blending. What was significant about the Congo was that the Portuguese, in trying to impose their own legal system on the native Congolese, found that they already had a remarkably sophisticated legal code, similar to the Portuguese except in so far as the Congolese were less possessive about material goods and therefore did not make theft a capital offence, as did the Christian Europeans.

It is important to recognise that while the history of Africa in this period is still obscure, it should not be assumed that the European slave-traders who developed contact with its peoples were entering an ethical desert. We have already seen the examples of native Congolese law. There were also advanced (though as yet ill-studied) systems in other African states. Benin was the centre of a culture which was reaching its peak around 1450, with a strong discipline and a tendency towards mass suicide at important funerals; for instance, 285 women committed suicide at the funeral of Bissa in 1774. Later, as commercial pressure undermined morale, the priests of Benin resorted to human sacrifice—Le Grand Custom. Similarly, the Ashanti and Masai were developing strong military ethics with solid codes of loyalty and self-control. The Masai in particular cultivated a remarkable ability to resist pain, stoic endurance of difficulty. Many of these cultures were to suffer corruption by contact with the bribes of European slave-traders, and were long underestimated by European commentators.

While the conquerors brought the cult of Mary to America, they did not bring many white women except for camp-followers. It was, therefore, a period of great male permissiveness even amongst the clergy, except for the Jesuits. The conqueror of Chile, Francisco de Aguirre (*fl.*1550), boasted of his fifty bastard children; but women were illogically expected to be virtuous while being condemned as incapable of it. One of the remarkable Spanish women of South America was Catilina de los Rios (1604–65), a cultivated sadist, daily flogger of her slaves and murderer of at least forty victims. Wealth, power over a subject people and geographical disorientation all contributed to the corruption of the Spaniards in the West. Also witnessed by Las Casas, and just as brutal an expression of Renaissance lust for self-glory, were the Spanish conquests of Mexico and Peru. Before reviewing those sadistic but darkly glamorous events, we should consider the two empires which were Spain's victims.

The Aztec Empire of Mexico had not lasted particularly long, and its short history was one of extraordinary cruelty. The year 1389 saw the foundation of Tenochtitlan, the first settlement of the wandering Aztec mercenaries who were renowned for their brutality. It expanded under Tezozomoc (1356–1426), leader of the chosen people, whom Davies tells us pronounced: 'At last we have been worthy of our god'. Tenochtitlan became a conquering power in its own right, with its prime objective obtaining enough prisoners of war to sacrifice to their insatiable god, Huitzilpochtli.

The inspiration behind this rapid and dramatic expansion of Aztec power was the remarkable Tiacaellel (1400–80), the male snakewoman prophet known as 'the Macchiavelli of Mexico', who preached the necessity of mass human sacrifice fed by conquest. Hearts were torn from living victims with obsidian knives, heads were slashed off female dancers and children drowned to please the rain god in one of history's cruellest societies. In certain cases, ritual cannibal meals followed the sacrifices. There may have been an economic reason behind the culling of hostages and prisoners in that the Aztecs' food supplies were notoriously unreliable, and there were a series of famines culminating in a particularly bad one in 1450. This may be borne out by the fact that in other respects their regime was relatively humane. Rulers were regarded as having the duty to look after poor widows and orphans, there were public hospitals, and Davies also tells of an Aztec adage:

Feed the poor, clothe the naked, cherish the sick for they are nigh to God.

The main ethos of the Aztecs was, however, based on an élitist concept of military knighthood which encouraged a fatalistic view of life, submitting to expected disasters like famines and earthquakes which seemed always on the horizon, and with a good after-life which, as for the Vikings, depended more on how you died than on how you lived. There was an automatic passport to heaven for soldiers in battle, victims of human sacrifice, mothers and children, and victims of earthquakes. Chastity was highly regarded and adultery a serious crime. They believed in the value of confession of sins, but punishments for offences were extremely harsh; an adultress who killed her rival was roasted and had salt poured over the wounds, disobedient army officers were flayed alive, even soldiers who surrendered and then escaped from the enemy were executed on their return, as were priests caught drinking too much. Executioners were, in fact, at the top of the social scale. Training of young warriors was precisely disciplined, with total concentration on producing highly competitive, glory-hunting officers. Trainees could be executed for drunkenness, but after their first successful appearance in battle were entitled to a concubine. Successful soldiers were able to lead a life of enormous luxury and wealth, and, at this level, prostitution was common, including transvestite boy prostitutes. Consumption of the local stimulant drug, peyote, was tolerated.

In 1486 came the climactic mass human sacrifice at the dedication of Huitzilpochtli's new temple. According to the records, 70,000 prisoners of war had their hearts cut out in one monstrous ceremony. Tzompantli, the huge wall of skulls, was built. During this period, Prescott estimated that in a typical year there were around 20,000 human sacrifices. Allowing even for tenfold exaggeration, it was still one of humanity's most barbarous single acts. But the warrior priests of Mexico were masochists as well as sadists, in the name of their religion. They would, for example, pass hundreds of sticks through freshly drilled holes in their tongues before singing hymns. Self-castration was practised, fasting, bleeding and freezing in a frenetic lust for priestly promotion.

The last ruler of this unsavoury empire was Montezuma II (1466–1520), who has earned subsequent sympathy as the bewildered victim of the conquistador Cortes (1485–1547); but his record was not a particularly attractive one. He had usurped the throne and made himself very unpopular by the harsh treatment of his relatives and others, which he had felt necessary to protect his insecure position. So the Aztecs fell an easy prey to the Spaniards. In the recorded words of Otomi: 'There is none who can surpass the Mexican in evil'.

The Inca Empire to the south was even more remarkable, though much less cruel. The expansion of Peruvian power began under the Inca Pachacutu (1420–71), taking in the areas now known as Ecuador and Bolivia, plus northern Argentina and Chile. Unlike the Aztecs, the Incas relied largely on apparent benevolence, immediately freeing all conquered prisoners of war so that they became loyal recruits to help conquer the next victim country. Cuzco was a remarkable, precision-built city of amazing architecture at the centre of a road system worthy of the Romans. Human sacrifice did occur but on a much smaller scale than in Mexico, mainly with young girls under ten as the victims of the gods. The Incas were themselves treated as gods, so it was customary when they died to execute their wives and staff, after first doping them with drugs or alcohol, and so provide for the comfort of the dead monarchs. Chastity seems to have been highly regarded, as shown by the convent of the Virgins of the Sun, and the motivation for good behaviour was, as in so many societies, the promise of a better after-life, although members of the noble class had the privilege of an automatic passport to heaven. Like the pharaohs, the Inca royal families allowed incestuous marriages. A hard work ethic was fostered with a low all-round level of material comfort, as so much resource was put into empire-building. A high birth-rate was also encouraged by compulsory early marriage.

The last independent Inca before the Spanish conquest was, like Montezuma, a usurper. Atahualpa (d.1533) had killed his own brother to reach the throne, had then (according to legend) drunk from his skull, and exterminated most of their relations. And, like Montezuma, the last real Inca succumbed somewhat naïvely to the conquistadors, in this case Francisco Pizarro (1478–1541).

Las Casas, in his history of the invasions, estimated that in the Aztec and Inca conquests by the Spaniards some 12,000,000 people died. He may have exaggerated, but the Spaniards did have a destructive confidence in their cause and more than half the deaths are attributed to European diseases or to disruption of food supply. The efforts of Franciscan friars, who used portable ovens to roast small animals as a hell demonstration and to help convert the American aboriginals to Catholicism, were crude but effective. The conquered peoples were rapidly converted. The deliberate encouragement of alcoholism was another tool used both to debilitate the aborigines and make money for the conquerors. Finally, the Spaniards were also guilty of massacring large numbers of Chinese traders in the Philippines in 1603, while the Portuguese conducted appalling massacres in China from 1522. Barbarians everywhere were fair game. The females, in particular, became members of slave harems for Europeans. Boxer tells us that, of the overseas Portuguese it was said in 1550:

> The sin of licentiousness is so widespread . . . men buy droves of girls and sleep with all of them and subsequently sell them again.

In Europe and the Middle East, the mantle of Islam was now firmly in the grip of the Ottoman Turks who, in 1453, at last captured Constantinople. Power fairly soon corrupted the Turks, but like most great bureaucracies they could sustain amazing corruption at the top without much apparent damage to the main structure of their empire. The regime had some remarkable characteristics: there was the levy of slave children from the large number of Christian families throughout their empire, including the luckless Armenians. There was a 20,000 turnover of slaves in the market at Constantinople alone. The élite of these slaves were chosen for training as the robotic crack troops of the sultanate, the janissaries. Not only were they fearless soldiers but, as compulsory celibates deprived of all forms of family ties, they found what Gibbon described as

> ... gratification for violent, sensual and sordid passions of their animal instincts amid the customary atrocities of war.

The reign of the sultan Bajazet I (1347–1403) was 'marked by a general corruption of morals and manners, propagated by the example of the court', especially Bajazet himself. His idea of justice was to order the belly of his chamberlain to be cut open because of a complaint that he had drunk the goat's milk of a poor woman.

The seraglio at the palace of Topkapi generated corruption: love affairs between an excess of bored concubines and frustrated eunuchs, lesbianism amongst the odalisques, opium addiction amongst the celibate army of janissaries, impoverished Georgian prostitutes of both sexes and drunkenness amongst the sultans. Since the seraglio kept producing so many potential heirs to the sultanate, there was within the royal family an accepted law of fratricide whereby the eldest son had to murder all his brothers and rivals in order to have any security, or at best imprison them for life. In general, the immensity of the wealth and power of the sultans made them rather like the worst emperors of Rome or Greek Constantinople. For example, the sultan Murad IV (d.1640) cut off his gardener's legs as a punishment for smoking, and massacred 60,000 rebels in Baghdad. In 1526, some 200,000 prisoners of war were massacred after the Battle of Mohacz. Generals like Lala Mustafa, who conquered Cyprus, tortured and flayed a Venetian counterpart. They were enervated by the challenges of the seraglio and driven to alcoholism: as the proverb put it, 'when a sultan takes to drink it is permissible for all to do the same', even in an Islamic state. Many sultans were prodigal and irresponsible, yet the Turkish war machine remained remarkably effective, and discipline was certainly very strict. Treacherous officers were flayed alive, and a gulp of red-hot lead was a not uncommon punishment for lower ranks.

Permissiveness was probably, as so often, confined mainly to the richer class. It was Sheik al Nafzawi of Tunis, a city where one of its sultans had a harem of 500 boys, who wrote *The Perfumed Garden* in the sixteenth century, maintaining an Islamic taste for soft pornography evident since *The Thousand and One Nights* of the Caliph Haroun al Rashid. The strange Turkish poet, Ishak Tschelebi, as Gibbon put it, 'indulged an infamous passion not rare among the Turks'. The new public baths on the Bosphorus 'appealed to the voluptuous passions of the Turks' and after their victories armies were 'as happy to carry off the pretty boys as the girls'. Drug consumption too remained significant. The traveller Raoulf, visiting Aleppo in the 1570s, is quoted by Inalcik as commenting: 'the Turks and Moors are in the habit of taking opium not alone during wars but also to give good heart and courage', and some respectability was given to this habit by the use of opium amongst the holy dervishes.

Further to the East was the resurgent Persian Empire, with its spectacularly beautiful capital in Ispahan. Shah Abbas the Great (1557–1628) expanded all his frontiers from a court where Islam could not restrain the self-indulgence. He prided himself on his ability to turn his slaves into eunuchs, had a reputation for pederasty as well as a massive harem, yet was surrounded by devastating poverty.

In India, the pattern of moral contrast continued. Kabir (1440–1518) began an attack on the caste system. His pupil, the guru Nanak (1469-1533), founder of Sikhism, ushered in one of the most profound new movements for many centuries. Sikhism had certain similarities with European Protestantism in that it placed more emphasis on individual conscience and less on religious ritual.

> Follow virtue and humility along the path to God . . .

> Hereinafter there is no caste . . .

> The beauty of the lotus is not diminished by the filthy water that may surround it.

It also sought some kind of reconciliation between Hinduism (from which it sprang) and Islam, condemning unnecessary conflict but accepting the idea of the just war. It rejected some of the eccentricities of the fashionable yogis and ascetics, although its own ethical standpoint was firm and has retained a tenacious grip right up to the present day, with over 6,000,000 adherents. Their response to persecution in 1699 was to become a fighting brotherhood—'the exaltation of the sword'—which added a strong military tradition to their creed. Their five evils, all beginning with 'k' in Hindu, were anger, greed, lust, materialism and pride; their five virtues were faith, charity, righteousness, humility and uprightness. Their recognition of the equality of women and classes was significant, and their five special symbols were unshorn hair, bangle, comb, knife and breeches. All full members of the sect added Singh to their name.

By contrast, the guru Vallabah (1479–1521) developed the hedonist cult which suggested that all the pleasures of the world should be enjoyed to the full in order to please Krishna. In the view of his followers, all forms of self-indulgence were virtuous; vices of the flesh, even homosexuality, were praiseworthy; music and dance were especially excellent and the only real sin was the sin of self-denial. A third prominent guru, Chaitanya (1485–1534), developed the purer cult of Vishnu, with its emphasis on devotion and ritual made more exciting by the constant rhythm of cymbals and drums. *The Lake of the Story of Rama* by Tulsilas (1532–1623) became the favourite book of 100,000,000 people.

The contrast remained. Kalyanamalla (fl.1200) produced *Ananga Ranga*, a guide to physical love, the objective of which was to prevent marital boredom and so discourage adultery. Temples like Konarak were decorated with enormously permissive statuary, as sex received religious blessing. Bengali Buddhism, also on its last legs, went permissive and magic, but in one year the puritanical Aurangzeb (1640–1707) destroyed 200 of the obscenely decorated temples and castrated the nude Jain statues of Gwalior. He revived the department of moral censorship in Mogul India in 1668, employing snoopers to enforce his puritanical standards, persecuting the Hindus and successfully eliminating Buddhism in India. Various forms of human sacrifice persisted: the Khonds of Orissa conducted seasonal sacrifices in front of big crowds, and at the funeral of General Kuava in Mysore, 1,000 warriors were persuaded to commit mass suicide, while 500 were buried with the King of Narsynga in 1576.

Within the Islamic part of Indian culture, the most innovative ruler of this period was without question the Mogul emperor, Akbar (1542–1605). Although a devout Moslem, he was substantially more tolerant of other religions than his Christian counterparts; in particular he was tolerant of Hinduism, and even developed his own new eclectic creed, a mixture of what he thought best in Islam, Hinduism and Christianity, called Fah-din-i-Ilahi. The well-intentioned Akbar, like so many philosopher-kings, was blessed with the misfortune of two alcoholic sons, the eldest, Jahangir (1506–1627), keeping a harem of 5,000 ladies and 1,000 young men, as well as indulging in opium. Akbar made huge efforts to curb alcoholism and even attempted a form of prohibition. The drink of Mogul aristocrats was 'charburgha', a mixture of cannabis, opium, wine and spices. In fact, both alcohol and drug excesses marred the careers of the highly creative Mogul emperors. Babur (1483–1530) took a drug called 'majun', and Himayin enjoyed opium in rose water. Prostitution also flourished and the Sufis, under the Moguls, had a reputation for condoning homosexuality. Though outwith this period, it is perhaps just worth recalling that it was one of Akbar's grandsons, another tolerant Moslem emperor, Shah Jehan, who built for his wife that sublimely beautiful monument, the Taj Mahal.

One of the remarkable features of this period is that despite the Moslem conquest of India, Islam failed to convert more than about a quarter of the Indian population. This is particularly remarkable in that Islam was casteless and might have been expected to appeal, although of course it did both veil and reduce the status of women.

In 1364, China had seen the foundation of the remarkable Ming dynasty, whose first emperor had begun his career as a mendicant Buddhist monk. The Ming period was essentially one of a stable ethical background, with a revival of the Confucian doctrines of respect for elders, ritualised bureaucracy and mannered routines. The Ming were well known for their exceptionally brutal forms of corporal punishment for government officials, which kept corruption at a very low level. The Emperor Hung Wu (1368–98) was specially noted for his violence.

It was the great period of the Chinese morality play, with colour make-up codings for actors: green for bad, pink for lovable, white for patient, black or red for loyal. The only two significant ethical abnormalities were the continued habit of female infanticide, and castration of young males to provide eunuchs as recruits for the imperial service. The second of these two methods of population control had the effect, as it did on so many imperial courts from Constantinople to Peking, of encouraging palace corruption and intrigue, which from time to time undermined the Ming system. This period also saw the birth of a new vice in China, which was in due course to reach enormous and dangerous proportions in subsequent centuries—opium smoking. Introduced and commercially exploited by Moslem and European traders, specifically the British East India Company, it was significant that the great British hero of India, Robert Clive (1725–74), became an opium addict.

Meanwhile, the highly creative Khmer regime of Angkor had become less aggressive, almost pacifist, altruistic and permissive to the point where it succumbed to conquest by the more aggressive and puritanical Thais. The topless temple dancers of Cambodia were transferred to Bangkok and forced to dress more prudishly.

That small and intensely religious country, Tibet, also at this time produced one of its outstanding religious reformers, Tsong-ska-pa (1358–1469), who reformed Tibetan Buddhism and developed a new élite of yellow-hatted lamas with a creed based on celibacy, abstinence from alcohol and the monastic ideal. Lhassa was soon surrounded by a ring of monasteries, and the high ratio of yellow hats made it one of the most spiritually active countries in the world.

Japan indulged in a hugely destructive civil war (1466–77), which led to a period of great gloom and pessimism, with unrestricted violence and a loss of ethical standards until, of their own accord, the new local leaders or 'daimyos' began to introduce their own local codes of behaviour. Even these, however, condoned treachery and cheating in warfare, which was quite unlike the earlier samurai attitude. By contrast, in the older samurai tradition, the forty-seven dispossessed samurai or 'ronin' killed their dead master's murderer and then submitted themselves to voluntary seppuku.

Overall, there was a trend in these two centuries towards ruthlessness and intolerance, with the revival of religious persecution, slavery and misdirected warfare. The worship of appearances and contempt for realities was not just confined to those areas affected by the

Renaissance, but appeared in different guises in other parts of the world as well. If anything, the human species was growing ethically more stupid: exhibitionistic obsessions were admired more than ever, cloaked in the most brilliant artistic finery so that their lethal effects might escape notice.

1600 — 1700

Sin is reputed to be no sin.

John Knox

MANY OF THE WORST aspects of religious squabbling in Western Europe continued into the seventeenth century. In 1619, the Dutch libertine Vanini was burned at the stake for pronouncing that there was no sin except the sin of thinking that society was sinful. The Emperor Ferdinand II (1578–1637) was the first imperial Jesuit, and was totally dedicated to the persecution of Protestantism. C.V. Wedgewood said of him:

> Few men so honest and pious have brought on the world such an avalanche of misery.

Not that Ferdinand alone was responsible for the Thirty Years War, or that religion was the sole subject of disagreement, but this war was so bitter, was fought so much over the heavily populated lands of the peoples involved, that it is estimated that some 7,000,000 lives were lost as a result. The devastation was particularly bad, and so was the moral breakdown that went with it. When the city of Magdeburg was captured after a long siege, 20,000 men, women and children were killed because the Count of Tilly's army was allowed to get out of control. Savage reprisals were a regular occurrence. At Wieskirche in Bavaria, the entire population was massacred just for refusing hospitality to the Count Mansfeld's passing army. At the siege of Breisach, the starving garrison resorted to eating their dead companions. At Fuerstenfeld and Diessen, monks and citizens were tortured and killed, while after the imperial capture of Kempten, men, women and children were all slaughtered. Glamorous but callous irresponsibility was typified by the dashing cavalry commander Count Pappenheim (1594–1632), who, in the great tradition of this type, knew neither fear for himself nor pity for others: his was the responsibility for the massacre of Magdeburg. War was still the only means by which a gentleman could make money, and the custom of capturing for ransom persisted until 1848. As Wedgewood put it, King Gustavus Adolphus was

> One of those born conquerors . . . who never made any conclusion to a war that was more than an armistice.

This particular war did, however, bring its own specially high level of brutality. When it was over, in 1648, so many men had been killed that the Nuremberg Kreistag voted to legalise bigamy.

It was an intolerant and violent century. Matthew Hopkins (d.1647), the most infamous English witch-hunter, arranged for the execution of several hundred in Norfolk alone between 1645 and 1647. In fact, he was so obsessive that in 1647 he was accused of witchcraft himself, tested to see if he would float bound in water, succeeded, and was hung. Elsewhere, similar persecutors were at work: at Treves in France, 7,000 witches were burned, and in Warzburg in Germany, 900 in six years by Prince Adolf von Ehrenberg. Prince Bishop Johann Georg II at Bamberg burned 600 between 1622 and 1633. King James VI and I of Britain (1566–1625) was petrified of witches. In 1670, seventy witches were condemned in Sweden and 4,000 in one session of the Toulouse Inquisition. The Spanish Inquisition, while past its outrageous peak, was still active and this was the era of the great ceremonial *auto-da-fé*, special days of inquisitional activity, often ending in execution at the stake. In 1690, Charles II of Spain was compelled to watch the formal burning of heretics as part of royal protocol. On the other side of the Atlantic, the Massachusetts non-conformist minister, Cotton Mather (1663–1728), wrote his hysterical *Memorable Providences relating* to *Witchcraft and Possession* in 1685, which did much to fan the cruel persecution mania that came to a head in the Salem witch-hunt of 1692. So persecution of eccentric women and vicious cruelty to them was prevalent for most of the century throughout Europe and New England.

It is possible that witch-hunting was an extension of the male sense of insecurity brought on by the increasing confidence of Renaissance women. What began as the ducking stool and the charivari to humiliate bossy wives may have grown imperceptibly into a violent form of persecution. Both the Puritans and the Catholics were certainly concerned to maintain male dominance.

In New England there was also persecution of aboriginal Indians; the Pequot, for instance, were exterminated in 1637. Cotton Mather Senior said they should be 'treated like rattlesnakes'. In 1641, the pious Samuel Maverick proposed the commercial breeding of negroes on Noddles Island near Boston, another aspect of Christian racial élitism. Admittedly, some of the Indians had mores unlikely to appeal to Europeans: the Iroquois and Cherokee had a reputation for sadism, and the Shawnee indulged in the slow roasting of captives. But according to Father White, in 1630 the Indians in Maryland were very chaste and kind to children, and William Penn (1644–1718) commented that 'the Redskins were particularly unselfish'; nevertheless, the killing of whites by Indians in Virginia in 1622 was turned into a permanent atrocity-image used to justify a slow genocide.

Much more advanced, in many respects, was the remarkable republic of Paraguay, which was set up by the Jesuits in the vast area south of Brazil and flourished from 1607 to 1768. Inspired originally by the ideas of Padre Diego de Torres (*fl.*1610), these were the first colonists to reject slavery—no more enslaving of Indians in their territories was allowed after 1612. They ran a tolerant, paternalistic regime, with mild punishments, excellent administration, good training and sound planning for economic growth and welfare. Only the political collapse of the Jesuits led to the end of this worthy experiment in Christian government. Against this must be contrasted the totally amoral behaviour of the Mamelucos, a people of mixed Portuguese and Indian stock, who founded a base in São Paulo from which they conducted a most ruthless slaving operation—they provided Brazil with over 2,000,000 slaves, and led a life of frontier license. In Nueva Granada, where slavery persisted, control was so poor that large numbers of slaves (the Cimarrones) escaped, so that society became an unstable mix of expatriate Spaniards, expatriate Africans, dispossessed Indians plus various mixes and classes of all three. One other figure stands out from the sad record of slave ill-treatment—St Peter Claver (1580–1654), who in 1610 pronounced that he was forever 'the slave of the negro', and devoted himself to the recuperation of newly-transported Africans.

In Europe, intolerance was (to some extent) a feature of the height-ened religious consciousness arising from the Reformation. Puritanism was an English form of Calvinism which began to surface in the reign of Queen Elizabeth I. Because it placed all human beings at such a low level compared with God, it tended to pour scorn on earthly inequalities, and so was a source not just of moral reform but of a desire for political and social equality. The *Marprelate Tracts* of the 1580s had shown signs of this. In 1625, Hugo Grotius (1583–1645) published his *Law of War and Peace*, which was not just one of the first great intellectual condemnations of national wars, it also made one of the earliest statements on the natural rights of human beings. In 1628, the English Puritans were the force behind *The Petition of Right*, the first request for a formal recognition of the rights of subjects and a foundation of modern democratic theory. On the theoretical front, this led on the one hand to the version of the social contract propounded by Thomas Hobbes (1558–1679) in his *Leviathan* of 1651, where morality was seen, in the tradition of Dante, as part of obedience to a properly appointed monarch. But Hobbes regarded good and evil as inconstant whims, varying between different groups, with the human right of aggression as the one which should most sensibly be suppressed under a legitimate government. The other (differently inclined) English theorist on human rights of this period was John Locke (1632–1704), who in his *Essay on Human Understanding* (1690) brought a whole new emphasis on human welfare as opposed to national success as criteria for political morality. It was Locke's view, developed from Grotius and reacting somewhat against Hobbes, which was to be the foundation of French and American radicalism in the next century, and became the springboard for the Western democratic ideal.

Meanwhile, the political struggle which came out of English Puri-tanism's dislike of Stuart absolutism developed into the English Civil War. In moral terms, there was at this stage no great difference between the two sides. Under Charles I (1600–49) a reaction had already set in against the permissive trends of his father, James I. The latter had himself exhibited increasingly homosexual tendencies in his middle-age and, according to Ashton, 'protected sodomy and incest'. Already, in the last years of Elizabeth, there were London brothels providing girls aged from seven to fourteen. Aphra Benn, in her *To Fair Clorinda*, had pled the harmlessness of lesbianism. The high necklines of the Elizabethan era had given way to the plunging, Jacobean fashion. Bawdy songs known as 'jiggs' were all the rage, and Jacobean drama was obsessed with evil, for example in John Webster's *Duchess of Malfi* (1623) and John Ford's *'Tis Pity She's a Whore* (1639). Male fashions had grown unusually extrovert, with jewels, earrings and elaborate ruffs. In 1618, James had issued a proclamation encouraging 'dancing, leaping and other harmless recreations' on Sunday afternoons. With James's death in 1625 the mood changed.

Archbishop Laud (1573–1645), who attempted to suppress Puritanism, was himself almost Calvinist in his ethics. Adultresses had to stand in public in a white sheet; Lady Purbeck, who had lived 'in comfortable adultery' for fifteen years, had to go into exile. Idlers went to the 'House of Correction' and drunkards to the stocks, while unmarried mothers faced prosecution. Charles I was one of the most pure-minded of all English kings. It was Stuart despotism and episcopal ritual which men like Oliver Cromwell (1599–1658) found intolerable; Cromwell's army of Ironsides was one of the most strictly disciplined and idealistically motivated armies ever known, and very successful.

Bloodthirsty preachers, like Stephen Marshall, recommended 'the slaughter of the Amalekites'—'cursed is every man that holds his hand from shedding blood'—and at Drogheda in Ulster, Cromwell's troops were responsible for the massacre of between two and four thousand survivors of the siege. Cromwell described it, in a letter to Parliament in 1649, as 'a righteous judgement of God upon barbarous wretches'.

The government of the Cromwellian Commonwealth attempted to apply to a whole country the type of moral regime which Calvin had eventually asserted over the city of Geneva. Pleasure was believed by the Puritans to be sinful, so dull clothes, Sunday observance, work rather than play became the dominant features of the period. The pamphlet *St Hilarie's Teares* (1642) recorded the decline in business for London prostitutes:

> Before ten or twenty pound suppers were but trifles to them . . . they are now forced to make do with a diet of cheese and onions; the ruination of whoreinge.

Adultery was made a capital offence, and indeed several executions actually took place. Fornication was made a felony in 1650. The duty of women was to bear children and do the housework. Bear-baiting was abolished, not (as Macaulay pointed out) because it was cruel to bears but because it was believed to be fun for the spectators. Every form of entertainment was suppressed, including the theatre, and in 1648 stage performers were whipped in the streets. Horse-racing was abolished. Commerce, on the other hand, flourished because not only did the new ethic approve of hard work, it also recognised the possession of wealth as a sign of divine approval.

The ideal was of the godly servant with the ascetic compulsion to save, of hard frugality, while the members of the 'Diggers' sect went even further and had penalties for idleness. On family life the Puritan moral revolution perhaps had only modest real effects: Peter Laslett has shown how the figures for bastard births or prenuptial pregnancy varied hardly at all in English villages between 1600 and 1700, but there were cycles of change. In the village of Terling, for instance, bastardy shot up to nine percent in the years 1600 to 1610, then back down to two percent between 1620 and 1630 as the village worthies cracked down on loose living. They also made marriage much more difficult, particularly for the young and poor. On the fringes, the 'Shakers' adopted a posture of ascetic celibacy even more extreme than normal Puritanism, whereas the 'Ranters' went in the other direction, condemning conventional marriage as 'a horrid hyprocisy' and advocating polygamy or communal love: 'to the pure all things are pure', property was theft and love free. As Richard Baxter (1615–91) put it in *The Saints' Everlasting Rest*:

> They conjoyned a cursed doctrine of libertinism which brought them to abominable filthiness of life; and many of them committed whoredoms commonly.

Another commentator pointed out that the Ranters had a tract in which they opined: 'adultery, drunkenness, swearing, whoredom may be committed without sin ... such acts are acted by the true God'. Naturally, in Cromwellian Britain, the Ranters and their orgies were of short-lived duration.

Since the American colonies had been from the start a refuge for Puritans and other extreme non-conformist sects like the Pilgrim Fathers, it was hardly surprising that a similar Calvinist theocracy developed in Massachusetts. Great preaching families like the Mathers achieved the same kind of Sabbatarian, pleasure-avoiding regime in New England, and a very strict Presbyterian outlook dominated the colonies until it was displaced by newer sects after the War of Independence. The influence nevertheless lingered on, as it did in Scotland, where extreme Calvinism persisted long after it had become unfashionable in England. The values prized in early Massachussets, according to Ziff, were 'contrition, humility, repentance'; the accent was on suppressing natural affection and overcoming nature, although it was an important if distasteful duty to propagate the human species. The Puritans there disapproved of luxury but soon began to make money out of luxury products, particularly beaver skins (which brought them into conflict with the native Indians) and rum. They began to justify violence against the Indians, whom they ignorantly regarded as satanic; their massacres of the Pequot began in 1637, while in 1659 they turned their wrath on the Quakers (who seemed commercially disruptive) and on witches, who were everyone's scapegoat. In addition, from 1640 they began their own independent slave-trading with Africa, helped by the currency of their rum.

One great literary work summed up the new Protestant fascination with the individual's dramatic struggle against the temptations of evil. In 1678 there appeared *The Pilgrim's Progress* by John Bunyan (1628–88), a brilliant allegory of the moral trials of the ordinary man.

> I saw a man clothed with rags, with his face from his own house, a book
> in his hand and a great burden upon his back.

In Scotland, where Calvinism had penetrated earlier, fornication became
a crime in 1569; the Church of Scotland dominated government from
1640 to 1690 with a particularly anti-permissive regime. Before John
Knox (1513–72), Scottish society had been so permissive 'that sin
is reputed to be no sin'. Knox attacked 'immoderate dancing and
whoredom' but was milder than his successors who mounted a very
strict drive against 'harlotrie'. It has even been suggested by some
historians that the regime was so sexually repressive that it may have
led to an increase in infanticide and homosexuality, but inevitably the
statistics are far too unreliable to prove or disprove such a theory. There
was also a certain cruelty which sometimes accompanied Presbyterian
intolerance, like the 'nailing of luggies and boring of tongues' in 1649
when Montrose's Royalist army retreated.

Another creative branch of the Protestant ethic flourished in the
Dutch republic, with vigorous commercial enterprise and political
individuality. The Dutch were thrifty, peaceful and tolerant, even
of Jews. The wealthy citizens of Amsterdam cultivated a deliberate
modesty, and enjoyed the saying:

> Jesus Christ is good but trade is better.

They had produced the original libertines, such as the tailor, Quintin
(*fl*.1525), who had declared that nothing was sinful except thinking
things sinful, but the majority were less extreme. Round about 1650,
however, it was a Dutchman who invented gin, a drink which, over
at least the next century, contributed significantly to problems of
alcoholism and marital distress in Western Europe. In the American
colonies its counterpart was 'the demon rum', fiercely attacked by
Cotton Mather.

The Dutch-Jewish philosopher Baruch Spinoza (1632–77), the professional lense-grinder, expounded in his *Short Treatise* of 1660 a new
humanistic view of human behaviour. His aim was to discover

> . . . a true good, capable of imparting itself by which alone the mind could
> be affected to the exclusion of all else . . . a joy continuous and supreme to
> all eternity.

He took an almost Stoic view that all evil could be overcome by
understanding and love. In 1672, he risked his life trying to defend
the two de Witt brothers when they were being murdered by a Dutch
mob for their opposition to the House of Orange.

Typical also of the Dutch spirit was the painter Rembrandt (1606–69),
who painted old men and beggars to the detriment of his career as
a fashionable artist. The depth of his human understanding and

simple approach contrast with the gilded sophistication of post-Renaissance Italian painters. Simon Schama has described brilliantly the seventeenth-century Dutch promotion of the domestic virtues in which the image of cleanliness was linked with that of the faithful marriage. Jan Liutcen's emblem books of the godly household, and Jacob Cats' image of *The Christelyke Huyswijf*, combined with the visual arts to project clean living in its fullest sense. The Dutch illegitimacy rate (at around one percent) was much lower than in the rest of Europe.

The greatest moral innovator of the new Protestant sects was George Fox (1624–91), founder of the Society of Friends or the Quakers. Fox, that great respecter of 'the inner light', hated all priests, lawyers and soldiers, denounced all forms of amusement, as had the Puritans, but also began the most unequivocal and long-lasting stand against warfare adopted by any group of people in human history, except the Jains. His utter rejection of class inequality was symbolised by his refusal to allow the raising of hats to superiors and his insistence on the personal 'thou', instead of the respectful 'you' plural. In 1671, he urged the freeing of the Barbados slaves, and the Quakers were at the heart of the anti-slavery movement in the years that followed. Quakers like John Buller were also very prominent in the prison reform movement, and the moral influence of the Society spread well beyond its own membership. That other great Quaker, William Penn (1644–1718), in 1682 had his famous parley with the Indians which resulted in the foundation of Philadelphia, the ideal city, where all sects were to be tolerated. In the Puritan tradition, Fox's *Journal* has card-playing and theatres condemned as 'evil sports and games'.

It was the Quaker diaspora throughout the United States who won credit for the long-enduring Puritan outlook of so much of American life, long after the Calvinists of Boston had lost their popularity. One of Penn's final achievements was the release of some 1,200 English Quakers from prison in 1686. Although he attempted to mitigate the effects of slavery, he was a slave-owner himself so his contribution in that area was hardly radical. In Maryland in 1676 it was commented that 'all notorious vices are committed so that it is become a Sodom of uncleanliness and a peat hag of iniquity.'

Catholic versus Protestant confrontation was the norm for centuries throughout most of Europe, but for over a hundred years the German-Polish town of Thorn managed to maintain good relations between the two denominations, which amazed a Spanish diplomat in 1674; but even here a student disturbance eventually upset the peace, which ended in 1724 when the Jesuits imposed torture and execution, 'the Tumult of Thorn'.

In the Catholic world the Jesuit domination continued, and one of the most significant humanitarian movements was begun by Vincent de Paul (1581–1660), the ex-galley slave who founded the Confraternité of Charity (to feed the poor and sick), a hospital in Marseilles and the Paris Foundling Hospital. Mère Angelique was in the same mould, while St Victoria Fornari Stati (1562–1617) founded the Order of Blue Nuns, and St John Eudes (1601–80) the Sisters of Our Lady of Charity to care for the poor. In the Portuguese Empire, charitable work of great value was done by the Santa Casa da Misericordia, with branches from Macao to Mozambique. Nevertheless, this was offset by the flagrant promiscuity of the male Portuguese settlers, who bought and sold their slave harems, leaving many mulatto bastards to an insecure future. Goa had a reputation for particular turpitude.

In 1617, the Jesuits conducted a drive to reform the morals of Ireland, where polygamy had apparently become popular, where wakes became orgies and there was talk of bestial rites amongst the peasants. In Italy too they had problems: the traveller William Lithgow, author of *Rare Adventures and Paineful Peregrinations*, commented in 1632: 'sodomy is rife here as in Rome, Naples, Florence, etcetera . . . a monstrous filthiness and yet to them a pleasant pastime'. Archbishop Della Casa had written *De Laudibus Sodomiae seu pederastiae*. The papacy, more concerned with heresy, maintained its support for judicial violence; in Rome between 1634 and 1790, 2,000 Jews were forcibly converted to Christianity.

France, on the whole, was less influenced by the anti-permissive fashion of the first half on the seventeenth century, because the Calvinist Huguenots were politically out-manoeuvred by Cardinal Richelieu (1585–1642), the workaholic arch-priest of *raison d'etat*. He did, however, succumb to compulsive ostentation, insisting that his coat of arms was inserted in every window in the Sorbonne. Louis XIII (1601–43) had begun his career as something of an ascetic, reading Joinville's *Life of St Louis* and the Greek Stoics, which were fashionable. He announced: 'Please God adultery shall never enter my house.'

Theophile de Viau, who died prematurely in 1626, was the leading libertine and an advocate of 'gallantry' (which meant adultery and the playboy life), paralleled by the hedonistic English envoy, the Duke of Buckingham (1627–87).

Spain was, perhaps, affected more by the Puritan fashion. Philip IV (1621–65), an enemy of baroque over-indulgence, enforced austere fashions on the Spanish court, made black the only acceptable colour and established new standards of prudery. For a period, court life was so restrained that there was a popular saying:

Better to be a nun in Graz than the Queen of Spain.

In later seventeenth-century Spain, adultery became more frequent and marriage was mocked. There was a rise in the illegitimacy rate in Valladolid. Honour remained the national motivating force, and the Spaniards maintained a very weak work ethic. They employed large numbers of slaves and vast numbers of servants—the palace of the Duke of Alba had 400 servants' bedrooms. The torpid indolence of Castille, the vice of Cadiz, the mania for display, the cheerful tolerance of prostitution, all argued a loss of ethical direction in the country at this time.

In Russia too the anti-permissive mood had been evident. Tsar Alexis (1629–76) announced in 1648 'the righting of morals', and launched an attack on fiddlers, dancers and the traditionally transvestite bear-keepers, all of whom were identified with permissiveness. His puritan legislation outlawed singing, dirty jokes, swings, card-playing and games. This does not seem to have prevented a rise in alcoholism and possibly homosexuality. According to Wittek, the traveller Krifanic commented:

> The drunkenness is disgusting and as to unnatural offences go and learn temperance from the Turks! They at least have some shame.

Dreadful poverty, violence, hopelessness and lack of education made sub-human behaviour in Russia so common as to excite little comment. Human life was very expendable; in 1662 alone the tsar executed 7,000 and mutilated 15,000. The Zaporozhni Cossacks, constantly having to fight for their survival, worked out an ethic rather like that of the Spartans in which warriors were not allowed to marry, lived in an all-male barracks but could take mistresses outside and father children which, if they were boys, were brought up communally in the barracks.

It was in England in 1660 that the big reaction to the suppression of fun erupted. The Restoration of the Stuarts was not just a putting-back of the political clock, but a moral reversion as well. As Macaulay put it,

> Men flew to frivolous amusement and to criminal pleasures with the greediness which long-enforced abstinence naturally produces.

King Charles II (1630–85), for long the wandering playboy under the influence of the flamboyant, self-indulgent French court of Louis XIV, 'encouraged the ostentatious profligacy of the court', while the 'modish vice' of the cavaliers was tolerated by the established Church which they had helped to restore.

> Natural virtue was at its lowest ebb when the Church of England was at its zenith.

Duelling, which had been successfully outlawed by Cromwell, now made its return; the word 'gallantry' came to mean adultery—'Hard-hearted shameless, swaggering licentiousness', in the words of Macaulay. The theatre also enjoyed defeating the censor, and 'took care to put the coarsest verses in the mouths of women'. In 'the profane and licentious pit' the dissolute audience required every year stronger and stronger stimulants. This reached its nadir with the decadent Lord Rochester's *Sodom or the Quintessence of Debauchery*. This was the age when Pepys read *L'ecole des filles*, and Nell Gwynne was one of the king's many mistresses; when the notorious Sir Charles Sedley (1639–1701) was fined for dropping his trousers in public in 1663, the king paid his fine for him. So, as Macaulay summed it up:

> An age of hypocrisy is in the regular course of things followed by an age of impudence.

In France, the changes were less abrupt, but Louis XIV (1638–1718)— with his huge palaces, numerous mistresses and enormously wasteful wars—was the most damaging (if elegant) king in Europe, obsessed totally with his own glory. He was served by men such as the remarkable Marquis de Martinet (d.1672) who gave his name to a whip with twelve thongs used to maintain discipline in the army. Louis was proud to announce that 'nobody shall be uncertain of his daily bread', but in fact his wars led to widespread hunger, nearly starvation. In 1667 he limited the use of torture, and his 'Code Louis' even included a section on the rights of negro slaves. The mood of his later years did become more sober under the influence of the Jesuits and the severe royal mistress, Madame de Maintenon. This was the era of what Mitford called 'sweated hypocrisy'. A number of sorcerers were burned to death for witchcraft; a clique of homosexuals at Versailles, led by the composer Giovanni Lully (1632–87), 'the king of Sodom', was rooted out in 1682. In 1685, 300,000 Protestants were hounded out of France with the repeal of the Edict of Nantes, but burning at the stake was at last outlawed. In 1703, Jean Baptiste La Salle, founder of the Christian Brothers, wrote his *Rules of Propriety and Christian Civility*, which went to 126 editions and became essential reading for middle-class parents.

In 1664, Dom Rancé (1626–1700) founded the Trappists, a new Cistercian community with one of the fiercest codes of discipline ever inflicted on a monastic brotherhood, an odd return to asceticism in the midst of the *ancien régime*, a strange idealisation of the value of silence, austerity and manual but not intellectual work.

Jean Racine (1639–99), brought up in the puritan atmosphere of the Jansenist Port Royal, rebelled and turned to libertinism. Perhaps the new concentration on wordly pleasures was assisted by or contributed to the general boom in the retail trade which Braudel has recorded throughout Europe, the vast expansion in the number of shops for luxury goods, restaurants and international trading. Ostentatious expenditure, even deliberate wastage, was a key component of the upper-class ethos. War too was such a gentlemanly affair that when the French captured secret papers travelling from London to Marlborough, they courteously passed on the letters without opening them and, of course, lost the war.

In England, it was also an age of some cruelty, as was shown in the hanging, drawing and quartering of General Harrison in 1660 and suppression of the Monmouth rebellion of 1685. Colonel Kirk became known for his sadistic cruelty and massacres of prisoners, Judge Jeffreys (1648–89) for the crude savagery of his sentences. This last condemned Lady Alice Lisle to be burned for harbouring a fugitive, though the sentence was later changed to hanging. More than 3,000 rebels were hung and 841 transported to the plantations of the West Indies, where it was the heyday of piracy. Port Royal was described by H.J. Hurwitz as the 'wickedest city in the West, a most ungodly and debauched people', until it was destroyed by an earthquake in 1692. In Campeachy Bay, however, the semi-legal British colonists managed (of their own volition) a well-ordered society without the need for capital punishment.

A few years later the moral pendulum began to swing back again. In 1698 came *The Royal Proclamation on Immorality* from King William III. Queen Anne (1665–1714) a few years earlier began a drive against obscenity in the theatres which were just 'more commodious brothels'. Macaulay says:

> Before 1685 it was reckoned to be breeding to swear, gallantry to be lewd, good humour to be drunk, wit to despise sacred things.

The Society for the Reform of Manners was set up and supported by men like Richard Steele (1672–1729) of the *Spectator*, one of the great champions of the new bourgeois family ethic in his *The Christian Hero* (1701).

Italy was particularly noted at this time for its violence and the harshness of punishment. One traveller reporting the rows of public gallows along the road sides commented: 'We see so much human flesh along the highway that trips are disagreeable'.

During this period Eastern Europe also saw a spread in self-indulgent frippery for the aristocracies, and a slide away from liberty for the agricultural masses. In Prussia, there was the ominous rise of the Junker class and parallel decline in the status of the peasant; and in Hungary, the peasants became serfs and could be whipped. Most serious of all (mainly because the country was so large) was the Russian imperial ruling of 1649 which began the rapid decline of the Russian peasant into serfdom. Freedom of movement was made illegal. Soon the serfs could be flogged by their masters, and by 1660 the vast majority of the Russian population were serfs. It was to be a mass suppression with very long-lasting consequences.

In Poland, the growing Jewish population, pushed eastwards after their expulsion from Spain, were segregated and thrust into ghettos. By

1648 their unpopularity had escalated, as they were the rent collectors of the kingdom, and large numbers of them were massacred by the Cossacks.

The vastness and relative backwardness of Russia meant that sadistic violence remained an important tool of social control. Torture by batog, knout and fire was normal practice. In 1704, when the Streltsi Regiment mutinied against Peter the Great (1672–1725), nearly 2,000 soldiers were tortured for six weeks. The Russians even had Torture Societies, where members submitted voluntarily to torture so that they would be better equipped to resist confession under the real thing. Peter, though a deliberate user of planned violence, did achieve some ethical reforms, notably his virtual ending of the practice of infanticide, the method by which most illegitimate or deformed babies were got rid of up till then. He also improved the status of women, ending their social seclusion and pre-arranged marriages. In 1717 he produced *The Honourable Mirror of Youth*, a guide to gentlemen on how to behave, ranging from dissuasion against dirty habits to not speaking anything so crude as Russian in front of the servants. All this character improvement need not, of course, affect the tsar himself, who liked to be surrounded by dwarfs and jesters at his regular drunken orgies; he enjoyed making people sick, fancied himself as an amateur surgeon and reputedly, like his favourite Alexander Menshikov (1660–1729), indulged himself with both sexes. He was also credited with causing the death of his own son.

It was hardly surprising that the Russians should at this time produce a number of escapist religious sects. Several of them stemmed from the extraordinary seventeenth-century Volga hermit, Danilo Filipov, including the pacifist Dukhobors, who refused to do military service and believed in universal love, hard work and abstinence. These 'Russian Quakers' were persecuted and eventually driven into exile in the nineteenth century. In Canada in the 1930s, they were still being persecuted for objecting to compulsory education and formal clothing. In 1932, 5,000 were gaoled for indecent exposure. Two other sects tracing their origins back to Filipov were the Skoptsi, who practised self-castration and had a well-known eunuch prophet, Selivanov, in the 1770s; and the Khyst, who were flagellants and horse-whipped each other.

This century also produced the first major Jewish prophet for many years, Sabbat ai Z'vi (1626–75), the self-styled messiah born in Smyrna who was the founder of modern Zionism. In later life he became a Moslem, but his ideas were to linger on and simmer as the focus for Jewish expectations for the recreation of Israel.

In the Middle East and beyond, this was the great era of the much-persecuted Armenians. From their base at Julfa, these people became the commercial travellers of the world, adhering to a dynamic work ethic, achieving success over a huge area but winning unpopularity because of their wealth, their vegetarianism and other seeming oddities of behaviour.

Many parts of the Ottoman Empire and its offshoots showed signs of increasing permissiveness. In Istanbul, the right of concubinage made up for the absence of prostitution. The Mecca pilgrimage circuit and the Shiite priests had a reputation for homosexual tolerance if not practice, yet the busy whores of Mecca never appeared without veils.

In India, the seventeenth century saw the rapid rise of the Marathas, led by Siragi, who got rid of his main enemy in a steel-claw embrace in 1659. At first the Marathas were tough but merciful, then they became ruthless, greedy and unpopular.

Though the main tenor of Chinese ethical history remained pacifist, China did have one of its many civil wars in this century and the rebel Chang Hsien Chung (1605–47), who is estimated to have caused 1,000,000 deaths between 1630 and 1640, was particularly noted for his brutality. His career was one of the symptoms of the decline and fall of the eunuch-ridden Ming dynasty, which ended in 1644. The Jesuit Matteo Ricci (1552–1610) estimated there were 10,000 eunuchs in Peking, noted the widespread female infanticide, and public suicide by despairing adults. Thereafter order was restored once more under the vigorous new Ching dynasty. Permissiveness in China went out of fashion under the new regime, and the vast number of sex manuals tolerated by the Ming disappeared. The pigtail was imposed as a symbol of submission and China moved into a period of relative prudery. Increased comsumption of alcohol became fashionable.

Japan also returned to a more puritan phase as Yamago Soko, the new high priest of bushido, encouraged female samurai to keep a dagger and commit suicide in defence of their chastity. The problem was that Japanese wives were so chaste that their husbands sometimes resorted to alcohol or prostitutes as an easier alternative. The Tokugawa Shoguns had encouraged a revival of Japanese Confucianism to help mould behaviour patterns which emphasised loyalty and filial piety. Helped by Seika Fujiwara (1561–1619), they put across the image of the emperor as a caring father and censored out the elements of Confucianism which condoned justifiable rebellion by oppressed subjects.

In many respects, the seventeenth century worldwide was a century of ethical disorientation. There were more civil wars than international ones, more divisions within religions than between religions, more erratic fluctuations between permissive and puritan, very little moral creativity. The species seemed to be losing its way.

1700 — 1800

Morality thy deadly bane,
Thy tens o' thousands thou hast slain

Robert Burns

THE EIGHTEENTH CENTURY was to produce in Europe one of the most profound and lasting changes in moral attitudes. It began as a century of rakes and turned into the century of the Wesleys, the 'sea-green incorruptible' Robespierre (as Carlyle called him), and the upright George Washington. It saw the middle-age of Casanova and Pompadour, but ended with Wilberforce.

In France, the final century of the *ancien régime* got going with the regency of Philippe Orleans (1674–1723). Orleans, an alcoholic and transvestite who wore rouge, was suspected of poisoning his way to power; he consorted with coquettes and those called (in the slang of the Regency) 'roués', addicted to an interminable round of petty orgies. The homosexual Duc de Vendome lost his nose from syphilis.

The French upper class was in reaction against the dowdy later years of Madame de Maintenon and Louis XIV. The fashion now shifted towards brighter colours, hooped dresses and greater permissiveness. Aphrodite Clubs were a form of organised promiscuity, and the masque a cover for something only slightly more casual. Versailles had its own rustic brothel, the Parc des Cerfs. Jean Antoine Watteau (1684–1721) was the fashionable painter of stagey court parties, Fêtes Galantes, the world in which no woman of fashion could be virtuous and no man honest, the world of Pierre de Laclos (1741–1803), author of *Les Liaisons dangeureuses*, of fictional heroes like the renegade priest Manon Lescaut, and the impudent Gil Blas. It soon also became the world of Madame de Pompadour (1721–64), who symbolised for a number of years the ephemeral cult of beauty and 'objets d'art', who visited her goldsmith to buy something every week for ten years. There was perfection in cuisine, wines and cheeses, tapestries and chinoiserie, complex dances performed by the minority, the fringe of rococo self-indulgence. Francois Boucher (1703–70) became the painter of the spoilt mesdames of the court, creating a whole mythology of nude Greek goddesses to reflect the mood of the time. Charles Couperin (1638–79) provided the musical background. Mothers handed their babies over to wet nurses at birth, and the royal minister Turgot (1727–81) muttered about the reduction of family feeling— 'there is no more affection for women and children'. Marriage in France reached a very low ebb.

One of the more fickle sycophants of the Pompadour entourage was the hugely talented Voltaire (1694–1778), whose real revolt against the *ancien régime* did not mature until he was in his fifties. His own sudden ejections from court society into the Bastille, or into exile, perhaps gave him more understanding of injustice than other members of his class, and in his later years he became the great champion of the oppressed. Gradually there developed amongst the French intelligentsia a horror of the inefficiency of the *ancien régime* and an urge for rational analysis. Denis Diderot (1713–84), the immensely hard-working compiler of the *Encyclopaedia*, used it as a vehicle for the first comprehensively argued case against superstition and persecution. Simultaneously, he was developing the view that reason was the means of achieving a better world and a new, rational approach to morality: 'if laws are good, morals are good'.

Francois Fenelon's *Telemaque* (1699) provided a fashionable attack on absolute monarchy. What Locke had begun in England, Voltaire and Diderot developed, and Rousseau (1712–78) brought to a climax with the publication of the *Contrat Social* in 1762. It was the most dramatic and comprehensive attack on greed and force as the basis of the state; the basis of society should, Rousseau argued, be a voluntarily agreed ethical code with responding rights:

> Man was born free and everywhere he is in chains.

As early as 1703, Lahoutan had promoted the idea of 'the noble savage' and later Captain Cook's discoveries in the Pacific in 1770 developed the theme. Man, to Rousseau, was born naturally virtuous and only tended to be corrupted by the artificial institutions of Church and state. The idea that there was a general or common will which, once purified by voluntary withdrawal of all sectional interests, would automatically lead to liberty and equality was the foundation for the two great Revolutions of 1776 and 1789.

One of the remarkable effects of the Rousseau influence was a new belief in the innocence of young children. Whereas the Calvinists had regarded them as born sinful (and even the Wesleyans recommended regular flogging), the British in the eighteenth century began to show their children far more affection, gave them pet names, bought them toys and treated them more kindly. This was observed as being in marked contrast to the French, who still terrorised their children: on the other hand, only the British used children as chimney sweeps and the very harsh treatment of them in factories was just beginning to strike the collective conscience.

Also in Britain, the early Hanoverian period was one of relative permissiveness, particularly in London, where George I (1660–1727) set a new fashion for adultery. In 1724, Lady Wortley Montagu wrote that

> The appellation of a rake is as genteel in a woman as in a man of quality.

Horace Walpole (1717–97) predicted 'the art of courtship will soon be reduced to the words lie down', and Charles Churchill (1731–64) observed the British appetites with the verses

> With Island vices not content
> We rob our neighbours on the continent.
> Women are kept for keeping the breed,
> For pleasure we must have Ganymede.

Upper-class homosexuality was fashionable, and brothels known as 'molly houses' flourished. There were 10,000 prostitutes in London (25,000 according to Baron Uffenbach), including 'Moors of both sexes hawking their bottoms'. Smollet commented in 1748, through the lips of his hero, Roderick Random, that homosexuality 'gains ground apace and in all probability will in a short time be a more fashionable device than fornication'. There was even a flagellant brothel at Theresa Berkeley's. Both sexes of the upper class wore very heavy make-up, face patches, perfume and powdered wigs. Female necklines plunged; masked balls were for mistress-swapping, maid servants were fair game, illegitimacy common and bastardy only a minor stigma. Lord Coventry, the governor of New York in 1702, was a transvestite, and there were several such cliques in London. 'Posture Nan' was a highly popular 'exotic dancer'.

This was the era of cheap gin production— 'drunk for 1d., dead drunk for 2d.'—and spirit consumption in London rose from 3.5 to 4.4 million gallons between 1727 and 1735. According to Samuel Johnson (1709–84), 'all the good people of Lichfield got drunk every night and were not the worse thought of', and as Porter puts it, 'to get a reputation as a blade one had to be at least a three bottle man'. Hygiene was not regarded as close to godliness, as earlier Pepys had not been unusual in relieving himself in his lounge fireplace. Cleanliness did not come into its own until later in the century. Gluttony was regarded as honourable, and a portly figure was acceptable in both sexes. It was a period of great British self-confidence, based partly on victories in three wars, imperial expansion and slavery.

By contrast, the debtors' prisons were full, and spectators went to jeer both at public executions and the madmen in Bedlam. Highway robbers like Dick Turpin and Sheppard were heroes, so were smugglers who contravened the Excise Bill. Hogarth (1697–1764) was the great portrayer of urban decadence in *The Rake's Progress* and *The Harlot's Progress*. James Boswell (1740–95) boasted that he had had sixty prostitutes, three mistresses, four actresses, seventeen doses of venereal disease— 'he could roger for 6d.'—and on top of it all, he was a chronic alcoholic. This was the age of those eccentric, amoral gangs of young squires known as the Mohocks and Bold Bucks, all taking extreme delight in as much violence and rape as they could manage. Also dabbling in experimental evil were the Hell Fire Club, and Sir Francis Dashwood's Monks of Medmenham. Alongside the sadistic streak came masochism in the shape of fashionable flagellation, with a new guide on the subject published in London in 1777.

At the other end of society, the new industries encouraged a new ethos. At Wednesbury, Staffordshire, in the 1750s, a population of colliers and nail-makers became 'Nicolaitans' and lived a promiscuous, pleasure-seeking life. Wife-selling, cockfighting, bear-baiting and drinking were their hobbies. Similarly, at churchless Edale in Derbyshire, a contemporary commented 'everyone just does that which is right in his own eyes . . . perfect licentiousness'.

In 1750 appeared *Fanny Hill, the Memoirs of a Woman of Pleasure* by John Clelland (1709–89), a 'success de scandal'. The sales of pornographic pictures by artists like Thomas Rowlandson (1756-1827) in London were substantial, and customers later included the Prince Regent. Daniel Defoe (1660–1731), who had earlier produced *Robinson*

Crusoe, the classic demonstration of how man could live happily with-out the fripperies of civilisation, went on to produce *Moll Flanders* in 1722, the biography of a prostitute. Henry Fielding (1707–54) produced his two bawdy but cautionary tales of the fate of aging libertines, *Tom Jones* and *Joseph Andrews*. In 1724, Bernard Mandeville wrote his *Modest Defence of Public Stewes*, the case for legal prostitution. Lord Chesterfield (1694–1773) in his famous *Letters to his Son*, having warned about 'the vices of the heart, lying, fraud, envy, malice and destruction', then went on to indicate some ideas on how a gentleman should master 'the humane refusal of a beggar, the reproof of a footman'.

It was an era when the most heinous sin was to cheat at cards. Debts of honour must be paid, but not debts to tailors. A gentleman could fight a duel with his equals and thrash his inferiors. The British slave trade was peaking, with 50,000 crossing the Atlantic every year, and a lot of money was being made.

Generally, it was in Britain a period of brutality in which, with average life-expectancy still at thirty-five, the under-privileged were maltreated and the over-privileged maltreated themselves. As the rate of illegitimate births rose towards fifty percent, new foundling hospitals were made harsh enough to reduce the life-expectancy of orphans, helped by over ninety percent infant mortality in workhouses of this period. The flogging of soldiers and sailors was normal, and sailors would boast their endurance of thousands of lashes. 'Our fleets are defrauded with injustice, marred by violence and maintained by cruelty', wrote Admiral Vernon (1684–1757), and recruitment was by press gang.

Up to 1789, women could still be burned alive for murdering their husbands, and crowds came to see convicted whores being whipped. There was a permanent wooden grandstand round Tyburn Tree to help onlookers enjoy the hangings. Blood sports like cockfighting were intensely popular, and cudgelling was a favourite in the West Country. There were numerous riots in London—Drury Lane was wrecked six times between 1743 and 1776. Homosexuals were sometimes stoned to death on the pillory, and witches were still persecuted, as were Methodists (who enjoyed it), the Irish and, significantly, the Jews. In 1753, there was a succession of anti-Semitic riots in England.

Elsewhere in Europe, Augustus the Strong of Hanover (1670–1733) boasted 354 bastards; and in Poland, the wealthy Prince Radziwill made a spectacle of providing free wine to a whole town, condoning spillage as an additional demonstration of his power and extravagance. Braudel says: 'Wastage was a rational act in a given social structure'. In Poland, persecution of witches was just begining to peak, with fifty percent of all those charged between 1500 and 1525 actually being burnt. The total number of victims there was 10,000, and around 20,000 in Silesia. This did not end until 1776. One of the most remarkable sects was that of

Jankiel Lejbowicz (1727–91), who offered the Polish Jews an exciting new variant on their own religion, which, according to the Bishop of Kamienec, allowed gross debaucheries.

Meanwhile, the redoubtable Venetian playboy, Casanova (1725–98), was writing his *Memoires ecrite par lui meme*. The outburst of license in France which followed the death of Louis XIV had spread to Italy, and the city of Venice (in its final century as an independent republic) had the wealth to be hedonistic in the new fashion. Whereas Venetian women in the previous century had been made to wear high, wobbly clogs to restrict their mobility, they now came out of hiding with low necklines and face-patches, accompanied by that remarkable Italian invention the 'cicisbeo', the hired male wife-minder or surrogate husband. In 1600, Venice had had 11,654 prostitutes for a total population of 100,000, but in the eighteenth century top courtesans were put out of business by the number of wealthy amateurs. The Italian father would advise his son to buy sex in the years before marriage; boys like Casanova clubbed together to share their favours, sometimes in groups of six. Venetian males wore elaborate clothes with frills and tassels, wigs and rouge. Gambling and adultery were their adventure substitutes; as Casanova observed, 'They do not taste their pleasures, they swallow them'.

Carnivals and regattas occupied half the year, a glittering world recorded by the painter Giambattista Tiepolo (1727–1804). Venice, which had long been known for its military and commercial ruthlessness, was now still successful but idle. In Rome, Goethe (1749–1832) observed the same kind of libertinage. It was the age of confetti battles and the castration clinic near the Vatican, which turned out the falsetto singers for the opera, the 'sacred capons' of Italian musicality.

In the American colonies, the eighteenth century saw a permissive trend, in which chattel slaves fulfilled the role of prostitutes. Benjamin Franklin (1706–90) was, in his own words, 'a bit of a blade': yet in due course he wrote his *Poor Richard's Almanac*, which became one of the most influential moral text books for the next few generations.

The moral reaction to this period of leisure-class permissiveness began in England in the 1730s. In 1729, General Oglethorpe began a campaign to improve debtors' prisons; Captain Coram was helped by the painter Hogarth to start a foundling hospital in 1745, and Thomas Guy built his hospital in 1792. By 1752 naked bathing in the River Ouse at York was forbidden. In 1735, the Society for the Reformation of Manners took out 99,300 actions in London alone, as the newly-literate lower-middle class began to assert itself. The Freemason's movement was growing rapidly, a humanitarian brotherhood which spread throughout Europe and to America. In 1731, the romantic novel *Sethos*, by Abbe Jean Terassou, helped spread the positive image of

Freemasonry, as did Mozart's *Magic Flute* (1791) and the work of the showman Count Alessandro di Cagliostro (1743–95):

> A mason is a man of benevolence, charity, not sitting down contented while his fellow creatures but much more his brothers are in need.

The Masonic movement also provided new victims for the morbid paranoia of the Inquisition, which was running short of targets, and the Masonic leader Goustos was tortured in 1743.

In 1748, Samuel Richardson published his novel *Clarissa*, in which the rape of a woman was seen as a moral indictment of the age; in fact, Richardson's stated objective in writing was to cultivate in his readers principles of virtue and religion. The eighteenth century in Western Europe was generally a period during which marriage for love actually began to become fashionable, reducing the dichotomy between dutiful wife and exciting mistress.

By the late 1720s there were already signs of a Christian revival in the American colonies, the great awakening when Jonathan Edwards (1703–58) led huge crowds to public repentance, and Mother Anna later founded the American Shaker Society in New York.

The burning of witches was stopped in Prussia in 1713, and there were no more Russian witch trials as Christianity struggled to be rid of obscurantism. In Eastern Europe, Count von Zinnendorf (1700–60) gave new life to the Moravian sect, the main survival of Anabaptism, and was a remarkable pioneer of the ecumenical concept for reuniting the branches of Christianity.

In 1739, John Wesley (1703–91) began the movement in Bristol which was to be known as Methodism. This was to revive the reality of hell-fire, to create a new moral inspiration amongst a wider cross-section of people, and a strictness of moral censorship which was as strong if not as harsh as that of the Calvinists. Wesley had a unique grasp of the techniques of emotional crowd control as an aid to conversion, and single-handedly laid the foundations of 'the non-conformist conscience'. By 1791 the *Gentleman's Magazine* could say 'we are every day becoming more delicate and without doubt at the same time more virtuous'. There was also at this time a greater awareness of cruelty and suffering. Porter quotes Richard Dean writing about bear-baiting and similar habits in 1768: 'Cruelty is exercised in all its hideous forms and varieties'.

Bedlam was closed to the public as a source of entertainment in 1766; in 1773, John Howard began his campaign of penal reform. Branding of prisoners was abolished in 1779. The 1770s saw a middle-class surge towards benevolent virtue, and George III seemed (if nothing else) a model of domestic virtue. Steele had written 'delicacy in pleasure is the first step in reformation of vice'.

The other great change happening in the second half of the eighteenth century was the onset of the factory system. It was in 1771 that Richard Arkwright went into partnership with Jedediah Strutt, the improver of the stocking-frame, to set up a large water-powered factory at Cromford, Derbyshire. This was the first step in the compression of humanity in what William Blake (1757–1827) soon afterwards called 'the dark satanic mills'.

It was the beginning of a new drive towards profit and mass production which seemed at that time, to moral thinkers like Adam Smith (1723–90), to offer an opportunity for the perfection of human morality, and could be seen as a symptom of natural moral evolution justifying freedom rather than demanding any interference.

Smith was a friend and admirer of the most influential of all the modern British moral thinkers, David Hume (1711–76), whose *Treatise on Human Understanding* attacked not only the traditional religious justifications of morality but also the Locke and Rousseau view that naturally-evolved conventions were necessarily good just because they had come into existence—because something *is*, it does not follow that it *ought to be*. The so-called natural laws, the traditions of society, could be just as artificial and invalid as the institutionalised moralities of Churches and states. To Hume, the only realities were human instincts and therefore the only genuine basis for any morality was 'enlightened self-interest'. Immanuel Kant (1724–1804), brought up as a Prussian puritan, responded to Hume with his 'categorical imperative' which postulated the existence of an objective standard, and in *Perpetual Peace* he argued for a world federation.

The new liberal morality was not without heartless adherents: the amiable cleric Thomas Malthus (1766–1834) blessed ill-treatment of factory workers on the grounds that it was part of nature's method of population control, and a still more unfortunate example of the new commercial free-for-all was the British East India Company's takeover and monopolisation in 1765 of Indian poppy-growing, leading to a massive sales drive on opium in China.

In pre-Revolutionary Europe, this was the age of the so-called enlightened despots. Certainly a number of the great monarchs of the period were intrigued by the teachings of the French philosophers and showed some interest in humanising their regimes. Frederick II of Prussia (1712–86), Charles III of Spain (1716–88) and Louis XVI of France (1754–93) all abolished torture in their kingdoms, and in Britain the use of 'peine forte et dure' was abandoned. Joseph II of Austria (1741–90) abolished serfdom and made a genuine (though largely unsuccessful) attempt to overhaul his archaic empire. Frederick II, while piously pronouncing himself 'the servant of the state', nevertheless followed a career of determined military expansion which resulted in the virtual doubling of the size of the kingdom of Prussia, an achievement justifying his epithet of 'Great' in traditional imagery, yet laying the foundation of long-term Prussian militarism, a major contribution to the destruction of Polish freedom.

The apparently least-enlightened of the enlightened despots must have been Catherine the Great of Russia (1729–96), the allegedly promiscuous 'Messalina of the North' and developer of Russian imperialism, who allowed the confirmation of Russian peasant serfdom and actually donated 800,000 serfs to her friends and retainers. She had, however, attempted to tackle the huge problems of her massive country, and quietly encouraged the immigration of Jews from Poland and Germany to help create a middle class. Russian women of the upper classes, brought out of seclusion by Peter the Great, now adopted a very dominant role: Catherine picked her own partners, and men were often degraded at the Little Hermitage. The level of promiscuity is shown by the exploits of the Physical Club in Moscow (a venue for partner-swapping), and by the fact that St Petersburg boasted Europe's largest orphanages.

The Russian aristocracy (though they had been superficially changed) still, according to Radishchev (1749–1818), observed 'immoderate luxury and indulgence in all forms of corruption'. Though they now followed the French fashion of no longer spitting in public or picking off their lice, they still drank heavily, gambled, and regarded soldiering as the sole source of honour. Radishchev commented on the 'impudence, the crude and offensive jests of the audacious gentry against the village maidens who were creatures of their lordly pleasures'.

Many of them treated their serfs with great cruelty. The serfs themselves, while often degraded by poverty, did preserve 'the primary virtues'. They were 'kind, cheerful, honest, brave and religious'. They enjoyed their weekly visits to the public saunas, drank a lot, and their habit of wife-beating seems to have been borne without rancour. After the Pugachev rebellion, Radishchev and others developed the first upper-class conscience, preaching that serfdom was an evil in both directions, creating arrogance amongst the aristocracy and debasing the serfs. In addition, as the Russians became more conscious of their ethnic identity they turned against the Jews, who had been slowly pushed eastwards into their lands, and thrust them into pales or ghettos. Twenty-five year compulsory military service was just one of the hardships imposed. In Poland, the lash and the knout were also standard tools for the control of the somewhat debased peasantry, although the Polish nobility did profess a code which encouraged love and social harmony on the land.

The culmination of British idealisation of the law and precedent as the permanent rule of life came with Sir William Blackstone's *Commentaries on the Laws of England* in 1765, and the greatest practical assertion of the right to natural justice came ten years later with the drafting of the American *Declaration of Independence*. The somewhat stagnant Puritan ethos of New England had been replaced by a rather more flexible Unitarian creed as the driving force of the new American leadership. There was the intensely upright moral posture of George Washington (1732–99) and Thomas Jefferson (1743–1826), though Jefferson, like most eighteenth-century leaders, accepted the inevitability of prostitution and recommended the inclusion of a brothel in his plans for the University of Virginia.

The non-conformist conscience, combined with the frontier ethos of self-help, was to remain the dominant viewpoint of the northern states, though inevitably it must eventually collide with the ethos of the slave-owning plantations of the South. There, thanks to 'King Cotton', the need for slave labour was perceived to be growing, and slaves were still regarded as sub-human.

> Duplicity is one of their strongest traits ... they are liars and thieves, insolent, selfish and dreadful ...

said a typical southern planter later quoted in David Christy's *Cotton is King* (1860). Thus maltreatment was rationalised, economically and anthropologically.

The eighteenth century has been described as witnessing the birth of modern racism, with its increased contact between blacks and whites in situations where the black was nearly always disadvantaged or misunderstood. The English anthropologist, Edward Tyson (1657–1708), had defined African pygmies as animals in 1699, and the great Swedish scientist, Carl Linne or Linnaeus (1707–78), ranked the races in classes, with white at the top and black at the bottom. Obscure new studies of the shapes of heads and of noses were used to argue the inferiority of blacks and, of course, Jews.

It was in France that there occurred the most dramatic reversal of attitudes, and the most overt assertion of freedom from political and religious constraints. It was the great test of the theoretical view that human virtue would flourish if allowed proper freedom, which had been developed by Locke, Diderot, Rousseau and the rest of the Enlightenment.

Maximilien Robespierre (1758–94) was the most articulate practical advocate of the new theme that 'the application of natural moral principles to government is the only cure for political evils'. Robespierre was a genuine idealist who believed that the state could create the right atmosphere for naturally moral behaviour. In practical terms, he was faced with numerous problems which made the Utopian end-product almost impossible. Believing (in the attempt) that 'le salut public est la loi supreme', Robespierre felt obliged to resort to ruthless persecution. He and the rest of the Committee of Public Safety conducted the cruel suppressions of Arras and Nantes, the execution of some 2,000 political opponents. His colleague, Saint-Just (1767–94), recommended a Spartan-type educational system in which boys would be taken away from their parents at the age of seven and raised as Jacobin clones. The new Religion of Reason was on its way, but the regime stumbled over its own paranoia: both Robespierre and Saint-Just went to the guillotine.

The French Revolution did achieve, albeit temporarily, a number of significant ethical breakthroughs. The streets of Paris were cleared of prostitution; even the Jews were emancipated. The work of the 'Societe des amis des noirs' did result in the abolition of slavery in the French colonies, though it was soon after restored by Napoleon. The same was true of the rights of women and of young adults, as well as the broad spread of libertarian rights, which were the foundations of the Revolution and from which no subsequent French government could entirely retreat. The movement was so full of vigour that the assertion of rights began to bubble up in most other European countries as well.

In France itself, the latter days of the Revolution saw not only a new moral justification for violence, wars and persecution for the sake of ideals as opposed to political caprice, but also a rejection of many traditional moral restraints. Both Robespierre and the Directory recommended showing no quarter to British and German prisoners in the Revolutionary Wars. After Thermidor, the anti-Jacobin reaction resulted in numerous massacres, particularly in the south. Not only had the political establishment been removed, so had the Church. Perhaps there was also a feeling that the palace frolics of the aristocracy should now be available to the 'sans culottes'. By 1791 the brothels of Paris had reached unprecedented size and their temptations were on very open display. Three years later Madame Tallien (1773–1835), the Thermidorean women, the 'merveilleuses' or 'incroyables' were flaunting themselves in skin-tight satins; the 'decolletée' of women like Madame Récamier (1777–1849), 'la Reine du Directoire', and Josephine Beauharnais (1763–1814) was the new fashion, and revolution was becoming identified with permissiveness. For a brief period, Paris saw a massive moral collapse.

The concept of the liberation of women gained its most serious and influential European prophet in Mary Wollstonecraft (1759–97), whose *Vindication of the Rights of Woman* (1792) was a pioneering work. Her views involved a certain amount of flouting of marital convention, which unfortunately linked the idea of women's rights with permissiveness and the personal misfortunes of her own life, but her influence was to be substantial. Her husband, William Godwin, wrote *The Adventures of Caleb Williams* in 1794, with its aggressive 'general review of the modes of domestic and unrecorded despotism'.

It was this perceived association of political with moral breakdown which stimulated the amazing swing back to rectitude which occurred in Britain at this time. In 1788, William Wilberforce (1759–1833) had founded his Assocation for the Reformation of Manners, and in the last years of the century the evangelical 'seriousness' of the Clapham sect spread with remarkable rapidity. Despite the death of Wesley in 1791, recruitment to Methodism increased steadily. Even the established Church enjoyed a huge revival:

> It was a wonder to the lower orders to see the avenues to the churches filled with carriages.

It was in this atmosphere that Hannah More (1745–1833) moved to Cowslip Green to do good works for the poor, Wilberforce and Thomas Clarkson (1760–1846) began their drive to abolish the slave trade, and in the 1790s there was a major attempt to clean up vice in the streets of London, suppressing books like Harris's *List of Covent Garden Ladies*. In 1770, Josiah Wedgewood was forced to put fig leaves on his classical figures, while the middle class were churning out tracts like *The Story of Sinful Sally*. They attacked swearing, cards, fairs and skittles; they preached thrift, sobriety, the bible and self-help. *The Times* in 1799 had attacked 'the fashion of nudity'. As Arthur Young has said, 'by 1800 virtue was advancing on a broad invincible front'.

By this time there was not just the pressure of revolution and moral breakdown, but war as well. The French Revolution marked the beginning of a dangerous new moral justification for war: the defence of ideals. The invention of conscription by the French war minister, Lazare Carnot (1755–1823), created the first mass armies and was to lead to a disastrous escalation in the death tolls of European warfare. Instead of the elegant little chess games in which Louis XIV had moved small mercenary armies from one square to another, condoning the gentlemanly, bloodless surrender of castles or battles as soon as a commander recognised that he was outmanouevred, we now move into an era where huge armies slogged it out with massive casualties on both sides, and with too much at stake to contemplate surrender until the situation was completely hopeless. It was the French Revolution's ideological justification of war and its creation of a new desire for conquest which provided the raw material for the destructive bellomania of Napoleon.

Islam also produced two distinct explosions during the eighteenth century. Nadir Shah (1687–1747), the Napoleon of Persia, came to prominence when he drove out the conquering Afghans and created briefly a new Persian Empire. At home he tried to impose the Sunni doctrine on his own people, and in his conquests he was barbaric. He instructed a massacre at Delhi in revenge for a riot against some of his men, and 110,000 were killed.

The other remarkable Moslem was Abdel Wahhab (1708–87), who advocated a return to Islam of the first generation, rejecting all the mysticism, additional saints and ideas that had been grafted on to Islam since the death of the prophet. He founded a small, puritanical, conservative state in Arabia, and in subsequent years Wahhabism became the focus for revivalist Islam and the Moslem protest against European infiltration. It was to be a focal point in the Indian mutiny and many other situations of Islamic protest against European conquest, producing the 'Mujahadin' or holy warriors of India and (later) Afghanistan.

The Jews also produced a great new prophet, Israel Baal Shem Tod (1700–60), founder of Hassidism, which gained a wide following especially in Polish Ukraine, promoting contentment based on long-suffering humility.

Indian civilisation went through a major crisis of confidence after the British expansion under Clive. The last years of the century saw an epidemic of gang robberies, the rapid rise of assassination cults like the Thugs and Pindari, an escalation in widow-burning, masochistic swinging from hooks, suicide in front of the Jaganatha of Puri and armed ascetic bands. This was paralleled by the systematic exploitation of India by the British.

In China, the Manchu Ching dynasty survived throughout this period, in some ways puritanical but with very cavalier treatment of women, who could be divorced or sold at will and who, by tradition, felt compelled to bind their feet to a painfully small size. It was under the Manchu that the pigtail became the compulsory symbol for peasant servitude, and punishments for even minor misdemeanors were sadistic. The Manchu were also guilty of a major act of genocide when they exterminated around 200,000 Elleuths in the 1750s, and caused such devastation that a further 250,000 died of smallpox.

Although the Confucian system and the mandarin bureaucracy based on competitive examinations still dominated imperial life, China was beginning to be exposed to foreign interference, particularly (from 1780) to the import of opium, the only trading product the British East India Company could find to help reduce its balance of payments deficit in the China trade. This was exacerbated by the fact that the Portuguese had introduced tobacco smoking, and when the two were put together the habit was much more addictive. By 1729 the problem was serious enough for the issue of an edict that all opium traders should be strangled. By 1840 it was reckoned that there were 2,000,000 opium addicts in China, a situation attributable largely to British commercial exploitation, which in turn led to further corruption. According to Peffer, 'nothing was so squalid, so culpable as the opium evil forced on China' which provided a tenth of the revenue of British India.

Chinese life, even at its worst, was always characterised by the Confucian attention to details of etiquette which kept society functioning like clockwork. A pedestrian meeting a labourer carrying two buckets on a bamboo pole should step aside; the labourer would have to step aside if he met a sedan chair carried by two labourers; the sedan-bearers would give way to a horseman, and all four would have to give way to a wedding or a mandarin's procession. The slightly permissive trend was fed by the availability of both concubinage and prostitution to those who could afford them, and open homosexuality appears to have been tolerated.

Japan moved into a permissive period, the age of Ukiyo, the floating world of tea houses, highly trained geisha girls, the nude paintings of Utamaro, the permissive novels of Saikaku, like *The Mirror of Manly Love*, transvestite theatre companies of dubious repute, bath-houses and homosexual monks. Instability reigned in a nation still hiding from the rest of the world.

Africa still suffered the attentions of the slavers. Throughout this century the trade persisted, and between 1795 and 1805, 381,000 were transported by ships from three main English ports—Liverpool, London and Bristol. The British plantations alone required 10,000 new slaves every year and, as Dorothy Marshall put it, 'no Liverpool or Bristol merchant felt the need to blush for the source of his wealth'. On the tomb of Foster Cuncliffe, the owner of five slaving ships, was the inscription: 'A Christian devout and exemplary in the exercise of every private and public duty.'

But the African ethos survived. Westermarck tells us that Charles Wheeler commented in 1744:

> The African is never tempted to rape as European men are and all the time I lived there I never once heard of those detestable and unnatural crimes of sodomy and bestiality so much practised among Christians.

In 1810, Mungo Park, exploring the Niger, wrote: 'I found African women uniformly kind and compassionate.' Similarly, the Englishman Francis Moore, of the Royal Africa Company, described Gambia in 1738 thus:

> The Fula people are hospitable, generous to neighbouring peoples in famines, strict Muslims who never touch alcohol, are rarely angry yet very brave.

The sufferings of negro slaves in the Americas had, if anything, grown worse with the increasing commercial pressure to produce tobacco, sugar and coffee as European demand grew. The death-rate of sugar slaves in Cuba rose to ten percent as they worked a twenty-hour day and had three hours' sleep. On the coffee plantations of Brazil the owners wanted a very quick return, and the death-rate was as high as twenty-five percent. Mass suicide was not uncommon as the only sure means of escape. When the Jesuit order was suppressed in the Portuguese colonies in 1759, it was the largest single owner of slaves in both Brazil and Angola.

In most of the world's societies the eighteenth century was a period of spectacular inequality, in which the upper classes tended to be permissive and insensitive, and the middle classes (where they existed) were so impressed that they wanted their share, wanted to take over and mimic the value systems of those in the layer above. This competitive urge caused a significant deadening of ethical sensitivities. In many respects the human species had reached the lowest ebb of ethical maturity since the founding of the great religions, yet by the end of the century there were hints of a new revival, the first thrust of middle-class sensibility.

1800 — 1900

A man who moralises is usually a hypocrite . . .
Oscar Wilde

T HE NINETEENTH CENTURY IN EUROPE alternated between romantic idealisation of the arrogant superman and a greater sensitivity to the pain and suffering of the masses than had ever been seen before.

The century began with the well-publicised dramas of Napoleon's military success. Napoleon Bonaparte (1769–1821), whose image was turned into that of a superhuman legend by the publicists of the empire, sacrificed the lives of 5,000,000 people, including 1,700,000 of his own nation, using the energy of the Revolution to pursue the objectives of the *ancien régime*. It may be argued that his individual egotism was the sole real cause of these disasters, but it has been pointed out that he came from an island whose social institutions were the banditti and the vendetta. In addition to being a product of the Corsican folk ethic and French revolutionary confidence, he nurtured himself on the stories of Alexander the Great and Caesar, the traditional superheroes. From this came his unquenchable thirst for power and glory, and his resultant extravagance with human lives, his favourite tactic being to hurl solid columns of infantry against the enemy head-on—he once observed that he could afford to lose 30,000 men a month. On the whole, he has not been found guilty of deliberate post-combat massacre, but he did slaughter 2,500 Turks at Jaffa. For a period he created a successful war ethic in France, where military success was the highest form of virtue and loyalty to 'la patrie' or 'l'empereur' came above all else. The anti-Bonapartist pamphlet, *Chronique Scandaleuse*, indicates the blind eye turned towards the behaviour of off-duty soldiers, who were allowed to gratify all their whims so long as they won wars. A true warrior was expected to be a gallant, promiscuous like Napoleon himself; but in such a period of prolonged warfare there were also signs of the development of sadistic, irrational behaviour as normal sensitivities were blunted. It was noted also that Napoleon was relatively tolerant of the outbreak of homosexual behaviour in his army during the Egyptian campaign, but not of the drug-taking habits which they copied from the local inhabitants.

The idea that the superhuman hero should be above conventional morality, that great endeavours mattered far more than bourgeois respectability, was made popular by Lord Byron (1788–1824), an advocate of liberty who made his name by cocking a snout at traditional values in his poems, *Childe Harold* and *Don Juan*.

In France, the eccentric arch-priest of the amoral hero was the Marquis de Sade (1740–1814), who pronounced that 'virtue is dull', and cultivated the pleasures of violence:

> Who else but nature whispers to us of personal hatreds, vengeances, wars, in fact all the everlasting motives for murder? It is impossible for murder ever to outrage nature.

In Britain, Thomas De Quincey (1785–1859), the romantic vagabond and self-confessed drug addict, wrote his *Murder Considered as a Fine Art*. The Berkeley Horse, a flagellating robot, did excellent business for London club-owners in 1828, catering for public school boys who had enjoyed a good beating from headmasters like John Keate of Eton (1773–1852). The novelist Gustave Flaubert (1821–80) promoted the sadistic Emperor Nero as a hero. In Germany, Hegel (1770–1831) presented the ambitious Prussian junker as the ideal man, while the

German historian, Theodor Mommsen (1817–1903), revived the cult of Julius Caesar as the great classical superhero, and Richard Wagner (1813–83) wrote the musical theme for Nordic empire-builders and made Bayreuth a centre for nationalist opera.

Friedrich Nietzsche (1844–1900) took the concept of the amoral superhero to its ultimate conclusion. Using Darwin as proof of the superiority of the higher races over lower ones, he argued that virtue was on a par with weakness and only the strong should survive:

> To the rhythm of my whip shalt thou dance and cry. I forget not my whip?
> Not I Zarathustra.

His exemplary hero was the totally amoral Cesare Borgia, whose motto was 'Either Caesar or nothing.' Nietzsche's *Beyond Good and Evil* (1886) argued that there was no absolute good or evil and people should give up both ideas.

Nietzsche's contemporary, Otto von Bismarck (1815–98), made his famous speech on conquest by 'blood and iron' rather than ideas, in 1862. Bismarck, more than any other single man, used his consummate diplomatic skill to disguise aggressive wars as apparent defensive wars, the crucial art of achieving moral respectability for conquest which had been the foundation of the Roman and, to some extent, the British Empires. Above all, he *won* his three wars, thus creating a widespread credibility for the military solution which was to have disastrous consequences when adopted by the naïve emperors of the next generation. Under Bismarck's influence the Franco-Prussian war saw the first deliberate use of artillery against civilian targets, with the bombardments of Strasbourg and Paris in 1870–71. Terror was being used as a tool of conquest. The value of war as a political tool was given intellectual respectability in Germany by the historian Heinrich Treitschke (1834–96), who developed the theory that expansion through warfare was good for a country, 'a medicine for the ills of the state', while Schlieffen (1833–1913) theorised the practical chess moves which formed the precise basis for a structured, aggressive war. Beside this must be seen the posturings of Wilhelm II (1859–1941), the warlord with the withered arm, descendant of generations of drill-sergeant emperors—his own father was a notable but short-lived exception—who posed in his glittering uniforms against the yellow peril and every other threat to Germany's *Weltpolitik*.

The whole military ethic of Germany is seen in miniature in their continued moral approval of the duel, long after it had been outlawed in other civilised countries. In 1897, there was still a moral compulsion on a German army officer who refused the gauntlet to resign from the service. In this atmosphere it was most unlikely that the state would itself turn away from conflict if there were any threat to its honour, however imaginary, however trivial.

Trapped in the same suicidal posture were Napoleon III of France, Nicholas II of Russia and Franz Joseph of Austria. Napoleon III (1808–73) was not a natural warlord, indeed he had pronounced that

> The Napoleonic ideal is not one of war but of social, industrial and commercial humanitarianism.

But as Bismarck shrewdly observed, he was also 'vaguely aware that he needed a war' to restore his domestic image. Tragedy was to lie in the compulsion which mediocre imperial leaders felt to maintain the pose of successful warlords, necessitated by the ethos of their time.

In the bitter Spanish civil war of 1836, Ramon Cabrera (1810–77), the Carlist general, carved an unsavoury reputation for the way he slaughtered prisoners of war and maltreated female hostages, and in South America the collapse of Spanish rule was associated with new republics in which lack of stability bred continuing political ruthlessness and violence. In 1817, Spain had used mass executions to maintain control of Nueva Granada: it failed, and between 1810 and 1929 there were to be thirteen outbreaks of internal violence in the republic of Columbia which replaced it. Similarly, in Argentina the dictator Juan Mamed de Rosas (1793–1877) used savagery cultivated as a deterrent to sustain his power. Violence as the first solution to political conflict became a feature of South American history.

The British cult of the military hero was kept more modest by the 'team comes first' theme cultivated by Dr Arnold of Rugby (1795–1842), pioneer of the British public school ethic, whose meditations by Lake Como had led him to his belief that corporal punishment was the key to education. Rugby, the game, taught a mindless, dogged obedience and, according to Dr Norwood of Harrow,

> Cricket has added a new concept of fairness and chivalry to the common store of our national ideal.

Manga deduced that

> In a large part through games . . . Britain had gained the physical and moral strength to acquire and govern its vast empire.

Mayo College was the Eton of India. Cricket, pipe bands, and later the Boy Scout movement, all helped create proper manliness and obedience throughout the empire. Hence the shock when the Indian army, reacting against the trampling on its traditional ethos by the British, mutinied in 1857. Suttee had been abolished, the Thuggee eliminated, as was infanticide of daughters and the burying alive of lepers, all seen as immoral by Victorian Britain. When the sepoys were threatened by their British generals with compulsory sea travel, a sin in the Hindu ethos, and compelled to use cow-fat cartridges, the resentment exploded.

The British public school ethic was the source of what Disraeli called 'muscular Christianity'. Jingoism, though orchestrated by Disraeli, was a response to empire rather than a desire for it. Richard Cobden remarked in 1836:

> The aristocracy has converted the combativeness of the English people to its own sinister ends.

Thomas Hughes, in *Tom Brown's Schooldays* (1857), castigated bullying and cribbing, while Tennyson had begun to put across the new chivalry in the *Idylls of the King* (1842). In due course, Rudyard Kipling (1865–1936) became the literary high priest of those who carried 'the white man's burden', of stoical and honourable resistence to all forms of aggression:

> If you can keep your head when all about you . . .

Rider Haggard, in *King Solomon's Mines* (1855), wrote of the decent Kaffir who would naturally sacrifice his life for his white master. Africa was the great victim of nineteenth-century militarism. The French boosted their flagging confidence by conquering one easy area after another from 1830 to 1880. The carve-up was sanctified by the Congress of Berlin in 1884, and other countries took their portions. Referring to his conquest of Ghana, the British general, Garnet Wolseley (1833–1913), said 'It was the most horrible war I ever took part in.' The other British oddity was transference of the ethos of the slave trade, now illegal, to the transportation of white British criminals to Australia—between 1787 and 1868 some 160,000 were forcibly exiled, in less than comfortable conditions.

Although the moral approval of militarism in Britain had a quite different tone from its approval in France, Germany or Russia, all four were without question paranoically sensitive to the white feather, and ready for mutual self-destruction. To add to it all, there was also the romanticisation of some of the small but successful wars of liberation in which military action was glamourised, particularly the success of Guiseppe Garibaldi (1807–82) and his Red Shirts in Italy.

Another bitter war which was readily romanticised was the American Civil War, in which, despite an apparently noble cause, the ethics of warfare sank remarkably low. William T. Sherman's famous march through Georgia in 1864 was a deliberate attack on non-combatants and termed by Liddell Hart 'a major step away from the concept of moderation in war'. Similarly, the Confederate massacre at Fort Pillow was an example of the extermination of garrisons who were either 'niggers' or whites fighting alongside them and therefore people unprotected by the rules of war.

There were three other areas where the military ethic dominated. The Turks, a nation under severe pressure as their system decayed, won themselves an unsavoury reputation as the practitioners of genocide. In 1876, some 15,000 Bulgars were massacred in the incident which so riled Gladstone; more seriously, nine years later 180,000 Armenians were killed by Sultan Abdul Hamid, who was deposed in 1909. Within twenty years the number of Armenians killed had risen to over 500,000 under the leadership of Enver Bey (1881–1922), the first major example of systematic genocide in modern times, and an act inspired partly by the nationalist writings of Zia Gokalp (1876–1914). There was a further area of violence, the Levant, where in 1860 the Druzes, a Moslem sect, massacred 30,000 Maronite Christians, leaving a bitter legacy for the future Lebanon.

Most dramatic of all was the spectacular revival of the military ethic in Japan. In 1882, the Meiji emperor resuscitated the old ideas of bushido, the ascetic military code linked with a new form of nationalism. 'Nippon Shugisha' was their version of the master race, and wars with both China (1894–98) and Russia (1904) seemed to prove that the idea was right, just as Sadowa and Sedan had done for the Germans. Notably the Japanese attack on Fort Arthur in 1894 saw savage atrocities, and the second attack in 1904 was launched with a lack of warning as startling as that of the attack on Pearl Harbor in 1941. In 1899, Dr Imazo Nitole wrote *Bushido*, spreading the concept of the samurai ethic (previously confined to the privileged élite) to all classes of Japanese society, and laying the foundations for a mass military ethic in the next century. This was to become, at its tragic peak, the ethic of the kamikaze:

> Live briefly but gloriously . . . the fall of the blossom is as moving as its beauty on the limb.

Thus a fanatical faith in the military solution became a strong motivating force in Germany, Japan, and to a varying extent in Russia, France, Austria, Britain and the lesser nations. The ethic was one which placed national success far above individual comfort, indeed took a pride in doing so; the virtues it bred were those of duty, service, courage, and contempt for the life of the individual. The image was of the parade ground, the spiked helmet, the monocle and the military moustache. Retreat, in whatever form, was the ultimate sin. The same was true of the new breed of anarchists like Ravachol (1852–92), who justified any form of violence, including terrorism, murder and body-snatching in the interests of revolution. A succession of political assassinations turned tyrannicide into a new art form.

In 1816, Shaka (1783–1828) seized the throne of the Zulus and instigated one of Africa's most aggressively expansionist regimes. Those who objected were impaled or disembowelled, and as he conquered neighbouring nations he used the phrase, 'sweeping up the rubbish', as quoted by Peter Becker. After his murder he was succeeded by the equally aggressive Dingane (d.1840), and the Zulus remained on a collision course with the whites.

Side by side with the new breed of nineteenth-century militarism there was developing also a more determined form of humanitarianism than the world had ever seen before. In its practical form, this movement took its origins from the religious revival which swept through many countries in the wake of the French Revolution. The first of a series of Christian pressure groups was led by William Wilberforce (1759–1833), helped by the Quaker Committee of Six. Nineteen years of campaigning procured the abolition of the slave trade in 1807, and the end of slavery in the British Empire itself came in the year of his death. As E.N. Williams says, it was 'one of the greatest propaganda movements of all time—the beginning of the end of one of society's greatest crimes'.

In the United States, the first anti-slavery society had been founded in Pennsylvania in 1777 and the number grew rapidly, but thereafter economic pressure pushed ethics in the opposite direction. By 1837 a hundred anti-slavery societies in the southern states had been disbanded because of the cotton boom. In the words of Gwendolyn Hall: 'the lords of the lash and the lords of the loom' were in harness. The Connecticut puritan, Harriet Beecher Stowe (1811–90), wrote the hugely influential *Uncle Tom's Cabin* in 1852. The fanatical abolitionist, John Brown (1800–59), conducted his strange raid on Harper's Ferry in 1859, and Abraham Lincoln (1809–65) had led the Illinois delegation against the extension of slavery since 1856. Abolition was on its way.

Around the same time in Russia, the novelist Ivan Turgenev (1818–83) wrote his *Sportsman's Sketches* (1852), as strong an attack on serfdom as Russian censorship would allow, and nine years later, as an act of political expediency, Tsar Alexander II (1818–81) ended serfdom. Some 40,000,000 peasants were freed, and though their economical burdens were far from lightened, it must rank as history's largest single act of emancipation.

Abolition of slavery elsewhere followed fairly rapidly. In Cuba in the 1870s, for instance, around 500,000 slaves were freed gradually; in 1888, some 700,000 were freed in Brazil. In 1865, David Livingstone (1813–73) wrote *The Zambesi and its Tributaries* to expose the continued existence of the Portuguese slave trade which allowed extremely high mortality rates, and gradually slavery was stamped out in the more obscure parts of the world. Abolition did not, of course, necessarily mean the end of exploitation, but it was a major achievement. Nor did it in some countries solve the racial problem created by years of mass transportation of blacks out of Africa. It is not insignificant that the Ku-Klux Klan was founded in 1865 by Civil War hero, General Nathan Bedford Forrest, the Confederate veteran who became the first Grand Wizard at Nashville, creating a new focal point for the idea of white supremacy and a justification of the cruellest violence against the negroes for a cause which had already cost 600,000 lives. Whipping, torture, arson and murder were basic tools in what was portrayed as a 'holy crusade'.

It is also significant intellectually that while white men had accepted that blacks should be free, they had not accepted that they should be equal. In 1855, Joseph Arthur Gobineau (1816–82), the French Orientalist, wrote his *Essay on the Inequality of Human Races* which paved the way for Nietzsche. The stereotypes of 'feckless blacks', 'evil little yellow men', 'hook-nosed Jews' and 'dirty dagos' were beginning to filter through into popular European literature, leading to the creation of long-term prejudices. Even in places like Cuba, the freeing of black slaves had an adverse reaction on white morale and relationships worsened. Conditions did not improve much, either. The new, free Chinese contract labourers, who to some extent filled the gap left by the end of slavery, had a suicide rate in 1855 as high as the blacks had had in 1834, when white reprisals had been near their height.

Apart from the abolition of slavery, there was a whole range of issues involving cruelty of which the middle-class conscience became aware during the nineteenth century. In 1854, Florence Nightingale (1820–1910) opened her hospital at Scutari in the Crimea; and five years later, after witnessing the untreated wounded in the battle of Solferino, the Swiss, Henri Dunant (1820–1910), began the campaign which led to the foundation of the Red Cross and later the Geneva Convention (1864). In Britain, female flogging was abolished as a punishment in 1820, the pillory in 1837, cockfighting in 1849, public hanging in 1864, army flogging in 1868, bull-baiting in 1870, chimney boys in 1892 and prison treadmills in 1895.

These are just a few examples of the many pieces of legislation which, in just one country, gradually reduced the atmosphere of physical cruelty which had for so long been an accepted part of life. At the same time there were the voluntary pressure groups aimed at achieving similar ends: the Royal Society for the Prevention of Cruelty to Animals was founded in 1824, Barnardo's Homes for orphans in 1867, the soup kitchens of the Salvation Army in 1865, Josephine Baker's campaign against the white slave traffic in the 1860s, the Society for the Prevention of Cruelty to Children in 1884. William Booth (1828–1912) summed up the uninhibited Victorian conscience when he wrote:

> We saw the need; we saw the people starving; we obliged; there was a compulsion.

It was clear to contemporaries like J.S. Mill (1806–73) that the new moral awareness was a reflection of the relative rise of the middle class, and the decline in economic significance of the land-owning aristocracy. Cobden, and the other opinion-formers of the Anti-Corn Law League, despised the old upper class—'the footpad aristocracy, gluttons and debauchers'—but were equally critical of the working class, with their 'utter recklessness of impure thought and living'.

The work ethic reached a new pinnacle of glory in the Victorian era with the idealisation of the self-made man, a fulsome belief in the automatic rewards of self-improvement, which was given literary stature in 1859 in the famous *Self Help* of Samuel Smiles (1812–1904), the perfect prize for good Victorian school-children. The work ethic went with the laissez-faire concept of competition, which linked up conveniently with Charles Darwin's (1809–82) concept of the 'survival of the fittest', itself almost a moral tale of the decline and fall of dinosaurs, which appeared in the same year in *The Origin of Species*. The suffering that went with it, what J.S. Mill called 'the trampling, crushing and elbowing' were soon to become evident. Yet with it came also the ascetic quality of the evangelicals, the disapproval of enjoyment. Sir James Stephen (1758–1832) so frowned on pleasure that after he had once smoked a cigar and found it delicious, he vowed never to do it again.

The third great train of thought dominating the moral ideas of this century was the socialist solution. The concentration of labour in the new, power-driven factories, the long hours, the heavy demands on the mining industry, the use of female and child labour on a new scale, all helped to make more visible the exploitation of the unskilled masses. Of all industries, coal mining probably had the most danger and the ugliest conditions. In the words of Ebenezer Elliot (*fl.*1830):

> . . . the inbacked slave
> Who laid face upward hews the black stone down,
> Poor living corpse; he labours in the grave
> Poor two-legged mole; he mines for half a crown,
> From morn to eve that wolves who sleep on down
> And pare our bones may eat their bread—tax warm.

By the middle of the century, reports and new legislation were beginning to flood through to halt the abuses of fast-expanding industry; but meanwhile a Utopian vision was being conceived which would replace capitalism. Robert Owen (1771–1858), a successful, philanthropic factory owner, published his *New View of Society* in 1813, adopted socialism, and by 1825 had founded New Harmony and eleven other Utopian communities in the United States, all unsuccessful. His basic creed—'Man's character is made for him not by him'—was, however, to be of fundamental importance. Owen also argued for a radical review of marriage. At his community in Orbiston they practised collective house-keeping, and at Meneaten experimented with communes; but he recognised the impracticality of some of these new ideas, as easy divorce was a difficult concept in the days before effective birth control. It would have to wait for 'the new moral world'.

The French enlightenment of the previous century had concluded that human behaviour would be moral and happy if men had political freedom; the nineteenth-century socialists added that the physical environment and economic pressures had to be right as well. John Pestalozzi (1746–1827) preached the moralising value of a rustic environment and simple agricultural labour, founding his orphan schools in 1798. François Fourier (1772–1837), the salesman from Besançon, preached the evils of capitalism and suggested the founding of small, phalange communities of 1,500 people each. Amongst his recommendations were a minimum wage, no marriage, constant changing of jobs and equal sharing of profits. Francis Place (1771–1854), the London tailor who contributed so much to the legalisation of trade union activity, was also a senior drafter of the rights claimed in the *People's Charter* of 1846, and a pioneer of family planning as a means of reducing urban deprivation.

Britain also produced that practical contribution to welfare, the co-operative movement. At first despised but later praised by Owen, the London Co-operative commenced in 1824 to help achieve cheaper food prices for the urban population by non-profit making production and distribution. *The Economist* was its original propaganda organ.

The next milestone in the rights claimed for mankind by socialism came in France, with Jean Louis Blanc's (1811–82) *Organisation du Travail*, the first major assertion of the right to employment. Ned Ludd (*fl.*1779), the Leicester village idiot, had accidentally given rise to a movement when he had destroyed some stocking frames in 1782. Luddite riots spread in 1811.

It was left to Karl Marx (1818–83) to give the fullest expression to the new form of industrial exploitation—unemployment. Particularly he was obsessed with the recent role of the bourgeoisie, which 'creates a world after its own image' and which, from a moral point of view, 'has resolved personal wealth with exchange value'.

> [For] exploitation veiled by religious and political illusions it has substituted naked shameless direct brutal exploitation ... It has left no other nexus between man and man than naked self-interest, than callous cash payment, it has drowned the most heavenly ecstasies of religious fervour, chivalrous enthusiasm, of Philistine sentimentalism in the icy water of egotistical calculation.

Marx observed that women were 'mere instruments of production' and he noticed

> ... the selfish misconception that induces you to transform into eternal laws of nature and of reason the social forms springing from your present mode of production and form of property.

Of private property, he commented it was 'the final expression of the exploitation of the many by the few', a concept which echoed the ideas of his French contemporary Pierre Joseph Proudhon (1809–65) who, in his *Qu'est-ce que la propriété?* (1840) had made the famous prounouncement that 'property is theft'. Marx, however, did not approve of Proudhon, and in one of his statements justifying war made the comment that he hoped the Prussians beat Napoleon III, as 'the French need a good drubbing'.

Thus nineteenth-century socialism created the sin of economic inequality, leaving to the next century the problem of finding a replacement motivation. For the time being it was left to the liberals, philanthropists and trade unionists to take the practical steps to improve what Charles Kingsley (1819–75) had called the 'forests of filthy poverty and disease'.

The swing back to religion at the beginning of the nineteenth century had also had its effect on attitudes towards the behaviour of the individual. Wilberforce and the evangelists typified it in Britain. In France, there was a new breed of saints like Madelaine Barat (1779–1806); and in the United States there was Elizabeth Seton (1774–1812) or Lyman Beecher, who in 1812 founded the Society for the Suppression of Vice and Promotion of Good Morals in Connecticut. In 1802, this Society began deliberations in London; and in 1805, Thomas Bowdler (1754–1825), the censor of Shakespeare's naughty bits, exposed a pornography ring with the help of Wilberforce. Miss Weeton (*fl.*1820) said children over seven should not be allowed to bathe naked, and coeducational schools were split up. King George III expelled his son's mistresses from the palace. In 1812, a toothpick-case producer was convicted of obscenity, but as the fear of Napoleon wore off a new atmosphere of materialism and permissiveness set in, led by the Prince Regent. Beau Brummell (1778–1840) was the hero of exotic male dress in the amoral years of the Regency buck: 'starch is the man'.

The Hell Fire Club flourished, and there was Mrs Prendergast's exotic Bal d'Amour. The English Regency was one of those periods, like the Restoration, when fashion definitely favoured promiscuity, the cad, the Corinthian sneer and ostentatious wealth. Byron preached the new amorality, which at times seemed almost suicidal. In Russia, the fashion took a significantly masochistic turn with a desire to fight pointless duels and suffer for love: Alexander Pushkin (1799–1837) and Mikhail Lermontov (1814–41) were two victims of this communal death wish, and Pushkin, like Byron, had taken permissiveness almost to the limit with his numerous mistresses and erotic poetry.

The new industrial towns in Britain were expected to be seed-beds for iniquity, especially when women went to work instead of rearing their children. J.L. Hammond quotes the 7th Earl of Shaftesbury (1801-85) as saying: 'Domestic life and domestic discipline must soon be at an end', but the decline was only marginal. The relatively easy-going attitude towards marriage of the early nineteenth century, the booming industrial towns where illegitimacy was a minor slur, the Cock and Hen Clubs, the rise in cohabitation, the persistence of wife-selling, all ended in the 1840s. The bureaucracy had backed marriage, and from then on the illegitimacy rate sank, not to regain the same level till the 1960s. The workhouse became a form of insitutionalised infanticide for unwanted children.

Lord Byron had been forced into exile on suspicion of incest with his half-sister, and the cad went out of fashion. By 1820 'working-class bawdry' was driven off the streets. Dandyism reared its head again briefly, with the Bulwer Lytton (1803–73) set which used perfume and hair oil, but was slapped down by Carlyle in *Sartor Resartus* in 1833, then by Thackeray and Dickens. The Victorian era was about to achieve a consensus morality. Parker tells us that it was commented with horror, in 1825, that education at Eton created 'a taste for gluttony and drunkenness, aptitude for brutal sports and a passion for female society of the most degrading kind'. But now Queen Victoria (1819–1901) reigned, and the example of disciplined domesticity which she set was profound, as (to a lesser extent) was that of Empress Eugenie in Paris.

In 1841, George Williams founded the Young Men's Christian Association in London to keep young city workers from being exposed to temptation. The Victorian values of chastity, prudery, piety, sobriety, thrift and punctuality began to assert themselves. Quinlan's *Evangelical Barometer* had fifteen grades of sin: drunkenness and theatre being curiously equated at four, novel-reading and neglect of prayer at five, adultery and parties on Sunday at six, and so on.

Without question the vice capital of the world was Vienna, where the waltz—'whose shameless embrace was not compatible with chastity'—was re-invented by Schubert and Weber in 1819, and in 1820 a population of 400,000 was matched by 20,000 prostitutes. The illegitimate birth-rate rose first to twenty-five percent and then, by 1847, to fifty percent, resulting in the presence in Austria of 1,000,000 foundlings between 1821 and 1840. Infanticide escalated. It took the sobering events of the 1848 revolution to bring the city briefly to its senses.

This period also saw the first entry of fashionable drugs into northern Europe, perhaps as a result of Napoleon's conquest of Egypt. Coleridge and de Quincey became addicts in England while, in the 1840s, the Hotel Primodan in Paris was the drug nightspot for Dumas, Baudelaire and others. There was to be a remarkable escalation of drug use in the United States later in the century, perhaps partly attributable to the over-liberal use of morphine for wounded soldiers in the Civil War, perhaps also to the large inflow of Chinese immigrants across the Pacific bringing opium to San Francisco in

1850. Cocaine was invented in Peru in 1858, as a development on their staple coca.

Oakley regards 1890 as the peak period for narcotics in the USA. In 1898, a new cure was announced for opium addiction, a 'heroic' antidote named heroin. As so often, the cure proved more dangerous than the disease. Less excitingly, the Irish and many other European peasants took to ether in the 1890s, as it was a cheaper escape than alcohol.

Meanwhile, the Jacksonian era in the USA had seen a number of efforts to improve urban morality: the American Tract Society, founded in 1825, was printing and delivering 5,000,000 tracts a year by 1850, projecting sobriety, diligence, piety, contentment with one's station and loyalty to the family. Paul Boyer records that, while in 1815 it was said of New York that 'vice is pouring into the city like a torrent', the 'haunts of wickedness' of Philadelphia were reported abandoned by 1822.

During the same period the Temperance Movement gathered momentum on both sides of the Atlantic. The Massachusetts Society for the Suppression of Intemperance was founded in 1813, though the first pledges were at least ten years earlier. By 1825 the movement had 1,000,000 adherents in the United States, inspired partly by Timothy Shay Arthur's *Ten Nights in a Bar-Room* (1854). Then came the even more aggressive Anti-Saloon League, which damned saloons as 'a most corrupt, fiendish and hell-soaked institution'.

The first European club was in Skitereen, Ireland, in 1818, and the greatest missionary of the movement was Father Matthew, whose frenetic campaign from 1839 to 1842 gathered over 4,000,000 abstainers and halved spirit consumption in the country within four years. In France, Emile Zola's *L'Assomoir* preached the same message. Queen Victoria was patroness of the British Temperance Society (1837–50)—'Lips that touch liquor shall never touch mine'—and in the United States, Carrie Watson, the Kansas prohibitionist, was famous for hacking up saloons with her axe for the Women's Christian Temperance Society of 1893. The idea was to peak in 1919 when the nineteenth amendment was passed introducing prohibition, which lasted until 1933. For over a hundred years alcohol had been blamed for virtually all that was bad in human behaviour, but in the end was discovered to be a symptom rather than a cause.

The religious revival in Britain swelled the numbers of the established Church, its evangelical branches and the non-conformist chapels, including the newly emancipated Roman Catholics. In 1830, the Plymouth Brethren were founded by the Reverend J.N. Derby (1800–82), and the influential Christian Socialist group by John Maurice (1805–72) in the 1850s; but the most dramatic and penetrating new British sect was the Salvation Army, with both its spiritual message and its practical ethical concern. The 'Great Revival' in Ulster 'was attended by the suppression of drunkenness and profanity, by a general reformation of moral character', as observed by G. Salmon. Similarly, there came the Welsh Revival, with the wild chanting of the chapels, and the fundamentalist Free Church of Scotland, later to be known as the 'Wee Frees'. In 1883, Scotland also produced the Boys' Brigade, with its motto 'Sure and steadfast', founded for the moral training of Christian youth.

Europe also had its revivals. France saw a big resurgence in Catholicism, with improved training for the priesthood, better organisation, a rise in recruitment to the religious orders from 37,000 to 190,000 between 1850 and 1870 (of whom the majority were nuns), and the appearance of St Bernadette and the new cult of the Virgin Mary centred at Lourdes in 1858. Other saintly models included John Baptist Viannes (1790–1859), the humble *curé* St Andrew Fournet (1752–1834), founder of sixty convents of Daughters of the Cross, Frances Cabrini (1850–1917), founder of fifty-four houses of the Sisters of the Sacred Heart, and Mary di Rosa (1813–55), founder of the Handmaids of Charity to help factory girls in Brescia. Rather more eccentric was the sect founded by Jean Antoine Boullan (1824–93) in Eastern Europe which attracted 600,000 members; it was strongly anti-Catholic, yet offered followers a mystic marriage which became a euphemism for widespread promiscuity.

It was the United States that was most prolific during this period in developing new Christian sects. This was the age of 'come-outism'; the Universalists of Boston in 1799 swung the emphasis away from orthodoxy and towards human behaviour. In 1825, Charles Grandison Furney founded a Perfectionist sect in New York with the emphasis on leading a useful rather than a holy life, and had his 'anxious seat for sinners'. In 1830, Joseph Smith (1805–44) first preached his thirteen articles at Fayette, Seneca County, and developed the Mormon ethic later extended by Brigham Young (1801–77) in Utah to become a highly effective lifestyle with the emphasis on co-operation and economic efficiency. The polygamy issue tended to assume exaggerated importance, and the controversy was ended in 1887 when the Mormons finally abandoned polygamy as a tenet. Soon afterwards they outlawed the even more controversial habit of allowing 'incestuous' marriage.

In the 1870s came both Christian Science, founded by Mary Baker Eddy (1821–1911), and the International Bible Students Association or Jehovah's Witnesses, founded by Pastor Charles Taze Russell (1852–1916), whose battle against the forces of evil in the new Armageddon was based on the Book of Revelation. This sect forbad divorce, smoking, drinking and military service, so it was in the great tradition of ascetic, pacifist sects. Also influential on the American ethos was the Unitarian pastor, Ralph Waldo Emerson (1803–82), the admirer of frontier individualism, preaching 'the infinitude of the private man' and 'conscience as the supreme judge'. The concept of backwoods self-reliance was taken to its extreme by Henry Thoreau (1817–62), 'the Hermit of Walden', who philosophised from the solitude of his log cabin:

> Any man more right than his neighbours constitutes a majority of one.

He refused to pay taxes to support slavery or the Mexican war:

> If the alternative is to keep all just men in prison or give up war and glory, the state will not hesitate which to choose.

A further odd sect was Theosophy, founded in 1875 by a Russian emigré, Madame Blavatsky (1831–91), and supposedly based on some Tibetan texts in her possession; it was an adaptation of Hindu guruism to Western palates which later attracted Aldous Huxley, Jaharawal Nehru and Rudolf Steiner. Less influential, but just as interesting, was the messianic leadership of the Iroquois chief, Handsome Lake, who preached a new, semi-Christian puritanism in the American mid-west.

There was an echo of Thoreau's theme of passive resistance from the Russian novelist Leo Tolstoy (1828–1910), who corresponded with Gandhi, and between them they founded a new tradition of non-violence. Tolstoy had some allegiance to the old Dukhobor sect, was a severe ascetic and propagandist (in *War and Peace*) of the follies of human glory-hunting. That other great product of Russian frustration, the nihilist concept, was coined by Turgenev in his *Fathers and Sons* (1862), in which Bazarov says:

> There is no single institution in our present mode of life, in family or in social life which does not call for complete and unqualified destruction.

The special quality of Russian despair was encouraged by the enormity of the problem, its oppressive regime and the huge scale of serfdom. The Romanovs of the nineteenth century were, on the whole, less permissive and better intentioned than their predecessors. Alexander I (1777–1825), founder of the Holy Alliance, believed that he was fighting the spirit of evil under the influence of the pious Madame de Krutener. His brother, Nicholas I (1796–1855), had a prudish streak, making it illegal to smoke in public or wear grey top hats, but he was the first ruler to use psychiatric wards as a form of unofficial punishment for those mad enough to suggest reform. Alexander II, the abolisher of serfdom, still ended up with a repressive reputation, assassinated for his pains.

The revolutionary Nechaev (1847–82) pronounced that 'Morality is anything which contributes to the triumph of the revolution.' Russian governments became obsessed with what Tolstoy called 'slavophile madness', the need for international glory to make up for repression at home. The anti-Semitic fashion had moved eastwards through Europe to Russia, and now reared its ugly head again; the Jews were blamed for the tsar's murder in 1881, thousands were murdered in Kiev, and 225,000 were expelled from Russia. The ascetic minister Constantin Pobedonotsev (1827–1907), the 'Black Tsar', and the homosexual, sadistic Archduke Sergei were leaders in this field.

Anti-Semitism was also on the increase in Austria and Hungary, where the Jews were seen as enemies of the downtrodden Christian peasant and of the new national movements emerging from the Austro-Hungarian Empire. The Jews were the successful capitalists of the area, the money-lenders of Galicia, the estate managers of Romania, the entrepreneurs and professionals of Vienna itself. The myths about their habit of ritual murder began to revive. The hostility simmered. Anti-Semitism reappeared also in the Islamic world, and there was regular persecution of Jews in Tehran and elsewhere in Persia in the 1890s.

The Eastern religions also at this time produced a ferment of ideas. In the Lebanon, the Maronites produced a new saint, the hermit Charbel Makhlouf, who died in 1898. In 1863, a new saviour appeared in Baghdad, Mirza Husein Ali or Baha Ullah (1817–92), whose new faith, Bahaism, became an Islamic off-shoot promoting equality, peace, unity, welfare and the right to work. It was a vigorous and very up-to-date religion in a would-be federal world. Hinduism was modernised first by Anya Sanaj (1828–83) and then more dramatically by Sri Rama krishna Para ma ham (1836–86), the 'Hindu Wesley' who pursued the ideal of compassion, reducing the challenge of rationalism against the relatively unsophisticated theology of traditional Hinduism. Most significantly, he spent some time as both a Christian and a Moslem, concluding that all the religions were really very similar. All the gods were

> The same Rama with a thousand names, just like water has a different name in different languages.

He preached the submissive, compassionate ethic in the best tradition with superb imagery:

> A tree laden with fruit always bends low
> A vulture soars high.

Sikhism also staged a revival in the nineteenth century, particularly with the foundation of the Singh Society at Amritsar in 1873. Meanwhile, on the Islamic side of India, Mirza Ahmad (1839–1908) was the liberaliser of Indian Islam. Buddhism also produced modernising leaders: a peasant woman called Kino (1756–1826) founded the faith-healing sect, Nyomi Kuo, in Japan, and there were monastic revivals in Burma and Thailand.

As ever in Western Europe in the second half of the century, there was the usual reaction against a period of puritanism and prudishness, what Ensor calls 'a reaction from puritanism to raffishness'. Flagellation was known as 'the English vice'. The 1840s had been the era of 'Colonel Spanker' and the flagellant brothels of London. In the 1860s, there were 9,000 prostitutes in Liverpool, one in six of them under the age of sixteen. The moral degradation of the slums (discovered in the course of the great sanitary inquiries of 1840 to 1860) aroused demand for a 'Moral Sewers Commission'. In the epidemic of 'magdalenism' in Edinburgh in 1842 there were reckoned to be some 2,000 prostitutes in 200 brothels, and opinion demanded reform, while Gladstone undertook his mission to rehabilitate the ladies of the night. Pornography was widespread, with *Betsy Thoughtless* for 'the floggers' and three-dimensional photograph shows called 'How Shocking' spreading in the 1880s; there was 'living statuary', which had been pioneered by the racy Emma Lady Hamilton (1765–1815), and by 1900 the craze for dirty mutoscopes, the scandals of Zola's *Nana* and Hardy's *Jude the Obscure*.

Algernon Swinburne (1837–1909), a flagellomaniac, wrote *Lesbia Brandon* for private circulation and 'the roses and raptures of vice!' George Reynolds (1814–79) published sadistic novels and William Stead (1849–1912), the journalist, bought a virgin of thirteen to create a press scoop. Oscar Wilde (1854–1900) was the literary lion of the new modish vice, and the Austrian novelist Sacher Masoch (1835–95), unconscious of his future fame, preached the pleasures of degradation and humiliation in *The Woman in Fur* in 1870. In Paris, Baudelaire's *Les Fleurs du Mal* in 1857 heralded the arrival of the new decadence, and Manet's *Déjeuner sur l'herbe* shocked France's Second Empire in 1863, with the whore *Olympia* following in 1865. Toulouse Lautrec (1864–1901) gave some artistic respectability to the twilight world of absinthe and prostitution; and in 1891, Gaugin escaped from civilisation to Tahiti. Copenhagen became the centre of a daringly liberal ethos by 1900. Stevenson's *Dr Jekyll and Mr Hyde* (1888) typified the 'fin de siecle' obsession with evil, and in the last year of the century Sigmund Freud (1856–1939) was completing *The Interpretation of Dreams*, which was to damn asceticism as a form of suppression and make self-indulgence respectable for the next century.

The years after 1880 also saw what has been called a 'revolutionary fall in human fertility in Europe', following the first mass production of contraceptives. The 'naughty nineties' held sway. In the 1890s, when the newly-invented pyjamas threatened to replace nightshirts, they were described as 'costumes for assignations'. By 1900, French insurance company records showed that between fourteen and seventeen percent of all deaths were due to syphilis. Louis Lépine (1846–1933), the Paris prefect of police, regarded prostitution as a perfectly normal activity, and even amongst Catholics in the 1860s it was estimated that nearly half the males had indulged with a prostitute—it was regarded as medically preferable to masturbation in the bourgeois ethos of the time. In the same period, male prostitution and resultant blackmail had expanded rapidly (according to Zeldin), and the Second Empire, as befitted its image, made strenuous efforts to suppress homosexuality.

In the United States, from the Gold Rush onwards, there was a particular drift towards lawlessness and permissiveness in the West. The jaded 'forty-niners' sought ever more exotic entertainment in expanding San Francisco, with its gawdy 'hook shops' and a thousand gambling joints, Mormon gunmen and deviant Turkish baths. According to Lonestreet, the Barbary Coast was 'Hell Yawning'. New Orleans had for some years been known as the United States centre for vice, but from the 1850s New York had a very substantial prostitute population. The 1860s to 1890s saw the subsequently much-romanticised amorality of the plain states—the wiping-out of the buffalo, the breaking of the Indians and an ethos that frowned only on shooting in the back. Similarly, in the eastern states rapid industrial expansion led to the idealisation of 'the robber barons', unscrupulous entrepreneurs, America's extension of the Samuel Smiles ethic of self-help.

The Ottoman Empire too was affected by the permissive fashion. Prostitution was almost unknown in Turkey as the allowance of concubines provided a useful substitute, but the 'ginks', or transvestite male dancers, were notorious, as was the open homosexuality noted by the traveller, Richard Burton (1829–90), and others near the holy places of Mecca. The trade in Abyssinian and Georgian slave girls was substantial. Kuwait had a particular reputation for both male homosexuality and lesbianism, while Egypt had its tribes of Ghawazee dancers, whose range of exotic performances was all-embracing.

In China, the nineteenth century saw one of its largest and most imaginative movements for political and moral reform. A village schoolteacher from the Canton area, called Hung Hsiu Chuan (fl.1840), became a Christian convert and was inspired to found a new ideal state called the 'Taiping Tien Kuo' or 'Heavenly Kingdom of the Great Peace'. His society was set up near Canton in 1843, promising freedom and equality in opposition to the unpopular Ching dynasty. It was based on the ten commandments and tolerant of both Buddhism and Taoism. The message to the peasantry was

> Where there is land we will till it together; where there is rice we will eat it together; where there is money we will spend it together. No place without equality, no one cold or hungry.

In addition to its political and economic aims, similar to all the great revolutions, the Taiping undertook a number of ethical reforms: the end of slavery, concubinage, infanticide, the opium trade, group punishment, torture, foot-binding, prostitution, adultery, bribery of officials, the inequality of the sexes. The pigtail, so long the symbol of inferiority, was no longer obligatory.

The result was a successful, revolutionary government which ruled about half of China for more than a decade. It might well have spread and continued but for the intervention of Anglo-French interests, offended by the Taiping clamp-down on the opium trade. There were also substantial vested interests from Europe and America in the tea and silk trades, plus the export of very cheap 'coolie' labour to plantations and mines all around the Pacific, a replacement for the Atlantic slave trade which created new racial pockets in places like Malaya and California. Despite the horror of some British radicals like Cobden and Bright, it was British military skill in the shape of General Charles George Gordon (1833–85) which helped the corrupt Ching dynasty to reassert itself. In the capture of Nanking, which finally broke the Taiping, 100,000 people were massacred in the streets, many virtually committing suicide rather than surrender. Pirates and mercenaries were given six dollars for every Taiping head they collected. China then reverted to the corruption of the Manchu court, dominated by the sadistic, opium-smoking dowager Empress Tzu Hsi until 1908. She prevented her son from instituting reform in 1898 by incarcerating him and cutting off all his followers at the waist. The same year saw the rebellion instigated by the anti-Manchu secret society, Yi Ho Tuan, known because of their physical training as 'the Boxers', but the old Empress used this as an excuse for yet another sadistic purge of her eunuch-ridden court and, with foreign help, kept her regime intact.

One other jarring note added to the dark clouds shrouding the end of the century. In 1895, the Spanish general Valeriano Weyler, attempting to restrain the forces of local nationalism in Cuba, introduced for the first time the idea of the concentration camp as a means of political control.

If there was one single dominating factor influencing the ethics of the nineteenth century, it was the massive technological and educational gap between the colonising nations and the colonies, the fact that it was so easy for the nations of the Old World to build their empires, for their dominant classes to make their imperialist values the norm. Even the substantial missionary expansion of Christianity at this time was no more than a facet of this imperialist ethos. The induction of many Third World countries into the mysteries of railway construction and Old World medicine was a questionable benefit compared with the massive worldwide conflict to which the whole process of such ethical posturing was bound to lead. The great tragedy was that such large numbers of the middle class, internationally, had swallowed whole the ethos and motivations of latter-day feudalism, thus creating a scale of conflict greater than any previously known. The middle-class conscience was sadly becoming infected with the aristocracy's paranoia.

1900 — 1992

*Love your country, tell the truth
and don't dawdle.*

Joseph Chamberlain

A S THE TWENTIETH CENTURY OPENED, the two main incompatible thrusts of the old century—the cult of the imperial superman and the relatively new concern for human suffering—were both still strongly in evidence. So was the regular ebb and flow of permissiveness and puritanism. At the same time, while the rise of science created ever larger numbers of people with a more confident disbelief in all things supernatural, there was no sign of any lessening of the extent to which human beings could be carried away by obsessions.

Socialist idealism was at its height, as yet untarnished by any of
the practical failures which philosophies suffer once they become
establishment creeds. This was the era of Socialist Sunday Schools
and new Labour hymns to justice and love. In 1902, there appeared
in Britain the ten commandments of Labour, quoted in Ensor:

> We desire to be just and loving to all our fellow men and women, to work
> together as brothers and sisters, to be kind to every living creature and
> so help to form a new society with justice as its foundation and love as
> its law . . .

But at the same time, darker clouds were looming. In 1902, 200,000
Boers were in Herbert Kitchener's (1850–1910) concentration camps in
South Africa. In 1903, the Russian minister Pobedonotsev (1827–1907)
organised a further pogrom of Jews in Kishinev, and other pogroms
were organised by a reactionary group known as 'the Black Hundred',
whose slogan was: 'The enemies of Christ are the only enemies of
the Tsar.'

In 1909, the platform of the National Democratic Party of Romania
was anti-Semitic. In Britain, in places like Stepney, Jews were pelted
with tomatoes because 'they always seemed to get on better than
anyone else'. Across the Channel in France, the affair of the maligned
Jewish officer, Captain Alfred Dreyfus, had stirred up a most unpleasant
hornet's nest of anti-Semitism and encouraged the paranoid militarism
of an army which had lost its last three wars in Europe. *The Protocols of
the Elders of Zion*, a make-believe plot by the Jews to become masters
of the world, engineered by Pobedonotsev on an idea dating back to
Napoleon, had recreated the great plot mythology. This development
was an ill omen of the racial paranoia which was to be one of the
least attractive features of the loss of ethical direction throughout
the whole century. It was to become the century's classic outlet for
pent-up frustrations, to seek revenge from minorities of different races
or religions, and to do so with a neurotic ruthlessness reminiscent of
the thirteenth century.

Meanwhile, Kaiser Wilhelm II, naïve enough to believe his own
propaganda, was posing in ever more exotic uniforms as the Hun
warlord standing up against the yellow peril. The macho posture of
the German hierarchy was perhaps forced to be that little bit more
aggressive by the hints of effeminacy and decadence which surrounded
it. In 1908, the Prince Eulenberg scandal climaxed: from around 1890
the Germans had been deeply worried that homosexuality was on the
increase, and that it was a portent of decay and destabilisation—in
fact, in France it was known as 'le vice allemand'. There is just the
suggestion that overcompensation for this fear, alongside the Kaiser's
overcompensation for his withered arm, contributed significantly to the
excessive admiration of warlike postures in 1914. Homosexuality had

been part of the tradition of the Prussian officer class, of their school, Gross Lichterfelder, going as far back (it is suggested) as Frederick the Great's ode in praise of homosexuality composed after his victory at Rossbach.

In Italy, the poet apostle of the new renaissance was Gabriele d'Annunzio (1864–1938), who preached the romantic beauties of war. His opposite number in Britain, much more jingoistic than Kipling, was Sir Henry Newbolt (1862–1938), who in 1914 published his *Drake's Drum* collection and *The Book of the Happy Warrior* (1917). J.A. Hobson (1858–1940), whose *Imperialism* came out in 1902, was a somewhat lone voice with his attack on the very roots of jingoism as no better than crude exploitation. There was a racist tone about the posturing of the Europeans. If Kaiser Wilhelm worried about the yellow peril, the Jews were universally disliked and the aspirations of the blacks increasingly resented. The year 1901 saw Act 1 in Australia—the 'White Australia' policy, excluding coloured immigrants. G.A. Henty (1832–1902) wrote of negroes having the mental ability of ten-year-old Europeans, and John Buchan (1875–1940) wrote of 'blue, black dagos' and 'fat Jews'.

The imperial war image was thrust on the young through cigarette cards, jigsaws, music-hall songs, board games, biscuit tins, lantern slides and picture postcards: 'Women Of Britain Say Go.' Throughout Europe the image of war stood high, and when Kitchener pointed his finger from the recruiting posters, the response of young British men— inured for some years to the idea of imperial patriotic war—was excellent. The Peacettes made little impact; few listened to the message in their tracts, 'the good soldier is a heartless soul-less, murderous machine'. Though in 1907 there had been an international convention signed against the military use of gas and aerial bombing, there was a strange naïvety about the capabilities of the new weaponry and an absurd confidence in their own invincibility amongst the professional soldiery. 'Audacity, audacity, always audacity' was the motto of 1914. Brought up on Lady Butler's *Roll Call*, Robert Gibbs' *Thin Red Line* and Mrs Heman's 'The boy stood on the burning deck', the new British heroes were Midshipman Easy, Lieutenant Daring, Richard Hannay and Biggles; the Prussian war cult lived on with Hindenberg and the legend of von Richthofen. The Americans took an idealistic stance against war, with the World Peace Foundation in 1910 and Andrew Carnegie's Peace Palace at The Hague. They were also influenced by Norman Angell's *The Grand Illusion* (1910), but German submarine attacks were to change their minds in the end.

The First World War was to cost approximately 12,000,000 military lives and some 20,000,000 civilian casualties. There were significant acts of mass sadism and breaches of the Geneva Convention, but this was modest compared with the way in which both sides condoned and accepted the extravagant and ineffective sacrifice of vast numbers of lives by their generals. The first aerial bombing of civilian targets began in 1915; indiscriminate sinking of merchant vessels occurred in the same year, with the 'sea atrocity' of the submarine attack on *The Lusitania*. With the introduction of mustard gas by the Germans in 1917, a particularly unpleasant new weapon was released. The Germans initiated the deliberate intimidation of the Belgian populace in 1914, with savage reprisals on disobedient villagers, such as the burning of Louvain and the shooting of 200 of its menfolk.

There was, naturally, a reaction to the huge slaughter, expressed most lyrically by the British frontline poets like Wilfred Owen (1893-1918) and Siegfried Sassoon (1886–1967). Owen was sorry for those who (like himself) were to 'die as cattle', trying to discredit 'the old lie: dulce et decorum est pro patria mori', and making the point in the preface to his poems:

> All a poet can do today is to warn. That is why the true poets must be truthful.

Apart from the massive slaughter which took place within the rules of warfare, there was also one major act of genocide—the ruthless extermination of a further vast number of Armenians by the racist regime of Young Turks in 1915. Probably about 700,000 were killed and about the same number forcibly deported. To this can be added the Turkish massacres of Nestorians and the Christians of Syria, as well as the expulsion from Turkey of the Kurds by Kemal Ataturk. On a considerably smaller scale, but illustrative the same mentality, was the massacre by the British General Dyer of more than 200 Indians at Amritsar in 1919, of whom Draper says:

> He had been brought up in a world where empires were expected to sustain themselves by occasional massacres.

Though condemned by his own government, he received wide support from the British public and believed till his death that he had been right in his actions.

The pre-war years of the twentieth century had also seen the usual tussle between the permissive and the puritan, but as expected in a period of militaristic confidence, the accent was not on the submissive virtues. In Britain, this was the era of the risqué music-hall, with Marie Lloyd as its elegant figurehead setting the hedonistic ethic to music: 'A little of what you fancy does you good.' Graves and Hodge's *The Long Weekend* (1940) speculated that

> Beneath a veneer of formality and beautiful manners the country house weekend must have throbbed with illicit sexuality.

Servants worked like slaves from 6 a.m. to 11 p.m. It was the period of saucy seaside postcards, of which 8,000,000 were sold in Britain in

1908, and twice that in Germany. There were the 'What the Butler Saw' Mutoscopes, night-club tableaux, cheap and salacious papers. Boyer describes how, in the United States, a succession of city vice commissions starting in New York in 1902 was shocked at

> ... the immoral movies, high divorce rate, dance halls where short-skirted girls competed in being tough as they whirled through the Turkey Trot and the Grizzly Bear, coarse and vulgar vaudeville shows, suggestive songs, scantily clad actresses, a repulsive homosexual sub-culture.

Round about 1908 came the swing away from permissiveness in Britain, a slight revulsion against the Edwardian hedonism of the naughty nineties. Lloyd George's Pensions Act was followed by his 1909 budget, which pointed to a new ethic for the fairer distribution of wealth and the protection of the old and the poor. It was also the year in which Baden Powell (1857–1941) founded the Boy Scout movement, which became one of the most important multinational movements for ethical training this century. The specific messages of 'a good deed every day' and 'paddle your own canoe' became an important part of the new, middle-class ideas of service and idealism. In addition, 1908 saw the revival of censorship in British theatre and its application to the new medium of film.

The result of the new climate was that by the time war was declared the illegitimacy rate in Britain was down to four percent, and average age of marriage was up to twenty-six, the highest it had ever been. The adulation of that new concept—the full-time mother—reached its peak, and in 1913 Mothering Sunday was revived as Mother's Day, borrowed from the United States. A kindly figure in a white apron was the dominant image, alongside the romantic idealisation of love and marriage, which was the universal propaganda for the nuclear family. Britain and the other countries were becoming more puritan, and chaperons were in. Kitchener instructed his recruits to 'avoid intimacy with women', but in due course the grim uncertainty of the war years led to a condoning of permissiveness for those about to die, and chaperons were out. In class terms, Marwick commented that the First World War 'spread promiscuity upwards and birth control downwards'; shorter skirts arrived in 1916 along with that new garment, the brassiere.

The war did, however, encourage the attack on Edwardian over-indulgence in alcohol. Taylor records that Lloyd George declared it to be 'a worse enemy than submarines', and the king himself took the pledge to set an example. The Prime Minister also commented that 'the great flood of luxury and sloth which had submerged the land is at last receeding'.

There was revulsion against war in 1918. The unfortunate thing was that this revulsion was exorcised by piling all the blame onto the old imperial regimes. The ethical content in Versailles, as embodied, for instance, in President Wilson's 'Fourteen Points', focused on national freedom with a bias in favour of ethnic, republican regimes, an ideal which had just as much (if not more) potential for conflict as the old empires. The other ethical ambivalence of the 1918 victors was their attitude to reparations, which punished entire nations for the belligerence of their governments.

The end of the war in Europe in 1918 inevitably led to a substantial anti-geriatric mood, a rejection not just of traditional military values but of general puritanism and discipline. The year saw the birth of a new craze in dancing, brighter music, brighter colours, women with more make-up and less apparent modesty. In Britain, necklines dropped and bare backs were in, referred to by the *Sunday Express* of that time as 'the climax of effrontery'. The Tango was 'a license to touch', and MacMillan tells us illegitimacy leapt by thirty percent.

In the United States, where the end of the war saw 300,000 divorces, there was a panic about the moral anarchy of the new generation, 'the lost generation', the flappers, the debilitating and decadent popularity of jazz, the world of F. Scott Fitzgerald's Jay Gatsby, the promiscuity of new, coeducational college life.

In Germany, a similar moral revolution characterised the Weimar Republic, with huge disillusionment in Prussian values, in parents, teachers, tradition and the Church, which had shown itself too slavishly patriotic during the war years. German women now abandoned the corset, smoked in public and cut their hair short. Berlin of *The Blue Angel*, Alfred Doblin's *Berlin, Alexander Platz*, Vicki Baum and Bertholt Brecht was 'Sodom on the eve of destruction'. The 'Nackttanz' (striptease) swept Berlin and homosexuality was more blatant than at almost any other time, as if in deliberate defiance of current mores, though surprisingly not all that far removed from the tradition of the Prussian army.

The reaction against the war ethic was rapidly overshadowed by new justifications for the use of force. In America, the war had hinted at a rise in the status of the black minority and the white backlash was immediate. In 1918, Colonel Simmons revived the Ku-Klux Klan, attacking blacks, Jews and Catholics so that by 1924 there were 4,000,000 members of the Klan in the southern states, Henry Ford's *Dearborn* newspaper contributing to the anti-Semitic strain.

In Russia, the violence took the form that might be expected after a revolution, particularly one following after so many years of severe repression, but there was also a particularly ruthless quality about the new Russian regime. Lenin (1870–1924) had not only suffered a long exile and substantial personal hardship, he had also demonstrated his antipathy to all forms of compromise and was totally dedicated to his own brand of Marxism. He announced his intention 'to purge the

Russian land of all kinds of harmful insects' and endorsed the theme of the new secret police, the Cheka, that

> We are going to bang our fist so hard on the table that the world will shake with terror.

The Russian people *en masse* were imbued with a quite remarkable sense of loyalty to the centre which, in some respects, was to be inherited by the new regime. The tsars had had an immense and apparently very naïve estimation of the obligations their people had towards them— 'No one is doing their duty in Russia these days', the Tsarina Alexandra had complained, somewhat unfairly. But the new Soviet sense of duty was to be remarkably similar, dedicated to success at national level rather than domestic or individual.

Apart from the obvious culling of the royals, there was the less predictable slaughter of the revolutionary Kronstadt sailors by Leon Trotsky (1879–1940). The civil war claimed 8,000,000 lives, most of them from starvation. By 1923 the first forced labour camp was set up on Solovetsk Island.

> Very, very great bravery was required to say no in the midst of that roaring chorus of approval

wrote Alexander Solzhenitsyn (b.1918), and the poet Vladimir Maya-kovsky (1894–1930) announced: 'He who swings not with us today is against us.' And again Solzhenitsyn warned:

> Don't ever be the first to stop applauding during a standing ovation.

Of the secret police, he observed that

> The Cheka was the only prosecuting organisation in history that combined investigation, arrest, interrogation, prosecution, trial and execution.

The Soviet regime had horrendous economic and social problems to solve in a very short time, and was committed to a specific ideology, but it was imbued from the start with the millennial ruthlessness of Marx. To this was added Lenin's carefully nurtured intolerance of deviation, so that for a period Soviet communism demonstrated a will to use force to convert all non-believers that was reminiscent of the first thousand years of organised Christianity. On the other hand, their beliefs often reacted against Christianity, as for example with their legalisation of abortion in 1920, long before this was considered in other countries.

Friedrich Engels (1820–95) had condemned marriage as a form of permanent prostitution, and after 1917 the reaction against bourgeois marriage led, particularly in the towns, to a breakdown of family moral-ity. The idea was mooted of 'free love', 'the nationalisation of women', but by 1935 Joseph Stalin had had enough of the permissive society.

By the time the torch was passed on to Stalin (1879–1953) in 1924, persecution was becoming part of the ethos of the state and its original purpose almost forgotten. In 1932, Stalin orchestrated the artificial famine in the Ukraine which eliminated (by his own admission) at least 10,000,000 kulaks as a class. About 3,500,000 went into labour camps and vast numbers died of starvation, as the collectivisation of agriculture was pushed through at all costs. The state ethic was given priority before the family: Pavlic Morozov, the teenage son of a peasant, was made a public hero for suffering martyrdom after betraying his own father to the government. Statues were erected to the boy, who was soon after murdered by other peasants, and for forty years he was put forward as a model of the collective ethos.

The ideological objective was the collectivisation of agriculture—but the kulaks saw this as a reversal of the emancipation of the serfs by the tsar in 1861. Differential wage motivation came to be needed to make the collective farms work. Huge administrative pressures on Stalin, combined with the geographical remoteness between the Kremlin and the steppes, might have excused him as a man trying to do his best within a newly established ethos. But by this time there was reasonable evidence of sadistic paranoia in the Stalin entourage. From 1929 onwards, the Trotskyists were mercilessly purged. In 1937 came the famous purge of 20,000 Red Army officers, including Marshall Tukhachevsky, and the grossly inhuman treatment of the vast numbers sent to the internment camps has been grimly described by Solzhenitsyn in *The Gulag Archipelago* (1973–75) and *One Day in the Life of Ivan Denisovich* (1962). There was a particularly high death-rate on the Volga-White Sea Canal.

Stalin did, of course, succeed in winning a war, in winning a new Russian empire of some eight satellite nations and in revolutionising Russian industry, but as yet there is no reliable statistic on the total human cost. One million Poles were forcibly deported before 1941, and there was the Russian massacre of Poles at Katyn Forest. In 1941, 132,000 leading citizens of the three Baltic states—Latvia, Estonia and Lithuania—were deported in a single night. Isaac Deutscher's biography shows Stalin's single-minded dedication to national ends, neatly illustrated by the Soviet leader's justification of the attack on Finland:

> Since we cannot move Leningrad, we must move the frontier.

He also reputedly remarked to Kamenev:

> To choose one's victims, to prepare one's plans minutely, to strike an implacable vengeance and then go to bed, there is nothing sweeter in the world.

Nikolai Yezhov, the Chief of Police until he was himself purged in 1939, wrote the NKVD manual on torture techniques approved by Lavrenti

Beria (1899–1953), including a wide range of different types of beatings which remained unofficial up to 1937 but were legalised thereafter, with such Russian specialities as 'stoika'—victims made to stand on tiptoe for hours until they confessed. The manual suggested that 'failure to confirm the evidence already obtained is indicative of poor work by the interrogator'.

The late 1930s and 40s saw the end of communism's permissive era. In 1936, abortion once more became a crime; the 1944 figure of 4,000,000 illegitimate children in Russia inspired Stalin to make divorce more difficult and thus discourage bastardy.

If idealism pressurised to the point of paranoia was the source of a mass sadistic ethos in Russia, then this was probably also true of Nazi Germany. The problems of controlling larger populations and the power of new media, new weapons and new wealth were immense; under these and other pressures regimes were brittle, conventional moralities easily swept aside. Adolf Hitler (1889–1945) was a product of the most corrosive of all pressures, reaction against defeat and humiliation. The obstacles in the way of his initial success were so enormous that it is hardly surprising that the new ethos he created was paranoid, vindictive and uninterested in human suffering.

> All the rubbish of the small states of Europe must be liquidated as fast as possible.

In 1939, the Germans shot 20,000 Poles at Bydgoszcz, later 9,000 Serbian Yugoslavs at Ravna Cora, just two examples of acts of mini-genocide against non-Jews.

The institution of compulsory sterilisation in 1934, to prevent the birth of abnormal children, had been followed by a euthanasia policy for the elimination of the congenitally insane, which led to some 70,000 deaths in 1939. This in turn was a step towards the elimination of Jews, homosexuals and gypsies. In 1940, as the Jews were rounded up in the first preliminaries of the holocaust, the Nazi cinema showed the propaganda film *Jud Suss* to create the right atmosphere. Physical violence and the threat of the concentration camp were, of course, also used to cow the Germans themselves; as Bullock put it:

> ... the contempt for justice and order shown by the state encouraged those impulses of cruelty, envy and revenge which are normally suppressed or driven underground in society.

Hermann Goering (1893–1946), product of the older, Prussian officer-ethic as transmuted into that of the biplane air ace of the First World War, obsessed with Blue Maxes and the Fatherland, was the main founder of the Gestapo and developer of concentration camps. Heinrich Himmler (1900–45), an obsessive racist who referred to Jews as *Untermennschentum*, took the most direct responsibility for at least

5,000,000 Jewish deaths and for medical experiments without the use of anaesthetics. Reinhard Heydrich (1902–42), who had a charismatic personality and a meteoric career, became known as 'the Hangman'. His version of 'the Final Solution' envisaged a plan for the removal of 11,000,000 Jews from the whole of Europe, and paralleled Hitler's 1941 project to reduce the population of Soviet Russia to 30,000,000 so that it could be recolonised by Germans. Joseph Goebbels (1897–1945) was the intellectual developer of the master-race ethos, and its greatest propagandist after Hitler himself.

This group of men and their followers were responsible for the establishment of a new ethos which admired courage, efficiency, national pride and the Nordic family unit, in fact many of the conventional virtues of contemporary Europe—but they also encouraged the most savage cruelty to those who stood in the way of their ideals. The rest of the German professional officer class had its own technical code of honour which shuddered at some of the Nazi techniques, but because its main objective was the same as the Nazis'—the military revival of Germany—it initially let the end justify the means. The traditional Prussian cult of sacrifice and duty in the military linked not too badly with the ideological fanaticism of the genuine Nazi. It was not until Hitler's methods began to show signs of failure on the Russian front, and the officer class was itself asked to join in the atrocities previously mainly left to the SS Einsatzgruppen, that they began to find fault with the Nazi ethos. With the attack in 1941 on the Russians, who were themselves regarded as sub-human, the holocaust moved up a gear; in two days in Kiev 33,000 Jews were killed, 16,000 in Pinsh, the real beginning of 'the Final Solution', which moved on to Auschwitz where 12,000 were gassed daily for the remaining years of the war. At the same time, the German army was increasingly brutalised by the hardships of the Russian front, by fear of its own officers and, ultimately, by fear of the Russians, as increasingly neither side gave quarter.

The Nazi period provides yet another example of a group of people in the grip of an ideological obsession doing what they believed was right, creating a new morality which for some time seemed both credible and admirable to large numbers of people, yet which viewed against any kind of objective standards seems to be in many ways diametrically opposed to normal standards of morality. The paranoid cruelty of the Nazis in pursuit of their master-race obsession can be compared with the religion of the Aztecs, the papal extermination of the Albigensians or the conquests of Tamerlane. Technology simply made the scale more devastating. Caused entirely by Nazi policy, the Second World War (together with its Japanese extension) was to cost at least 40,000,000 lives. Amongst other nations involved were the Croats, whose terrorist regime under the Ustasi leader Ante Pavelic (d.1945) massacred large numbers of both Jews and Serbs.

Japanese militarism was, like Germany's, the victim of its own success. It is one of the least arguable laws of history that countries which win wars tend to fight more wars. The militaristic ethic becomes more and more popular with success. Heideki Tojo (1885–1948) was a product of the Meiji revival of bushido, a teenager at the time of the elation surrounding the victory over the Russians at Tsushima, and a believer (like others of his generation) in Japan's role as the master race of the East. Prime Minister of Japan from 1941 to 1944, he authorised the destruction of Pearl Harbor, which, because it was done without formal warning, was a breach even of the conventional ethics of national warfare: it appeared as a very inexpensive victory and therefore morally very acceptable, at least to the Japanese. In 1937, according to the Chinese, 340,000 of their people were slaughtered by the Japanese in Nanking. The evidence of Tokyo military tribunals revealed a number of specific examples, including the mass rape and murder of 20,000 women in Nanking. Brackman's account shows that all ranks of the Japanese army were governed by an unusually sadistic ethos driven by militaristic hysteria. This had been well projected by the propagandists, such as the neurotic Shumei Okawa (1886–1957), Yosuke Matsuoka (1880–1946) and the racist Colonel Hashimoto (1890–1957). Not only did the ethic they advocated condone the vast number of atrocities ordered against the Chinese, but they deliberately encouraged growth of the opium and heroin trades to help raise funds. Labourers were paid with heroin cigarettes so that they would become addicts, and it is estimated that about 50,000 were addicted in the Nanking area. Similarly, the Japanese conquest of the Philippines was followed by an estimated 131,000 murders, many of them deliberately sadistic, such as the cruficixion of Luchas Doctolero in 1943. Brackman quotes the local Japanese military directive:

> When killing Filipinos assemble them together in one place . . . thereby saving ammunition and labour.

General Yamashita (1885–1946), the Japanese conqueror of Singapore, was not untypical of the many very able Japanese commanders whose ethos included a fairly low estimate of human life, and certainly did not include the expected Western ethos of fair play towards prisoners of war. He was hanged as a war criminal for his atrocities, but his reputation as a revered Japanese hero was to live on even in a country which underwent a major revulsion against the military ethic when it suffered severe defeat. General Tokutaro Sakurai was an effective commander, yet he always wore a string of valuable pearls and would entertain his troops by dancing naked with two lighted cigarettes in his nostrils. In 1945 he stuck to his principles and disembowelled himself in the traditional manner. This went along with the torture of prisoners of war, the brutal treatment of Japanese soldiers by their own officers and medical experimentation without anaesthetics. Most spectacular of all in Japanese ethical history were the kamikaze, practitioners of a concept conceived by Vice Admiral Onishi (1891–1945), which turned suicide on behalf of the fatherland into the highest military virtue.

The same ethic which inspired Hitler and Tojo also produced a number of other marginally less demonic leaders during approximately the same period. Gabriele d'Annunzio, pioneer of Italian fascism, postured in Fiume and boasted that he always went to war with a pro-phylactic in his pocket and was hated by a thousand husbands. Benito Mussolini (1883–1945) preached a more austere nationalist ethic:

> We are against the easy life . . . imperial ambition demands a sense of duty, discipline, self-sacrifice and the will to power.

His efforts as a warlord were relatively minor, his most famous conquest being over the backward Ethiopian Empire, where the Emperor Haile Selassie (1891–1975), popularly known as Ras Tafari, conducted a heroic resistance which made him a future focus for the new African Christianity. The Rastafarians believed that they were the true Jews, black because of their past sins, with Ethiopia as their promised land. They were particularly anti-permissive, anti-white and militant, although they regarded soft drugs like cannabis as quite accceptable. Their creed became one of the most generally appealing of the ethnic black sects of Christianity.

The other would-be fascist superhero was General Franco of Spain (1892–1975), victor in the Spanish Civil War, famous for the bombing of Guernica immortalised by Picasso as the symbolic use of modern air bombing against a defenceless civilian population. The Spanish Civil War was generally noted for the extreme brutality on both sides—over 100,000 troops were massacred after surrendering and 200,000 executed, this apart from massacres like Cuidad Real. MacMartin relates the words of Juan Garcia Olivar: 'Everbody created his own justice.' While Franco's Falangist terror squads conducted huge purges in Castille and Galicia, their comrades in the Catholic Carlist Requetés killed 200,000 leftists and liberals; but the republicans responded with a spate of convent-burnings and multiple murders of priests and right-wing sympathisers.

And just as the Spanish Civil War echoed the ruthlessness of Spain in the nineteenth century, so in the Spanish ex-colonies of South America the twentieth century saw a continuing of the quick-flaring violence evident since the Wars of Independence. The conflict of races, classes, economic interests, religious and political fanaticism formed the foundation: the weakness of central authority and a growing habit of violence kept the trend well fuelled. In 'La Violencia' of Columbia between 1946 and 1966, at least 200,000 people were murdered in electoral violence, guerilla activity, military coups or terror campaigns.

The Trelew Massacres of Argentina in 1972, the 'Dirty War', Trujillo, the Tonton Macoutes of Duvalier, Pinochet's tortures in Chile, the 10th May in Buenos Aires—all were features of the same disease, that is, chronic loss of compassion. The 1950s produced the idea of 'los desaparecidos' (the disappeared people), and the 1960s the 'esquadrao de morte' (the death squad). The survival of the various dictators and juntas took precedence over all normal standards of behaviour. Aboriginal peoples were still suffering economic genocide: the Ache of Paraguay were exterminated in the 1960s, as were the Amazon Peruvians and the few surviving native Brazilians.

Finally, in this review of the main proponents of the fascist ethic in the first half of the twentieth century, it was in 1942 that J.B. Vorster (1915–68), later Prime Minister of South Africa, became a member of the group known as the Ossevrabrandwag, a pro-Nazi, anti-Semitic organisation which became the focus for the idea of permanent white supremacy in South Africa.

The cumulative lessons of the two world wars were at least theoretically enshrined in the *United Nations Declaration on Human Rights* in 1948. While not exactly a new moral code, this was an agreed description of the basic conditions for human happiness and therefore, by the utilitarian concept of morality, a definition of the overall objectives for human behaviour. These basic rights of political, racial and sexual equality, of physical and spiritual freedom, of legal protection, the right of ownership of property, economic security, leisure, education and culture, attempted to create the world's first universal standard of treatment without any objective sanction other than the utilitarian concept of the avoidance of misery and pain for as many people as possible. One particularly significant addition which appears in the parallel document, the *International Convention on Civil and Political Rights*, is the statement that

> The family is the natural and fundamental group unit of society and is entitled to protection by society and the state.

Whatever the political criticism of the Chinese revolution of 1948, it without question aimed at and largely achieved one of the most significant acts of mass emancipation since the end of Russian serfdom. The level of improvement in the rights of the majority of males was perhaps arguable, although the first mass literacy campaign alone must be seen at least as the basis for improvement, but the reduction in the exploitation of females is incontestable. Up till that point they had still been liable to be sold as slaves or to brothels, were morally obliged to bind their feet to keep them small and had virtually no right to own property. All this was ended, and the new regime commenced the horrendous task of reorganising the food supply and economy of its massive population. The Maoist regime was at times ruthlessly cruel in purging its own middle class, the commercial and intellectual minority, which, however often stamped out, had a knack of reviving, particularly as it was almost impossible to run the country without it.

The Chinese also persisted with the communist, militarist ethic, the inevitability of war to spread the faith, long after that idea had been abandoned by the Russians in the famous speech by Nikita Khrushchev in 1953 at the 20th Congress of the Communist Party. The basic motivation of the Chinese people in the post-revolutionary period, as with the Russians, had been to put the state first and the individual second. To some extent, therefore, both these cultures had a higher appreciation of self-sacrifice inculcated into them than was the case in the Western bloc and, perforce, despite the official denigration of spiritual values, they were perhaps substantially less materialistic, less disillusioned and less subjective. Mao Tse Tung (1893–1976), mocking the old Chinese legend of the general who refused to take advantage of the enemy by attacking them crossing a river, referred to this as 'asinine ethics' in 1938. This persecution did result in massive casualties. The Great Leap Forward and the Cultural Revolution have each been calculated to have caused around 1,500,000 deaths by a combination of economic persecution and forced labour camps.

The Cultural Revolution of 1967 was associated with a temporary complete abandonment of conventional morality, with widespread rape, brutality and vandalism which proved quite hard to reverse. The last decade of Mao saw a reversion to more puritan ideals than the first permissive fling of the communist regime. China had preserved its above-average concern with moral training, except for that one respite; a major example was the group hero-worship of the young soldier Lei Feng (1940–1962), who devoted his short life to serving the elderly. When the myth of Lei Feng lost its credibility, a new Chinese saint was created in the guise of a young lady propagandist, Zhang Zhikin (c.1930–1975), whose honesty led to her martyrdom at the hands of the Gang of Four. The agricultural work ethic was also given mythological status with the cult of Dazhai, an obscure mountain region where the peasants had improved the soil with stakhanovite zeal. In Chinese primary schools moral training was strong, discouraging aggression, individualism and competition. Perhaps the one anomaly to Western eyes was the apparent tolerance of some mild homosexuality in the vast Chinese army, where it was allowed to help cement military morale in a not-unfamiliar pattern.

Intellectual minorities suffered acutely under communist regimes. In the Soviet Union, political dissidence was regarded as an abnormality, a disease. The Russian human rights activist, Vladimir Bukovsky (b.1942), in the labour camp at Pern in 1974, helped write *A Manual on Psychiatry for Dissidents* to cope with the problem of 'madness' cured. Solzhenitsyn also wrote at first hand of his persecution by a totalitarian regime, but a number of Western writers were obsessed by the same insecurity. In the United States, Senator Joseph McCarthy (1909–57) became a maniacal hunter of communists in the late 1940s, and was referred to by Harry Truman as 'a pathological character assasin'. Franz Kafka (1883–1924) wrote of overbearing but pointless regimes. Aldous Huxley (1894–1963) produced *Brave New World* (1932) on a theme of moral anarchy in an increasingly scientific world. Bertholt Brecht, the German dramatist, wrote *Mann ist Mann* (1926), a stark picture of inhuman soldiery, and *Dreigroschenoper* (1928), with its condemnation of indolence and greed. Perhaps two of the most popular and vivid attacks on the totalitarian state came from George Orwell (1903–50) in *Animal Farm* (1945) and *Nineteen Eighty-Four* (1949).

Most of these writers were concerned with the removal of oppression as an end in itself, and so long as the oppression existed they had the comfort of an objective target. The problem of emerging from the tunnel with nowhere to go is most evident in the works of Jean Paul Sartre (1905–80), particularly The *Roads to Freedom* (1945) in which, once the French Resistance has achieved its goal, the participants are left with the fresh problem of choosing new objectives. The problem of achieving human freedoms becomes one of what to do next. In *The Outsider* (1942) by Albert Camus (1913–60), the hero is 'an absurd man in an absurd world'. Samuel Beckett (1906–89) became the pioneer of the 'theatre of the absurd', his *Waiting for Godot* (1956) being an essay in 'cosmic meaningless'. Similarly, Eugène Ionesco (b.1912) persisted, in plays like *The Bald Prima Donna* (1950), with the portrayal of the pointless world, while John Osborne's (b.1929) *Look Back in Anger* (1956) caught the mood of the period in its attack on conventions and its portrayal of 'the angry young man', utterly disillusioned in society, heartless and amoral. Parallel to this was the impression made in 1953 by the American film *Rebel Without a Cause*, whose title epitomises mid-century dissatisfaction.

The fashion in philosophy was more and more to reject any objective standards or aims in life. Edvard A. Westermarck (1862–1939), in his *Origin and Development of Moral Ideas* (1906), had projected the idea of moral relativity, that moral codes were no more than the bylaws of particular tribes or peoples at particular times, while the logical positivist, A.J. Ayer (b.1910), in *Language, Truth and Logic* (1933) was saying:

> No morality can be founded on authority, not even if the authority is divine.

While science, reason and literature combined to read the funeral rites over objective moral ideas, the practical need to preserve something remained. Bertrand Russell (1872–1970) raked through the ashes.

> When the concept of honour is freed from aristocratic insolence and from proneness to violence, something remains which helps to preserve personal integrity and to promote mutual trust in social relations. I should not wish this legacy of the Age of Chivalry to be wholly lost on the world.

He added the belief that

> So long as social life survives, self-realisation cannot be the supreme principle of ethics.

J.K. Galbraith (b.1910), the Canadian economist, concerned about the loss of direction of *The Affluent Society*, argued the need for objective standards, even if philosophically they seem false:

> It is a far, far better thing to have a firm anchor in nonsense than to put out on the troubled seas of thought.

The problem remained essentially unsolved, except for those who did still have causes to fight for. One of the most significant causes in the whole of the twentieth century was the drive for sexual equality. Amongst the pioneers of this in Britain were Emilie Pankhurst (1837-1928) and her daughters, paralleled in the United States by women like Lucy Stone (1818–93) and Emma Wilmer. Political equality was achieved in the period between the wars virtually on a worldwide basis, with the first female votes in Britain in 1918, and with the Twentieth Amendment in the United States in 1920. In America, the women's movement was particularly associated with anti-alcohol movements, such as the Women's Christian Temperance Union founded in Ohio in 1873, so it was not surprising that almost at the same time as the advent of female political power came the Nineteenth Amendment, the prohibition of alcohol, not entirely the most successful of experiments in behavioural control.

The other major step forward in female emancipation was the development and eventual encouragement of family planning, pioneered in particular by Marie Stopes (1880–1920), who produced her *Married Love* in 1918, followed by Mrs Bertrand Russell's *Hypatia* in 1925. The ethic approving of large families was swept away in Britain after the Victorian era, as the demand for cheap labour declined. In 1928, the Archbishop of Canterbury referred to sex as 'joyous', a revolutionary change in attitudes.

In terms of numbers and basic human rights, the greatest single step in the liberation of women took place in China, culminating in Mao Tse Tung's reform of the Chinese family system in 1952. So deeply was the multi-generation family unit entrenched, that it was estimated that as many as 70,000 women may have committed suicide in that year due to the tensions of family squabbling when young wives first began, with Mao's blessing, to reject the authority of their husbands and mothers-in-law. From the economic point of view, the reform released some 70,000,000 young female workers from the family to help with industrial development. The Chinese word for 'wife' was abolished from the vocabulary, divorce escalated, and for a while the population grew rapidly until the danger signs showed and the post-Mao Chinese government began to promote the small family, one-child ethic to slow down the increase. Once the Maoist 'Great Leap Forward' had progressed beyond its first huge appetite for cheap labour, the danger of the population explosion was realised.

Female political emancipation has, therefore, been directly and inevitably linked with family planning and soon accepted by virtually all governments—Ireland was one of the few exceptions—and by most institutions, except the Catholic Church. The cause now moved on to the details of female equality in terms of careers, property, right to divorce (still not allowed in certain countries) and to the correction of attitudes. One of the most prominent campaigners in this third stage was Germaine Greer (b.1939), who published *The Female Eunuch* in 1970. Attention also moved to problems only indirectly connected with the cause, such as world peace, where it was believed that the influence of women had in the past been insufficiently felt.

Another great cause which occupied a large number of minds was ethnic emancipation. The massive achievement in this field, which set the pattern for many others, was the decolonisation of India. Mahatma Gandhi (1865–1948) was without question one of the most profound practical moralists of the century. Influenced by Tolstoy and centuries of Hindu mysticism, he began to apply his technique of passive resistance to help protect the Indian minority in South Africa. Ashe's biography tells us that Gandhi's word 'satyagraha', a social force which was a substitute for violence, developed the older concept that

> Ahimsa is not just a negative state of harmlessness, but also a positive state of love or good-will even to evil-doers.

In *The Story of my Experiment with Truth* he wrote:

> Truth is perhaps the most important name of God . . . I shall not bear ill-will towards anyone. I shall not submit to injury from anyone. I shall counter untruth with truth. In resisting untruth I shall put up with all suffering.

He used the threat of fasting to death, and the media blackmail which this provided, against the government to achieve the concessions he was looking for in India. But his philosophical ideals stretched much further than mere racial self-determination. He was a rigid opponent of caste, refusing to allow the Harijans to be treated as inferiors; he did not accept the split between Hindu and Moslem, arguing to the end in favour of an integrated Indian state, and applauded the value of the

Koran, Bible and Hindu scriptures with equal emphasis; he rejected alcohol, was almost Luddite in his obsession with hand-labour and detestation for mechanisation; he was a convinced ascetic, a vegetarian who believed in the protection of all creatures, even insects, and in his later years, like Tolstoy, disapproved of sex as a distraction. Gandhi's total commitment, the breadth of his ideas and his brilliant ability to put them across to a semi-literate population mark him out as one of the great prophets.

Not to be forgotten is his Islamic counterpart, Mohammad Al Jinnah (1876–1948), leader of 90,000,000 Indian Moslems, who up to 1946 conducted his barefoot trek with the same ascetic charisma as Gandhi, suggesting the two gods were one, preaching that greed should be replaced by love: Ispahani quotes him saying, 'change human motives rather than social structure'. The Moslem thinker Mohammed Iqbal (1876–1938) had been the pioneering moderniser of Indian Islam, pushing towards equality for women and rejecting Koranic mythology. In Vahid's biography, Iqbal preaches: 'Heaven and hell are states not localities'.

In practical terms, the movement for the unification of the new India (as opposed to its simple liberation) ended in the martyrdom of Gandhi and substantial bloodshed between the supporters of the two religions before the frontiers were finally fixed of the three states (later four) of the Indian sub-continent. It was estimated that between 250,000 and 1,000,000 people were massacred in what Lapping termed 'the most savage mass killing of all time'. While the Moslems probably began it in Calcutta, the Sikhs, particularly under Tara Singh, carried it to new lengths and the Hindus followed. Racial hostility continued: the break-up of Pakistan was accompanied by widespread massacres by the regime of Yahya Khan (1917–80) in 1971, resulting in the scattering of 10,000,000 refugees. Salmaan Taseer says that:

> Killing defenceless people became a habit like smoking cigarettes or drinking wine.

Bangladesh then witnessed the genocide of many hundreds of thousands in Chittagong in the late 1980s. Savage economic inequality also remained a feature of the Indian sub-continent, with many in a state of virtual slavery, including some 5,000,000 under debt bonds and large numbers of economically enslaved children in industries such as carpet-weaving. Excess children also became a problem in Brazil in the early 1960s, when there was an outbreak of delayed infanticide to reduce the hundreds of thousands of delinquent stray children. To property-owners this infanticide seemed morally justifiable—a form of pest control.

Racial or religious killings have been a feature of many of the other movements for ethnic independence in other parts of the world, local

hatreds rising in the wake of liberation. The reversal of the Jewish
diaspora and the creation of the new Israel has been a focal point
for Arab discontent, although in general terms the regeneration of
both Arab nationalism and Islam (helped by the wealth of oil) has
been a major feature of the twentieth century. Modern Islam has been
remarkable for the puritanical conservatism of a number of its regimes,
partly as a deliberate reaction against Western materialism. Some of
the would-be saviours of the previous century, the Mahdi Ghulam
Ahmad of Punjab (*fl.*1880) and Mohammed Ahmed, the Mahdi of
Sudan (1848–85), victor over Gordon, had had a strong puritanical
strain, as did the Wahhabi sect which dominated Saudi Arabia itself.
The Shiites believed in the twelve imams, the twelfth being Al Mahdi,
and had a strong tradition of spiritual leadership which blossomed after
the overthrow of the Shah of Iran in 1978. The Ayatollah Khomeini
(1900–1988) emerged as one of the most powerful religious leaders of
the century after Gandhi, the creator of a puritan state reminiscent of
Calvin's Geneva, where he fended off the evil influences of Western
youth culture, pop music, jeans and anarchism. Iran has a remarkably
high ratio of priests per head of population (1:150), with a tight grip over
local finance and welfare, a well organised propaganda machine and a
conservative attitude to female emancipation. In these strict Moslem
states the old prohibitions of alcohol, gambling, and so on, still held
strong. Khomeini's regime demanded strict sacrifice, as in Hiro's *Iran
Under the Ayatollahs*:

> The more people who die for our cause the stronger we shall become.

And many did die in the long war with Iraq, during which torture was
allegedly used. His 100,000 mullahs combined political and religious
control while the Supreme Islamic Propaganda Council disseminated
tracts and put on thematic plays supporting their ideology. Saddam
Hussein (b.1937) is believed to have massacred 5,000 of his own
Kurdish population with poison gas bombs in 1988. This was followed
by his invasion of Kuwait in 1990, with further major evidence of mass
brutality.

In contrast, and equally dedicated to Islam, were the new reformist
groups, including the Moslem Brothers of Egypt, founded in the tarika
tradition in 1927 by Hasan al Banna (b.1903), with a violent ethos which
came to the fore in the Arab-Israeli wars and became the model for
hardline nationalists like the Libyan leader, Colonel Gaddafi (b.1942),
and Yassar Arafat (b.1929), the Palestinian folk hero. The crude appeal
of this tradition was shown after the displacement in 1977 of Ali
Bhutto (1928–79), the Western-style democratic leader of Pakistan, by
General Zia al Haq (1924–80), who immediately decreed amputation
and whippings as punishment for relatively minor crimes. The ill-fated
revival of Sikh militarism came to a head in 1984 under Jamail Singh

Bhindranwale at Amritsar. Less violent and less popular has been the Brotherhood of Jamaat, founded in 1941 by Maulana Abul al Maududi (b.1903), an opponent of Pakistani nationalism whom Jansen quotes thus:

What is selfishness in individual life is nationalism in social life. A nationalist is naturally narrow-minded and niggardly.

Regrettably this was not a particularly popular message; a century of worldwide propaganda for the nationalist ideal, had exploited the very real and natural feelings of ethnic solidarity and made nationalism one of the most ineradicable facets of the twentieth-century inheritance. Often, because of the decline in other objective values, nationalism was for many people the only ethos which could be classified as anything but materialist and egocentric. The acute problems which it created (not just in the Arab world) lay in the numerous geographical areas where races had been muddled in the past, and where ethnic independence was not wholly practicable. This was the case with the Germans outside Germany in 1938, the Basques in Spain, the Armenians in Turkey and Russia, the Turks in Cyprus, the Ukrainians in Russia, the Serbs and Croats, the native Vietnamese, East Timor as a province of Indonesia, the Kurds in Iraq and the Biafrans in Nigeria

Africa had also seen vast strides in emancipation, often backed up by a superficial Western-style nationalism which sometimes rode roughshod over tribal minorities, allowing the dominant tribe to become the nation, with lesser tribes becoming dissatisfied minorities. This, together with the sheer administrative problems of rapid modernisation, has meant that the state has taken precedence over human rights in most of the emergent African regimes.

The pressure of heavy odds on small, militant groups has led them to accept very violent codes, condoning or encouraging terrorism, hijacking, kidnapping or other normally criminal practices. EOKA, Mau Mau, the PLO, the IRA, Action Directe, all followed an ethos justifying the murder of men, women and children in the cause of ethnic status. In the classic ethic of terrorism, the perpetrators believed themselves totally in the right, justified in their own eyes by the long-term suppression of their group. The three-sided civil war in Yugoslavia in the 1990s, exacerbated by ethnic hatred and laced with religious paranoia, evinced levels of brutality comparable with the Thirty Years War—mass murder, mass rape, forcible repatriation, and imprisonment with torture reveal the total failure of communism, Christianity, Islam and European educational standards to offset long-term racial paranoia.

The other minority overlap problem has been religious, the problem of two opposed religions in Northern Ireland, in the Lebanon, in India and Pakistan. In each of these areas religious difference has provoked violence, and the violence feeds the religious zeal, Ulster, for instance, having by far the highest church attendances of any part of the United Kingdom.

While Islam was not only militant but generally conservative and puritan, both in the Middle East and to some extent in northern Africa, the same trend was also visible in the Christian sects of Africa. Rastafarianism was inspired by Ethiopian nationalism yet began in Jamaica, with a cannabis farm as part of its infra-structure. The new sect founded in the Congo in 1921, by Simon Kimbangu (1890–1951), was in reaction to Belgian oppression and was puritanical, rejecting alcohol, tobacco, dancing and polygamy. Similarly, the Zulu prophet, Isaiah Shembe (1880–1935), set up his new church of the Nazarites in 1911 with a fundamentalist, puritan ethic. Oddly enough there was also a puritan and very intolerant strain about the Afrikaner dominant class in South Africa, which, like the Spartans, wanted to preserve its purity in every sense. Significantly, the Afrikaners allowed homosexuality between consenting adults (as most other governments do in the twentieth century) but in this case only so long as they were of the same colour. Nelson Mandela (b.1918) remained (until 1990) the dignified figurehead of imprisoned resistance to a regime whose fundamental ethic of apartheid was opposed to that of most other nations in the world. F.W. De Klerk (b.1933) rose above the prevailing ethos of his fellow Boers to release Mandela and begin the dismantling of apartheid.

Turning to the rest of the Christian world, one of the most remark-able achievements of the first half of the century was the revival of Catholicism, and the ability of the papacy yet again to rejuvenate itself after lapsing into a period of uncreative conservatism. The Second Vatican Council called by Pope John XXIII (1881–1963) in 1962 heralded an amazing modernisation without any concessions on basic doctrine; however, the number of adherents of established Christian Churches (including Roman Catholicism) fell drastically after 1950 and, despite the new papal extroverts, there were fundamental ethical divisions even within the Catholic establishment on issues such as birth control, divorce, abortion and homosexuality, where successive popes were reluctant to yield to the new permissive fashions.

One of the features of the scientific age has been that even sophis-ticated groups sometimes find it easier to accept a *highly* irrational faith than a *slightly* irrational one. The expanding sects have tended to be the fundamentalist ones—Jehovah's Witnesses, Seventh Day Adventists and Mormons. The new sects of the century have tended to be eccentric, like the Snake Handling Church of Tennessee founded by George Went Henley in 1909, a very puritan group, with handling of deadly rattlesnakes as a test of purity. The Native American Church of 1918 encouraged the use of the old Aztec drug, peyote, to strengthen its appeal. In 1977, the Reverend Jim Jones (1931–78), obsessed with the impending nuclear holocaust, moved his Peoples' Temples and many of his followers from Los Angeles to his new Utopia in Jonestown, Guyana, where he imposed a religious dictatorship under which slackers could have their heads shaven. When the regime began to crumble, there was an act of mass suicide. It was reported in *The Sunday Times* that Jones declared:

> If you love me as much as I love you we must all die or be destroyed from the outside.

The church founded by Sun Myung Moon (b.1920) has also been criticised for the intense way in which it tends to capture susceptible youths. Moon proved himself an enormously successful businessman who promoted a highly organised sect in which he focused attention on arranged marriages, which he conducted *en masse* for large groups of his followers. The couples surrendered most of their property to the sect, and often worked for it thereafter for minimal wages. Even more extreme was the sect founded by David 'Moses' Berg (b.1919), the Children of God, in which Berg promoted unrestricted sexual license and even used a form of religious prostitution as an aid to recruitment. His circulars to his followers, known as 'Mo's Letters', had titles such as *God's Whore*. More rational, but equally intense and possessive of the property of its adherents, was Moral Rearmament, founded by Frank Buchman (1898–1966) to promote four absolute virtues: truth, purity, love and honesty, which it did with dedicated evangelism. Scientology, which was originally founded as 'dianetics' by Lafayette Hubbard (b.1911) in 1948, was a pseudo-scientific religion in which the soul, called the Thetan, might be condemned to a kind of permanent hell unless psychiatrically purified. It was Scientology which mounted a pressure group in 1967 in San Francisco calling for sexual freedom.

Amongst the conventional Christians who maintained the humanitarian ethos were Martin Luther King (1929–68), the outstanding promoter of non-violence and racial equality in the United States; Albert Schweitzer (1875–1965), the paternalistic doctor of Lambarene; Mother Theresa (b.1910), the carer for the poor of Calcutta; and Abbe Pierre (*fl.*1950), the French homebuilder. Also of great significance was the work of the pacifist, Nathan Soderstrom (1886–1931), who developed the ecumenical movement which led to the first World Council of Churches in 1928.

Of the new Buddhist sects of the century, the most powerful was probably Soka Gakkai, the 'value creation' society founded by Makiguchi Tsunesaburo (1871–1944) in 1937, with a promise of peace and happiness for all mankind based on the Mandala scroll of a thirteenth-century Buddhist monk called Nichiren. After a period of suppression in Japan during the war, it sprang to life in the pacifist, post-war atmosphere of Japan alongside one or two other modern versions of Zen. In general, the Japanese, having shed the warlike aspects of bushido, transmuted their competitive zeal into a ferocious work ethic which helped them become the economic leaders of the world. Reminders of their darker side were typified by the hari kiri role model and novelist, Yukio Mishima (1925–70), whose work was redolent with repressed homosexuality and frustrated medievalism.

For the first time in its history, Hinduism managed to export itself outside the Indian race. Bhagwan Shree Rajneesh's (1931–90) sect of Orange People had begun as a seaside commune in Bombay in 1969, with a particularly permissive view of sex in the Tantric tradition. This attracted worldwide adherents, so the mission of unrestrained sexual freedom was moved on first to Poonah, then in 1981 to Oregon, USA. The code of total promiscuity and abandonment of the family unit was seen as a means of improving the breed, but the Utopian city at Big Muddy Ranch degenerated into corruption and murder. Hinduism also produced new sects such as Swami Prabhupada's (b.1896) International Society of Krishna Consciousness, with its radio and press advertising campaigns, conversion through hunger and exhaustion, rigorously ascetic and hard-working communities. With the perverse resilience of so many age-old prejudices, suttee was revived in the 1980s in Rajistan, despite being against the law, and self-burning as a protest against too many new rights for the Harijan became prevalent in 1990. Katmandu became a 'hippy Mecca' for disillusioned Western youth, while the new Moslem Sufis practised a pastoral asceticism. As Jansen comments, all these sects had in common the rejection of modern scientific logic, 'the diabolical invention, mind'.

The other great cause of the second half of the century was peace. On the one hand, the ethos of the just war tended to persist despite the huge amount of damage it had already done. While countries which had suffered a great deal, like Japan and Germany in particular, were relatively pacifist, many others still believed in the achievement of ethnic ends by force. The Arabs believed in the idea of 'jihad' or sacred war, as did the Israelis. Numerous other emergent nations in Africa, South East Asia and Central America sought their own form of justice from just wars, many of them involving considerable unnecessary cruelty and massacres. The nationalist movement in Kenya led to some 2,000 sadistic murders by the Mau Mau, a Kikuyu strike force resorting to orgiastic ritual as a bond in their fight for freedom; the French-Algerian conflict of the 1950s was extremely bitter, as was the war in Biafra (1968–9) and the savage reprisals of the Pakistanis in Bangladesh. The Marxist regime of Khmer Rouge in Cambodia (1975–8) used terror and torture for social control. In Phnom Penh some 20,000 were tortured and murdered, many by skull fracture, and Prince Norodom Sihanouk (b.1923) pronounced:

The Khmer Rouge are not criminals, they are true patriots.

The total Khmer genocide was estimated at 1,500,000 people. Then, as if to emphasise the continued immaturity of the human race, the three-sided civil war in the former Yugoslavia produced a new euphemism for induced genocide—'ethnic cleansing'.

De-colonisation in Africa produced a number of highly unstable regimes hampered by lack of training, corruption and ethnic rivalries. Idi Amin (b.1930) of Uganda was one of Africa's most violent leaders, a man whom Decalo has shown liquidated over 10,000 opponents within one year, possibly 85,000 two years later. The Karume Falls Bridge over the Nile became known as the Bridge of Blood. Much of this activity was genocidal, since the tribes of Langi and Alcholi were hated by the Nilotic tribes under Amin. Corruption and a tendency towards promiscuity marked his attitudes, though he preached to his officers that they were 'not to pursue each other's wives in the light of the abundance of other women'. Numerous other African regimes suffered from similar problems of corruption in the centre surrounded by racially-exclusive guard regiments in a position to snatch power quite easily. Similarly, many of the nominally Catholic regimes in Latin America continued to depend on terror for survival; the government of Jean Paul Duvalier (1907–71) in Haiti was just one example, with its sadistic guards, the Tonton Macoute.

In terms of the ebb and flow of permissiveness, both the world wars were followed by periods of disillusionment in the idea of self-sacrifice. Even in the United States, where prohibition appeared to begin as a major act of abstinence, the 1920s were essentially a period when self-indulgence was fashionable. Marcel Proust (1871–1922) published *Sodom and Gomorrah* in 1922, D.H. Lawrence (1885–1930) who had written *Sons and Lovers* (1913) produced *Lady Chatterley's Lover*, the antithesis of puritanism, in 1928, and Henry Miller (1891–1980) wrote *The Tropic of Cancer* (1934). Thomas Mann (1875–1955) produced his *Magic Mountain*, symbolising the moral disintegration of Europe, and his brother's novel was used for the film *The Blue Angel* in 1934. The Times on 1st January 1930 thundered: 'Moral debasement is the inevitable prelude of downfall.' Isadora Duncan (1878–1927), who died in an accident in 1927, had been doing her exotic dances; Gipsy Rose Lee (1914–70) had invented the American striptease; 'Nacktkultur' was spreading in Germany and France, the pornography industry was thriving and drug addiction was spreading, particularly in the United States where it had reached one per 4,000 of population in 1918. Cities like Berlin prided themselves on their decadence, and homosexuality became the great Berlin fashion, with gay night-clubs like the lesbian

'Silhouette'. In 1937, the French were apparently much more tolerant of homosexuality than they had been in the previous century and, according to Zeldin, it was claimed that there were 250,000 homosexuals in Paris, starting in the lycées, encouraged by writers like André Gide (1869–1951) and protected by a clause in the Napoleonic Code. At the same time, there was considerable growth in odd sects; for instance, the Buddhists opened their first European temple in Berlin at this time, and there were reckoned to be 3,000 occultist practitioners or astrologers in the city, including the alchemist Franz Tausend, who was not exposed until 1929.

The 1930s stock market crash and the Second World War brought a temporary halt in the decline of objective values. The defeat of fascism became a unifying cause and was followed by a period when the active confrontation between communism and capitalism seemed almost to take over the same role. The reduction in East-West tension after Khrushchev allowed the West to get back to indulging itself. The late fifties in Britain saw the famous Lady Chatterley case (which virtually ended literary censorship), the Street Offences Act, the legalisation of adult homosexuality and, in 1968, the end of stage censorship. This became the period of Vladimir Nabokov's (1899–1980) *Lolita* (1955), a novel about a man's love for a twelve-year-old girl, Fellini's (b.1920) *La Dolce Vita* (1960), the toleration of cannabis, the regarding of abortion as a human right, the founding of the Playboy empire in 1953, and rapid sales of Alfred Kinsey's (1894–1956) *Sexual Behaviour in the Human Male*. In France by the 1960s, the number of prostitutes had risen to about 400,000, but then went into decline as the young came to enjoy free promiscuity with each other. In Britain, the rate of pre-marital co-habitation rose from one percent in the 1950s to twenty-one percent in the early 1980s, by which time one child in four was born out of wedlock. After 1973, homosexuality in America was no longer classified as a personality disorder like other pathological forms of sex.

Even in the communist bloc objective values were under threat. As the puritanism of the later Stalin era in Russia, with its large-family ethos and strong work ethic, was replaced by a small-family ethos and reduced work ethic, alcohol became increasingly prominent as an escape route. In 1988, one report suggested that there could be as many as 30,000,000 alcoholics in the Soviet Union; in the USA there were about 30,000,000 regular users of marijuana and 500,000 cocaine addicts. The drudgery of life in modern, industrial states, combined with ready availability of escapist drugs, showed signs of reaching epidemic proportions. In the Western world objective values were disappearing rapidly.

In 1984, almost exactly 500 years after the first known appearance of syphilis, there appeared another new venereal disease, AIDS, which particularly attacked homosexuals. San Francisco, with 70,000 gay men, acquired the reputation once belonging to cities like Florence and Corinth. The general fashion for homosexuality was given a moral justification by the need to restrict population growth. Thailand, with an prostitute population estimated at 700,000, by the 1980s had developed an economy based on vice to maintain its balance of payments. Brazil had an estimated 4,000,000 prostitutes, and Gabriela Silva Leite (b.1947) began a movement to improve their status. But perhaps least savoury of all was the ethos of the Philippines, where corruption and economic inefficiency under the presidency of Ferdinand Marcos (1917–87) led to the justification of child prostitution, one of the worst examples in history of mass child abuse.

Despite the spread of general permissiveness, there remained issues which created considerable excitement—peace and the threat of nuclear war remained one. The Americans were obsessed with the Leninist-Stalinist doctrine of going to war to spread communism, and could not believe Krushchev's declaration that this was over; besides, this mantle appeared to have been partly taken over by the Chinese. Accordingly, the Americans were surprisingly more prone to war *then* than they were before either of the two world wars, until Mikhail Gorbachev's (b.1931) policy of 'glasnost' began to convince the world that Russia was no longer interested in world conquest.

Conflict in Korea was followed by Vietnam, and incidents like the My-Lai massacre were symptomatic of the brutality. The arms race with the Soviet Union continued with two-sided paranoia, making the nuclear problem into the most acute moral dilemma of the century. In 1945, it had been a relatively straightforward decision: President Truman (1884–1972) authorised the use of atomic weapons at Hiroshima and Nagasaki on the basis that it had been estimated that the gradual conquest of the Japanese mainland would cost around 7,000,000 Japanese lives, or ten percent of their population, whereas the instant destruction of the two towns would cost 120,000 lives and would extract a much quicker surrender. So, statistically, the tally in Japanese lives alone favoured the atomic bomb. In the twenty years that followed, the size and power of the bombs increased enormously, and they were provided with unmanned delivery systems; also, at least half a dozen nations had their own version of the bomb.

This situation required a new ethos. The bomb could not be abolished or ignored; no country which had it trusted the others enough to abandon it unilaterally. So there evolved the homeopathic ethos of the threat of evil to avoid evil. The problem with the deterrent theory, so far as public moral attitudes were concerned, was the technological complexity of the whole system—no lay person could be sure of how the controls and counter-controls might work, or of the true attitudes of the participants, or of the real danger of accidental firings. This blurring of the issues has meant that pacifism, as so often in its history, has had less support than might be expected. On the one hand, the world was in a position where a minor incident or accident could lead to the total destruction of the human race; on the other, the obvious moral imperative arising from that possibility was thrust into the sub-conscious by the complexities and uncertainties surrounding it. Thus, in the 1980s, anti-nuclear lobbies and peace movements remained minorities. The Campaign for Nuclear Disarmament, founded in Britain in 1958 when they began the Aldermaston Marches, made only slow headway despite mediagenic marches and demonstrations. Other groups, like the Greenham Common women protesting between 1982 and 1986 against Cruise missiles in Britain, the Greens in Germany, the peace movements in the United States, had relatively limited success. Greenpeace, founded in 1977 by David McTaggert (b.1933), received an ambivalent boost to its profile when the French secret service provided it with a martyr in 1985. The real beginning of reduced tension ultimately came from the top, when President Gorbachev took the initiative in disarmament.

The other major ethical issue in world politics has been sorting out the misery caused by economic chaos—cyclical booms and slumps, structural changes in industry, currency anomalies and debt. While the Old World has seemingly been at times wracked with guilt about its ever-increasing materialism, it has at the same time had to recognise that non-materialist puritanism would simply cause greater economic distress. As J.M. Keynes (1883–1946) put it:

> Whenever you save five shillings you put a man out of work for a day.

Thus thrift, one of the virtues of the nineteenth century, became tantamount to a vice in the twentieth. However, the competitive materialism needed to fuel a capitalist economy, nurtured by heavy advertising, created other pressures, such as the demand for higher wages and the demand for the right to work for both sexes, which (as Marx foresaw) would make capitalist economies even more fragile. At the same time, the problem of creating even subsistence economies in emergent nations, particularly those without major natural resources, seemingly remained insoluble. In 1936, President Roosevelt (1882–1945) was saying

> We have always known that heedless self-interest was bad morals; now we know it is also bad economics.

And twenty years later, John F. Kennedy (1917–63) named

> ... the four common enemies of the world; tyranny, poverty, disease and war.

But political leaders during this period have all tended to become rapidly preoccupied with practical problems of survival. The problem of the 'acquisitive society' is that it can find no escape from its self-consuming acquisitiveness, and the system is so inherently fragile that survival always seems to be more important than principle. Little heed can be taken of prophets like R.H. Tawney (1880–1962), who wrote:

> As long as men are men, a poor society cannot be too poor to find a right order of life nor a rich society too rich to have a need to seek it.

Contrast between abject poverty in some areas, and fragile affluence in others, presents an insoluble problem due to man's inablity to control the man-made chemistry of cash, credit and employment. Cities, despite slum clearance, have developed new forms of urban squalor, new polarisations of rich and poor. Nations with too much food are economically unable to share it amongst those with too little. Charity organisations to help Third World welfare or offset political oppression are not insignificant: Amnesty International (founded 1961), Oxfam (1942) and Bob Geldof's (b.1954) Band Aid (1984) are examples.

One of the effects of a major loss of credibility in objective values is that anyone can be right—one individual is as capable of creating his or her own inner convictions as another. Strange new minorities arise, claiming recognition for their own codes. A classic example in the late 1980s of the clash between the new subjectivity and the old objectivity occurred when a group of homosexual Catholic priests in San Francisco asked for approval from Pope John Paul II (b.1920). He refused, just as he refused to condone divorce, abortion and birth control, the other new rights of the majority of peoples.

Everywhere the strident demands were heard of groups claiming special attention for different codes which they thought all-important: saving whales, the rights of unmarried mothers, equal career opportunities for the sexes, racial tolerance, the urge to lose weight, the evils of acid rain, the nuclear winter, the abolition of fox-hunting, legalisation of soft drugs, the morality of euthanasia. Science had created new moral dilemmas, such as surrogate motherhood. As Russophobia receded in the era of Gorbachev, and the idea of the nuclear holocaust became more remote, the ethics of the world turned into a vast maze of subjective interpretations of fading objective codes. Continued increases in drug addiction, marital breakdown and suicide were symptoms of the continued loss of direction in the final decade of the twentieth century. Intensive levels of social research show the prevalence of wife-beating, child abuse and paedophilia, private sins previously kept secret. The massive revival in the image of liberty, and the collapse of the communist system in 1989, began to harmonise the ethical trends on both sides of what used to be the Iron Curtain, removing a whole battery of state values. In the 1990s, China remained the last huge bastion of objective values, crushing its youthful democratic movement with a display of ruthless conviction in Tianenman Square.

The dominant ethical trend in the twentieth century has been to reject the values of imperialism. Between the break up of the Austro-Hungarian Empire in 1918 and that of the Soviet Empire in 1991, there has been decolonisation on a massive scale, the gradual rejection of imperial stereotypes, including their ideologies, religions and ethical systems. The century has probably seen the biggest ever continuous rebellion against objective values. As with all rebellions, its success can only be judged by the quality of the new structures which replace the old, and the new subjective codes have still to be properly tested. While the old empires collapse, there are numerous national groupings still thirsting for the glamour of acquisitive self-determination, still imitating the post-feudal ethos. In 1992, there was a stampede of ethnic groups declaring independence whilst having little or no experience or infrastructure.

The other massive ethical shift worldwide in the twentieth century was in the increasing equality of the sexes, and in a lowering in respect for fertility, a concept worshipped for thousands of years, but now, like so many idols, treated with suspicion. The long-term effects of this trend have yet to be examined or assessed.

If the great tragedy of the first half of the century was that the middle class (if not the masses) had been affected with the self-destructive paranoia and racial élitism of the old aristocracies (and this cost at least 100,000,000 lives), the tragedy of the second half was that this spread to the emergent nations, possibly also to the last servile grouping on earth—women. This century had seen the human species as a whole reach its lowest depths in terms of utilitarian morality: the holocaust from 1914 to 1945, with its many subsequent extensions into the Third World, had been an infinitely greater demonstration of mass sadism than any in previous centuries. While there has been a surge of conscience in its wake, possibly probing tentatively towards greater perfection of utilitarian morality than man has ever previously managed, there has also been a great deal of subjective experimentation, the consequences of which are only vaguely understood. Mankind still has a lot to prove in terms of any evidence of serious progress in ethical development.

> The new young gangsters just don't have the same principles as the old Triad.
>
> Hong Kong business spokesman, 1991.

PART THREE

What Next?

Public crimes are committed by individuals who play roles in political, military or economic institutions . . . yet the crimes don't seem fully attributable to the individual himself.

Thomas Nagel

It is easier for a man to be loyal to his club than to his planet; the by-laws are shorter and he is personally acquainted with the other members.

E.B. White

Nature has placed mankind under the governance of two sovereign masters, pain and pleasure. It is for them alone to point out where we ought to go.

Jeremy Bentham

Nine of the ten commandments are negative.

Bertrand Russell

You have no choice. You are committed to socially acceptable acts, a little machine capable only of good. A man who cannot choose ceases to be a man. To turn a decent young man into a piece of clockwork should not surely be seen as a triumph for any government save one proud of its oppressiveness.

Anthony Burgess

The so-called new morality is too often the old immorality condoned.

Hartley Shawcross

The law of the fishes is that the large eat the small.

Indian proverb

What we witness is the shuddering, drunken tottering
of a social structure supported by an inadequate
philosophy.

Robert Ardrey

O NE THEME HAS already emerged regularly, from the Roman philosopher Seneca onwards: the greatest crimes in history have been committed by officialdom, by leading groups in particular societies, or by individuals convinced of their own rightness and abetted by ambitious aides apparently working with the blessing of their peers.

A second theme is that there is possibly some kind of underlying streak of sadism in human beings, particularly men, for whom the use of murder, torture or terrorism is an avenue to power or prestige. The result has been to rationalise this sadism in all kinds of ways. Historically, the first great rationalisation of sadism was the acceptance of the widespread habit of human sacrifice to the gods, including the early variant in which servants were killed or buried alive with their masters. This habit was almost universal in the pre-Christian era, from Norway to China, and later in South America. The second version was the mass slaughter of defeated armies or civilians as a policy of deliberate terrorism, as practised by the Assyrians, Egyptians, Vikings, Mongols and others. Then there came the frenzied persecutions of minorities starting with the Romans' toying with gladiators, the killings of Jews in the crusades and, after the Black Death, the massacre of the Albigensians and the frenetic attacks of the Inquisition on heretics and witches.

Next came the vast scale of exploitation and cruelty when the slave trade was revived in the early modern period, serfdom was renewed and followed by heavy industrial exploitation. The latest stage of institutionalised sadism has been that of the megalithic tyrannies from Napoleon onwards, with the hyperactive destructiveness of the new breed of self-made rulers who could use conscription and modern weaponry to increase greatly the scale of killing. In all these periods, individuals and groups have shown themselves capable of becoming mega-sadists willing to use almost any level of cruelty to foster their ambitions—the Mongol Khans, the fathers of the Inquisition, the Turks in Armenia and the Nazis among them. It is not satisfactory to blame these atrocities on small numbers; each of these groups had created an ethos in which it seemed moral for large numbers of their henchmen to carry out their orders, as executioners, torturers, witch-burners, slave-traders, gas chamber attendants, people who may well have gone home to be kind to their families and pet animals.

This leads to a third possible theme, which is simply that people are easily led. Throughout history we have seen numerous examples of populations who have been readily persuaded that what is normally black is white; not just that vendetta is justifiable, but that genocide and the deliberate mass-infliction of pain are acceptable.

Humans, as we have seen, can be led not only into sadism, but also masochism. The willingness to die (often quite pointlessly) in battle, to sacrifice life for glory or obscure causes, to suffer deliberate torment as a religious demonstration or self-deprivation for the sake of public recognition, have all been quite common. Inverted self-indulgence has been part of the regular pattern of mass movements from the earliest times.

A fourth theme is the oscillation between an emphasis on self-restraint, puritanism and the family virtues, and an emphasis on hedonistic self-gratification and abandonment of discipline. These swings may be due to the reaction of one generation against its predecessor—change for change's sake—or the fact that the very tendency to move towards extremes pushes habits to the point where a reverse swing becomes inevitable. There is no particular evidence that societies which become excessively permissive destroy themselves, though there have been examples where this form of decadence did presage the decline and fall of regimes. There are more examples of highly disciplined societies in which moral fanaticism has led to a level of intolerance or ruthlessness sometimes more damaging overall to human life than the less intense irreponsibility of the permissive regimes. In passing we can note how often intense moralities of whichever extreme are associated with periods of great creative energy in the arts, and also that strong codes are often, in the tradition of Arnold Toynbee, a response to adverse conditions. Amongst vices which have been in existence almost since the dawn of time, many have been greeted with surprise, as if they were new in each era, and as if they presaged a new downturn in human behaviour; but these vices have ebbed and flowed, the epidemics have peaked and receded and there has been no permanent relapse.

A more positive standpoint for reviewing moral history is to consider it in terms of compassion. It could be stated that if most of what is good in human behaviour relates to caring for human life and comfort, then the prime source of goodness is mankind's natural instinct for compassion. The characteristics of human compassion are that, at its best, it substantially outdoes anything similarly evident in the behaviour of other animals, yet at its lowest demonstrates a much worse behavioural pattern than is seen in any other animals. Many of the examples of mass human cruelty which we have looked at suggest that it was the obsessive leadership of small groups or individuals who, for a time, manipulated their peoples into ignoring normal feelings of compassion.

By contrast, many of the non-events of history relate to societies with low-profile leaderships and non-fanatical ideologies, who thus earned neither the glory nor the notoriety to feature in history. Westermarck provides numerous examples: how Kolben found the Hottentots 'the most friendly, most liberal, most benevolent people to one another that ever appeared on earth'. The people of Madagascar, according to Doury, 'treated one another with more humanity than we do'. The Tonga Islanders 'were not selfish but admired liberality'. The Arctic explorer, Nansen, commented: 'The Greenlander is the most compassionate of creatures with regard to his neighbours. His first social law is to help others'. The Dyaks were 'hospitable, kindly and humane'. The North American Iroquois observed 'kindness to the orphan, hospitality to all and a common brotherhood'. Amongst the Sea Dyak 'if any are sick or unable to work, the rest help'. These examples suggest, even if they do not prove, that natural human behaviour tends to be compassionate, and that a mass sadistic attitude is more of an artificial state of mind created by leadership or other pressures. We should therefore look at those conflicting emotions which tend to blunt compassion amongst both leaders and followers, because this clash has been the largest source of corporate cruelty in history.

Compassion can be blunted by a sense of competition. The competitive spirit, as we have seen, is easily aroused in human beings, can become obsessive, and in many cases directly contradicts the sense of compassion. Competitiveness is at its strongest amongst the élites of societies, but is readily passed on down through the classes. The compulsion to win replaces the milder instinct to co-operate, and charity is demoted. This in turn creates individuals who feel a sense of superiority. Competition leads to the idea of stratification, of superiority and inferiority on the basis of race, inherited rank, merit, wealth or ideology. A sense of superiority is habit-forming, turns into bigotry and prejudice, so that contempt for inferiors overrides compassion. And contempt is but a short step from violence.

Equally, compassion can be blunted by a sense of inferiority. If people feel that they have suffered injury or are threatened, the wells of goodwill dry up. If exposed to atrocity myths, tales of sabotage or usury, fear of war or famine, compassion is corroded and the undercurrent of violence can easily be tapped. It is more than possible that people maltreated or abused as children may grow up with sadistic tendencies or neurotic compulsions to regain equality or achieve superiority.

Third, compassion is blunted by superstition and prejudice, particularly a belief in a good or bad after-life. We have seen numerous examples of sadistic persecution in the name of religions, where fanaticism displaces natural feelings.

Finally, compassion can be blunted by overexposure—cruelty seen too often is not seen at all. We have seen examples of how major philosophers apparently ignored evils common in their own lifetime; Aristotle did not question slavery, and Thomas Aquinas accepted prostitution as necessary. Peoples used to the slave trade, witch-burning, human sacrifice, or mass slaughter barely noticed it. For centuries, infanticide was just a normal part of most people's lives. For millennia, women and children may have been abused with impunity, causing untold misery. Possibly the prime objective of education should be the fostering of natural compassion and the study of the forces that can destroy it; and perhaps that is little more than a restatement of the common core of the teachings of Christ, Buddha, Mohammed and the other great prophets.

For anyone rash enough to consider possible trends in moral codes for the next century, it is just possible that there are some lessons which can be learned from the past. History shows that there have been numerous periods when changes in moral codes led to greater human pain and misery, not less. To some extent this was due to the obsessive quality acquired by originally straightforward objectives because of the paranoia, ambition or over-enthusiasm of a society's leaders. Hence the world has endured so many periods of what Marc Bloch called 'collective error', such as the persecution of witches, heretics, Jews and Trotskyites. Most of the man-made suffering in the world has not been attributable to delinquents, criminals, deviants or other people who rejected the moral norms of their societies, but to those who followed the norm very diligently, who were heroes of their own time, who had the intellectual power or authority to rationalise the cruelties they were committing.

New measures to avoid or reduce individual delinquency or deviation are perhaps useful, but they are nowhere near as important as trying to make sure that 'collective errors' are consciously avoided in the future. The twentieth century has all too clearly been a century of massive 'collective errors'. We have seen that the study of the creation process of moral codes is not nearly scientific enough for anyone to be able to create 'clockwork oranges', morally perfect robots suited to the needs of the next century. But what is reasonable is to suggest that peoples should agree first on their corporate objectives, and perhaps thereafter consider the appropriate priorities in moral co-operation which would best achieve those ends.

The zoologists like Robert Ardrey and Konrad Lorenz addressed the subject in exactly this way. They have been concerned with what they see as the greater recent deviation away from nature, and in particular the reduced effects of natural selection which have affected man in the twentieth century. As Lorenz put it:

> Under conditions of modern civilized life there is not a single factor exerting selection pressure in the direction of goodness and kindness, unless the innate feeling for natural justice.

Lorenz offered a new list of eight deadly sins: overpopulation, destruction of environment, the decay of compassion and the cheapening of pleasure, the failure of parental training, the increased indoctrinability of the masses and the possession of nuclear weapons. In particular, he saw the over-crowded, obsessive inhabitants of the West as vulgarised by the pressures of mass industry, over-strained by perpetual contact and emotionally dried up by the endless sub-division of responsibility.

If we look at the likely pressures and thrusts evident in the last decade of the twentieth century, there is likely to be increased pressure against population growth, so the dominant ethic is likely to favour late marriage, late child-bearing, small families, possibly greater permissiveness. Because of worldwide economic and employment patterns, there will be even more pressure to foster the acquisition of material goods; to prevent the collapse of the commercial system, there will be a need for a further spread of the materialist, self-indulgency ethic. There will be the pressure of an ageing world population, blunting the edges of compassion for old age. There will be continued pressure for the development of technical skills or brainpower in a competitive world where the skilled are more likely to survive and the unskilled to be exploitable. As the world population shifts steadily en masse away from subsistence agriculture towards the competitive marketing of luxuries and services, there will be numerous frustrations and readjustments to resolve, and the likelihood of new types of civil war and violence as the only form of escape will increase. Throughout the world there will be increasing numbers of people brought up as children pressurised towards material affluence, with the emphasis on educational competition, neurotic about rights and status, light on duties and with little time for compassion, deprived as they are by modern philosophy and science of all objective standards or beliefs. Because the mass ethos is likely to be so subjective, so egocentric, so competitive and so materialistic, it will also tend to be very vulnerable. The higher the demand for achievement and physical success, the more frequent the inevitability of failure and the greater the susceptibility to create routes of escape or consolation.

The evidence of this century so far is that the abrogation of traditional, rational creeds (mostly the moderate ones like the great established religions) does not preclude the attraction of quite extravagant, less rational ones. The leap into unreason might as well be a big one.

The trappings of the extravagant can be more alluring than the simpler guises of traditional faiths. Amidst the mass of materialist, rational crowds there are likely to appear from time to time groups which are irrational to the point of eccentricity, if not danger and violence. This will include the revival of odd little nationalisms and odd little religions, plus new versions of both, as frustrated masses react against the increasing uniformity of the species.

The steady momentum turning the world's population into one vast, commercially-conformist middle class will create new challenges for each new generation's inevitable desire for rebellion and individual identity. As throughout history, violence will forever tend to offer itself as the easiest solution to mass boredom. The capacity to indulge in torture, persecution, even genocide is never totally eradicated from the human psyche.

Our tendency recently has been to define a sound morality as one which leads to the maximum possible elimination of human misery, but one factor has been neglected. We have been able readily to identify those aspects of physical misery—starvation, disease, neglect, warfare, genocide, persecution, slavery, torture and exploitation—which, it is fair to argue, moral codes should be structured towards preventing. But this is essentially negative, and if the physical discomforts are eliminated, history has shown often enough that we can still end up with a maladjusted, disgruntled, bored, demotivated society whose sheer *ennui* may sow the seeds of moral breakdown and consequential physical disaster in the generation to follow. The Caliph Abdul Rahman commented after a fifty-year reign in which he had enjoyed victory, peace and every material blessing, that out of his entire life he could only identify fourteen days of real happiness. The human spirit has other needs which may be referred to as emotional and spiritual, and which a purely rational moral philosophy may not satisfy. Human beings need additional goals, causes, ideologies; because happiness is a fluctuating emotion, a cessation of beating the head against a wall, it cannot be guaranteed simply by the permanent elimination of all pain. Successful moral ideologies of the past have tended, therefore, to be part of major spiritual packages or religions in which irrational components are added to lend charisma and motivation to the rational code. It is this irrational element which has often provided the fanatical strain which led to otherwise sound moralities condoning or encouraging extraordinary levels of persecution, thus almost defeating the original reason for evolving the code at all. We must still recognise, however, the need for charismatic packaging, for a supra-rational targeting of objectives, for a spiritual life structure.

Edward de Bono has made the point that 'the old religions including Marxism were designed for a world of suffering'. It is also true that most of the world's great moral systems were the products of hard times.

The Jewish code came from a dispossessed desert tribe, the Spartan ethic from an isolated fighting minority, Puritanism from an age of persecution by Catholic governments, Victorian values from the harsh competitive environment of the industrial revolution, and so on. Most of these systems were founded on a strong demand for sacrifice from the individual, so that energy could be directed towards corporate goals. This sense of suppressing self in favour of country or king, ideals or gods, is what gives many great ethical codes their feeling of altruism.

However misconceived the corporate objectives may be, the fact that society is thus not totally self-centred at an individual level does give it a certain positive quality. People who make these sacrifices may derive as much if not more happiness from sharing in corporate objectives as they do from indulging themselves. Even fighting lost causes together, or sharing persecution, may be more fulfilling than attaining materialist goals individually; perhaps even corporate goals which are intrinsically worthless do in fact have a value because of the self-sacrifice which they may demand.

Looking at the average moral codes of periods when life was less hard, there tended to be a lower requirement for corporate objectives and personal sacrifice. The later Roman Empire, the Renaissance, the Restoration and Edwardian eras were characterised by an aimless and never-quite-satisfied search for personal pleasure and contempt for impediments to it. For much of the world, the late twentieth century has set the greatest of all challenges in its low requirement and low credibility for corporate goals. Life (in all but the Third World) is too comfortable on the whole to encourage the co-operative thrust for survival which helps create the interlocking, surrendering self. Hence the loss of a sense of direction, the growth of self-destructive experimentalism and the low reputation of self-sacrifice typical of affluent societies.

The problem of developed societies with no obvious goals left to strive for, where there is long life-expectancy and little fear of the horrors of a punitive after-life, where there is no unifying inspiration for corporate objectives, is how to channel the motivational surplus with which most reasonably well-fed humans are endowed, so that they are less prone to self-destruction, or to escape into polygamy, alcoholism, violence and obscure obsessions. There then comes the problem of countering an awesome cynicism: the harsh realism of the mass media makes it much harder to create new mythologies, to justify new corporate goals in this world or the next. The great tragedy in moral history has been that the dominating ethos up to the present has nearly always been the self-aggrandising model of the land-owner, with its overtones of racial exclusivity, sometimes accompanied by religious élitism. This single factor has accounted for the vast majority of man-made misery throughout the centuries. In the last 200 years this model has been imitated first by middle-class regimes, then even by so-called working-class regimes, with horrendous results. In the second half of the twentieth century this essentially acquisitive, glory-hunting, compassionless ethic is to some extent being followed by women as well, the last great grouping to insist on equality. Men certainly have no right to complain, but it could have devastating results if women have not learnt from the long record of male folly.

Moral codes of the future should not fall into the trap of over-motivating their participants, of turning them into fanatics who may become élitist, intolerant and even violent in upholding their belief system. It also clearly makes sense to follow Aristotle and Buddha in going for 'the middle way', neither too puritanical nor too permissive, neither too ascetic nor too self-indulgent; history clearly indicates that the extreme societies have been the least stable. We have seen the importance of not allowing the state component in a moral system to become over-dominant; societies where patriotism and other macho virtues are regarded as the most important tend to thrust themselves into crises and disrupt the moral system they are supposed to protect.

Crucially, morality should not be regarded as a magical happening but should be thought through with the objectives which matter most to the time and place; for example, the conservationist content of moral systems should probably increase. Then we must recognise that the packaging of moral codes not only has historical precedent but is probably a present and future necessity—so we will need new or revised mythologies, new images, new dramatisations, even, perhaps, new 'tablets of stone', while at the same time being fully conscious of their purpose, functions and limitations. This leads to the final characteristic, the fact that moral codes do need to have some level of objectivity, some mixture perhaps of precedent, scientific validity and corporate ideology. The residual codes of the great religions can fit well into this, as does the observation of natural morality. The natural ethos which has persisted amongst some primitive peoples and many peasant communities, which survived as what E.P. Thompson identified as the 'deep-rooted crowd morality' of the eighteenth century, has qualities which often eluded the over-complicated moral systems of the great civilisations.

The lesson of history is to keep it simple: most successful moralities have been based on fear—fear of pain, punishment, ridicule, disapproval or everlasting torment. Remove these fears, as often happens in affluent communities, and the system slips into imbalance. Only when the imbalance begins to produce sufficient destruction to restore fear is there a sign of revival. The challenge for the twenty-first century is to construct a new, mature ethos based on positive instead of negative objectives; one it touch with the crisis facing both planet and population, a code built on compassion and not just fear.

Bibliography

A number of major works referred to in the main text are not included in this bibliography on account of the large number of editions available. These include the Bible, the Koran, Bhagavadgita Upanishads, Homer, Adi-granth, Havamal, Buddhist Tipitaka, Book of Meng Tzu and Analects of Confucius.

Aeschylus. *Oresteia*, tr. R. Eagles (London, 1976)

Agnellus. 'History of the Bishops of Ravenna' in *Monumenta Germaniae Historica* (Stuttgart, 1952)

Alcuin. *Works*, ed. J. Raine (London, 1879)

Arblaster, Anthony and S. Lukes, eds. *The Good Society* (London, 1971)

Ardrey, Robert. *Social Contract* (London, 1970)

Ariès, Philippe, and Georges Duby, ed. *A History of Private Life*, tr. A Goldhammer, vols I–IV (Cambridge, (MA) 1991)

Ariès, Philippe, and A. Bejin. *Western Sexuality* (Oxford, 1985)

Aristotle. *The Ethics*, tr. J.A.K. Thomson (London, 1953)

Ashe, G. *Mahatma Gandhi* (London, 1968)

Ashton, R., ed. *James I by his Contemporaries* (London, 1987)

Athanasius. *Life of St Anthony*, tr. R.T. Meyer (London, 1950)

Augustine, Saint. *City of God*, tr. John Healey (London, 1945)

Augustine, Saint. *Confessions*, tr. John Healey (London, 1945)

Aurelius, Marcus. *Golden Book of Meditations*, tr. Farquharson (London, 1945)

Ayer, A.J. *Language, Truth and Logic* (Oxford, 1910)

Barclay, William. *Ethics in the Permissive Society* (London, 1971)

Barnett, Corelli. *The Collapse of British Power* (London, 1978)

Barnsley, John H. *The Social Reality of Ethics* (London, 1972)

Barret, Michelle and May McInnes. *Anti-Social Family* (London, 1982)

Barrow, G.W.S. *William Rufus* (London, 1964)

Barthes, Roland. *Mythologies* (London, 1971)

Bartov, Omer. *Hitler's Army* (London 1991)

Baxter, Richard. *Reliquiae Baxterianae* (London, 1696)

Becker, Peter. *Rule of Fear* (London, 1964)

Belden, J. *China Shakes the World* (New York, 1949)

Benassar, Bartolomeo. *The Spanish Character* (London, 1969)

Bentham, Jeremy. *Introduction to the Principles of Morals and Legislation* (London, 1789)

Bernard, Saint. *Life and Teachings*, ed. A.J. Luddy (Dublin, 1937)

Berry, L. and R. Gurney. *Rude and Barbarous Kingdom* (Wisconsin, 1968)

Bismarck, Otto von. *Reflections and Reminiscences*, tr. A.J. Butler (London, 1898)

Bloch, Marc. *Feudal Society*, tr. L.A. Manyon (London, 1961)

Bloch, Marc. *Slavery and Serfdom in the Middle Ages*, tr. W.R. Beer (London, 1975)

Bonet, Honore. *L'arbre des Batailles* (Paris, 1515)

Booth, William. *Darkest England* (London, 1890)

Bosman, W. *Description of the Coast of Guinea* (London, 1814)

Boswell, James. *Life of Samuel Johnson* (London, 1791)

Bouquet, A.C. *Hinduism* (London, 1961)

Boxer, C.R. *Mary and Misogyny* (London, 1975)

Boxer, C.R. *Portuguese Seaborne Empire* (London, 1969)

Boyer, Paul. *The Urban Masses and Moral Order in America 1820–1920* (Connecticut, 1980)

Brackman, Arnold C. *The Other Nuremberg* (London, 1989)

Braudel, Ferdinand. *The Mediterranean World in the Age of Philip II*, tr. S. Reynolds (London, 1973)

Braudel, Ferdinand. *The Structures of Everyday Life*, tr. M. Kochan (London, 1981)

Breasted, J.H. *Ancient Records of Egypt* (Chicago, 1906)

Breasted, J.H. *The Development of Religion and Thought* (London, 1935)

Bristow, E.J. *Vice and Vigilance* (Dublin, 1977)

Brock, Peter. *Pacifism in Europe to 1914* (Princeton, 1972)

Brooke, Chris. *Popular Religion in The Middle Ages* (London, 1984)

Brooke, Chris. *The Medieval Idea of Marriage* (Oxford, 1989)

Brooke, R.P. *The Coming of the Friars* (London, 1975)

Broude, Norma. *Feminism and Art History* (New York, 1982)

Buckle, H.T. *Civilization in England* (London, 1904)

Bullock, Alan. *Hitler: A Study in Tyranny* (London, 1952)

Bullogh, V.L. *Homosexuality: A History* (New York, 1979)

Burchard, John. *Diaries 1483–92*, tr. A.H. Matthew (London, 1910)

Burckhardt, Jacob. *The Renaissance in Italy*, tr. S. Middlemore (Oxford, 1981)

Burckhardt, Titus. *Sacred Art in East and West* (London, 1967)

Burgess, Anthony. *A Clockwork Orange* (London, 1962)

Burke, Peter. *Popular Culture in Early Modern Europe* (London, 1978)

Bury, J.B. et al., eds. *Cambridge Ancient History* (Cambridge, 1936)

Butler, Joseph. *The Analogy of Religion* (London, 1736)

Campbell, J. *The Masks of God: Primitive Mythology* (New York, 1959)

Canetti, Elias. *Crowds and Power* (London, 1962)

Carcopino, J. *Daily Life in Ancient Rome* (London, 1956)

Carlyle, Thomas. *Critical and Miscellaneous Essays* (London, 1838)

Carr, E.H. *History of Soviet Russia* (London, 1950)

Carr, E.H. *What Is History?* (London, 1961)

Carsten, T.L. *The War Against War* (London, 1982)

Catlin, Gerry. *The North American Indians* (London, 1841)

Chartier, R., ed. *A History of Private Life and Passions of the Renaissance* (London, 1989)

Chesterfield, Philip, Fourth Earl. *Letters to his Godson* (Oxford, 1890)

Chesterton, G.K. *The Barbarism of Berlin* (London, 1914)

Childe, V. Gordon. *The Dawn of European Civilization*, 6th ed. (London, 1959)

Churchill, Charles. *Poetical Works* (Edinburgh, 1855)

Cillis, John. *For Better Or For Worse* (London, 1975)

Claridge, Gordon. *Drugs and Human Behaviour* (London, 1970)

Clark, Grahame. *World Prehistory* (Cambridge, 1969)

Clark, Kenneth. *Civilization: A Personal View* (London, 1969)

Clarke, Samuel. *Discourse Concerning the Being and Attributes of God* (London, 1738)

Clausewitz, Karl. *On War*, ed. A. Rapaport (London, 1968)

Cobban, Alfred. *History of France* (London, 1961)

Cobden, Richard. *Speeches on Questions of Public Policy*, ed. J. Bright and T. Roger (Manchester, 1870)

Cohen, A.R. *Attitude Change and Social Difference* (New York, 1962)

Cohen, Stanley. *Folk Devils and Modern Panics* (London, 1972)

Cohn, Norman. *The Pursuit of the Millenium* (London, 1957)

Confucius. *The Ethics of Confucius*, ed. M.M. Dawson (London, 1915)

Contenad, G. *Everyday Life in Babylon and Assyria* (London, 1954)

Cope, Gilbert. *Christianity and The Visual Arts* (London, 1964)

Couze, Edwin. *Short History of Buddhism* (London, 1975)

Davenport, R. *Sex, Death and Punishment* (London, 1990)

Davies, Nigel. *Human Sacrifice* (London, 1981)

Davies, Nigel. *The Aztecs* (London, 1973)

Davies, R.T. *Four Centuries of Witch Belief* (London, 1947)

De Bono, Edward. *Lateral Thinking* (London, 1971)

De Sade, Marquis. *La Philosophie dans le boudoir* (Paris, 1793)

Decalo, Samuel. *Coups and Army Rule in Africa* (Yale, 1976)

Dent, H.J.H. *The Moral Psychology of Virtue* (London, 1970)

Deschamps, Eustache. *Oeuvres Completes*, ed. Saint Hilaire (Paris, 1878)

Deutscher, Isaac. *Stalin* (London, 1966)

Dickinson, G. Lowes. *The Greek View of Life* (London, 1896)

Disraeli, Benjamin. *Tancred* (London, 1847)

Douglas, Jack D., ed. *Deviance and Respectability* (London, 1970)

Dover, K.J. *Greek Homosexuality* (New York, 1978)

Dover, K.J. *Popular Greek Morality in the Age of Plato* (Oxford, 1974)

Draper, A. *Amritsar* (London, 1981)

Du Boulay, F.R. *Germany in the Late Middle Ages* (London, 1983)

Duby, Georges. *History of Private Life: Revelations of the Medieval World* (Harvard, 1987)

Duby, Georges. *The Knight, The Lady and The Priest* (London, 1956)

Dupaquier, Helen et al., eds. *Marriage and Remarriage in Populations of the Past* (London, 1988)

Elkington, E.N. *New Guinea* (London, 1907)

Ensor, E.K. *England in the 19th Century* (London, 1965)

Erasmus. *Selections*, ed. R. de Molen (London, 1973)

Euripides. *Tragedies: Selection*, ed. J. Diggle (Oxford, 1981)

Fage, J.D. *Introduction to the History of West Africa* (Cambridge, 1959)

Fennell, J.L.I. *Ivan the Great of Moscow* (London, 1961)

Ferguson, John. *War and Peace in the World's Religions* (London, 1977)

Finlay, George. *History of the Byzantine Empire* (London, 1854)

Finley, H.I. *Ancient Slavery and Modern Ideology* (London, 1980)

Finley, H.I. *The World of Odysseus* (London, 1977)

Fliegelman, Jay. *Prodigals and Pilgrims 1750–1800* (Cambridge, 1982)

Flugel, J.C. *Man, Morals and Society* (London, 1945)

Foucalt, M. *History of Sexuality* (New York, 1978)

Frankfort, Henri. *The Birth of Civilisation in the Near East* (Chicago, 1948)

Frazer, J.G. *The Golden Bough* (London, 1914)

French, Marilyn. *Beyond Power* (London, 1985)

Fromm, Erich. *War within Man* (Philadelphia, 1963)

Fuller, Thomas. *Wisdom of Our Fathers* (London, 1863)

Gandhi, M.K. *The Story of My Experiment with Truth*, tr. M. Desai (London, 1982)

Gandhi, Mahatma. 'Non Violence in Peace and War' in *The Essential Gandhi*, ed. L. Fischer (London, 1963)

Genicot, Leopold. *Contours of the Middle Ages* (London, 1967)

Gibbon, Edward. *The Decline and Fall of The Roman Empire*, ed. J.B. Bury (London, 1896)

Gilbert, Martin. *The Holocaust* (London, 1986)

Glaser, K. and S. Possony. *Victims of Politics: The State of Human Rights* (New York, 1979)

Goethe, Johann Wolfgang. *Selections in English*, ed. Stephen Spender (London, 1958)

Goode, William J. *World Revolutions and Family Patterns* (New York, 1970)

Graham, Billy. *Answers to Life's Problems* (Dallas, 1988)

Gratian. *Decreta*, ed. S. Chodorow (Berkeley, 1972)

Graves, R. and A. Hodge. *The Long Weekend* (London, 1940)

Green, V.H.H. *Wesley* (London, 1964)

Greer, Germaine. *Sex and Destiny* (New York, 1984)

Gregory the Great. *Moralia*, tr. J. Bliss (Oxford, 1844)

Greyerz, Kaspar Von. *Religion and Society in Early Modern Europe* (London, 1984)

Guillaume, Alfred. *Islam* (London, 1954)

Gurney, O. *The Hittites* (London, 1975)

Haimendorf, C. Furer. *Morals and Merit* (London, 1967)

Haldane, J.B.S. *Fact and Faith* (London, 1934)

Hall, Gwendolyn Midlow. *Social Conditions in Slave Plantation Societies* (Baltimore, 1971)

Hallpike, C.R. *The Principles of Social Evolution* (Oxford, 1988)

Hamilton, B. *The Medieval Inquisition* (London, 1981)

Hammond, J.L. and L.B. *Shaftesbury* (London, 1939)

Harris, Marvin. *Cannibals and Kings* (New York, 1977)

Harris, Marvin. *Cows, Pigs, Wars and Witches* (New York, 1975)

Hays, H.R. *The Dangerous Sex* (New York, 1964)

Hebb, D.O. *Organisation of Behaviour* (New York, 1949)

Hegel, G.W.F. *Lectures on Philosophy of World History*, ed. J. Hofmeister (Cambridge, 1975)

Henriques, Fernando. *Prostitution in Europe and the New World* (London, 1963)

Herodotus. *Histories*, tr. W. Shepherd (Cambridge, 1982)

Herries M.S. *Soldiers of the Sun: The Rise and Fall of the Japanese* (London, 1991)

Hibbert, Chris. *Venice* (London, 1988)

Hiro, Dilip. *Iran Under the Ayatollahs* (London, 1985)

Hitler, Adolf. *Mein Kampf*, tr. R. Maheim (London, 1972)

Hobbes, Thomas. *Leviathan* (London, 1955)

Hobhouse, L.T. *Morals in Evolution* (Cambridge, 1979)

Hobsbaum, Eric. *The Invention of Tradition* (Cambridge, 1983)

Hoggart, Richard. *The Uses of Literacy* (London, 1958)

Hookham, Hilda. *A Short History of China* (London, 1964)

Hosking, Geoffrey. *History of Soviet Russia* (London, 1985)

Hsia, R. Po Chia. *The Myth of Ritual Murder: Jews and Magic in Reformation Germany* (Yale, 1988)

Huizinga, J. *The Waning of the Middle Ages* (London, 1924)

Hull, Isabella. *The Entourage of Kaiser Wilhelm II* (Cambridge, 1982)

Hull, N.E. and P.C. Hoffer. *Murdering Mothers* (New York, 1981)

Humana, Charles. *World Human Rights Guide* (London, 1983)

Hume, David. *On Human Understanding* (Edinburgh, 1739)

Humphreys, Christmas. *The Wisdom of Buddhism* (London, 1960)

Humphreys, Stephen. *Hooligans* (London, 1983)

Hunt, R.N.C. *Calvin* (London, 1933)

Hurwitz, S.J. *Jamaica: A Historical Portrait* (London, 1971)

Hutterbak, Robert. *Racism and Empire* (Cornell, 1976)

Ibn Batuta. *Travels in Asia*, tr. H.A.R. Gibbs (London, 1929)

Inalcik, H. *The Ottoman Empire* (London, 1973)

Ingram, Martin. *Church, Courts, Sex and Marriage in England 1570–1640* (Cambridge, 1987)

Ingram, Martin. *Religion, Communities and Moral Direction in The Late 16th and Early 17th Centuries* (Cambridge, 1990)

International Convention on Civil and Political Rights (New York, 1948)

Ispahari, M.A.H. *Quaid-e-Azam Jinnah as I knew him* (Karachi, 1966)

James, E.O. *The History of Religions* (London, 1956)

Jansen, G.H. *Militant Islam* (London, 1979)

Jesse, Captain. *Life of George Brummell* (London, 1844)

Johnson, Paul. *Enemies of Society* (London, 1977)

Jung, Carl Gustav. *Selected Writings*, ed. Antony Storr (London, 1983)

Kant, Immanuel. *Selections*, ed. L.W. Breck (New York, 1976)

Kei Kwei Sun. *Secret History of the Mongols* (Aligarh, 1957)

Keynes, J.M. *Collected Writings*, vol. 28, ed. D. Muggridge (London, 1982)

Kingsley, Charles. *Health and Education* (London, 1874)

Kitto, H.D.F. *The Greeks* (London, 1948)

Knowles, David. *Saints and Scholars* (Cambridge, 1962)

Knox, John. *History of the Reformation in Scotland*, ed. W. Croft Dickinson (Edinburgh, 1949)

Kohler, J.H. *On The Prehistory of Marriage* (Chicago, 1975)

Kroeber A.L. *Anthropology* (New York, 1923)

Labarge, M.N. *St Louis* (London, 1968)

Lang, D.M. *The Armenians* (London, 1981)

Lao, Tzu. *Tao Te Ching*, tr. D.C. Lau (London, 1963)

Lapping, Brian. *End of Empire* (London, 1985)

Larkin, P.J. *Reshaping of Everyday Life 1740–1840* (London, 1975)

Las Casas, Bartolomeo de. *Writings*, ed. F.A. MacNutt (New York, 1909)

Laslett, Peter and K. Ooskeveen. *Bastardy and its Consequences* (London, 1950)

Laurence, C.H. *Medieval Monasticism* (London, 1984)

Laver, James. *The Age of Illusion: Manners and Morals 1750–1848* (London, 1972)

Lea, H.C. *The History of Sacredotal Celibacy* (London, 1906)

Leach, Edmund. *Culture and Communication: The Logic by which Symbols are Connected* (London, 1976)

Lecky, W.E.H. *History of European Morals From Augustus To Charlemagne* (London, 1911)

Lecky, W.E.H. *The Rise and Influence of Rationalism in Europe* (London, 1910)

Lenin, V.I. *Selections*, ed. I. Deutscher (London, 1973)

Lentin, Antony, ed. *On the Corruption of Morals in Russia* (Cambridge, 1969)

Lessa, William and B. Lewis. *The Arabs in History* (London, 1950)

Levey, Michael. *A Concise History of Painting* (London, 1962)

Levine, D. and K. Wrightson. *Poverty and Piety in An English Village-Terling* (London, 1977)

Leyser, H. *Hermits and the New Monasticism* (London, 1984)

Liddell Hart, B. *Sherman* (London, 1930)

Liegeois, J.P. *Gypsies: An Illustrated History* (London, 1983)

Lindholm, Charles. *Generosity and Jealousy* (New York, 1982)

Lithgow, William. *Rare Adventures and Paineful Peregrinations* (London, 1814)

Lloyd George, David. *War Memoirs* (London, 1936)

Locke, John. *Selected Essays*, ed. I.C. Tipton (Oxford, 1977)

Longstreet, Stephen. *The Wilder Shore* (New York, 1971)

Lorenz, Konrad. *Civilized Man's Eight Deadly Sins* (London, 1971)

Lorenz, Konrad. *Motivations of Human and Animal Behaviour* (New York, 1973)

Lorenz, Konrad. *On Aggression* (London, 1966)

Lull, Ramon. *Order of Chivalry*, tr. E.A. Peers (London, 1929)

Lyons, D. *Ethics and the Rule of Law* (Oxford, 1973)

Macaulay, Thomas. *History of England from the Accession of James II* (London, 1848)

Mackie, J.L. *Ethics: Inventing Right and Wrong* (London, 1977)

Macklin, Ruth. *Man, Mind and Morality* (London, 1972)

MacMartin, Neil. *Spanish Fighters* (London, 1990)

MacMillan, James. *The Way We Were 1904–14* (London, 1978)

MacMillan, James. *The Way We Were 1914–34* (London, 1979)

MacMullen, Ramsay. *Corruption and the Decline of Rome* (Yale, 1988)

Male, Emile. *The Gothic Image* (London, 1961)

Malinowski, B. *The Psychology of Myth* (London, 1926)

Mallet, M. *The Borgias* (London, 1969)

Mandeville, Bernard. *The Grumbling Hive* (London, 1705)

Manga, J.A. *The Games Ethic and Imperialism* (London, 1980)

Maranda, Pierre. *Mythology: Selected Readings* (London, 1973)

Marcus, Jacob R. *The Jew in Medieval Europe* (Connecticut, 1975)

Marcus, Joyce. *The Cloud People* (New York, 1983)

Marcus, Steven. *The Other Victorians: A Study of Sexuality and Pornography in the 19th Century* (New York, 1966)

Mareff, R. *The Beginning of Morals and Culture* (London, 1963)

Margolis, M.L. and A. Marx. *History of the Jewish People* (Philadelphia, 1957)

Marshall, Dorothy. *Eighteenth Century England* (London, 1962)

Marwick, Arthur. *The Deluge: British Society and The First World War* (London, 1973)

Marx, Karl. *Das Kapital*, tr. B. Fowkes (London, 1976)

Mason, J.A. *The Ancient Civilizations of Peru* (London, 1957)

Mason, Philip. *The English Gentleman* (London, 1982)

Masson, Georgina. *Courtesans of the Italian Renaissance* (London, 1975)

Mattingly, H. *Roman Imperial Civilisation* (London, 1957)

McCall, Andrew. *The Medieval Underworld* (London, 1987)

Mead, Margaret. *Coming of Age in Samoa* (London, 1928)

Meeks, W.A. *The Moral World of the First Christians* (London, 1987)

Mill, J.S. *Liberty* (London, 1859)

Milman, H. *History of the Jews* (London, 1856)

Moore, Albert C. *Iconography of Religions* (London, 1977)

More, Sir Thomas. *Utopia* (London, 1938)

Morris, C. *Varieties of Human Value* (London 1932)

Morris, Desmond. *Manwatching* (London, 1979)

Morris, Desmond. *The Human Ape* (London, 1978)

Morse, George L. *Toward the Final Solutions* (London, 1975)

Mussolini, Benito. *Autobiography*, tr. R.W. Child (London, 1928)

Myers, J.L. *The Dawn of Civilization* (London, 1913)

Nagel, Thomas. *Philosophy, Morality and International Affairs* (Oxford, 1974)

Naguet, Vidal. *The Armenian Genocide* (London, 1926)

Nansen, Fridtjof. *First Crossing of Greenland*, tr. N.M. Gapp (London 1890)

Napoleon, Charles Louis. *Reveries Politiques* (Paris, 1836)

Neale, R.S. *Class and Ideology in the Nineteenth Century* (London, 1972)

Nef, J.U. *War and Human Progress* (New York, 1968)

Niebuhr, Reinhold. *Moral Men and Immoral Society* (New York, 1932)

Nietzsche, F. 'Beyond Good and Evil' in *Selections*, tr. R.J. Hollingdale (London, 1977)

Nietzsche, F. *Thus Spake Zarathustra*, tr. A. Tille (London, 1958)

Nikilananda. *The Gospel of Sri Ramakrishna* (Madras, 1947)

Nisbet, Robert. *The Morality of Modern Society* (Brighton, 1986)

Nowell-Smith, P.S. *Ethics* (London, 1954)

Oakley, Ray. *Drugs and Society and Human Behaviour* (London, 1978)

Oblonsky, D. *The Bogomils* (London, 1978)

Olearius, Adam. *The Travels of Olearius in Seventeenth Century Russia*, tr. S. Baron (Stanford, 1967)

Oquist, Paul. *Violence, Conflict and Politics in Columbia* (London, 1983)

Ordericus, Vitalis. *Historia Ecclesiastica*, ed. M. Chibnall (Oxford, 1976)

Origo, I. *The World of San Bernardino* (London, 1963)

Otis, L. *Prostitution in Medieval Society* (Chicago, 1985)

Owen, Robert. *New View of Society*, 4th ed. (London, 1918)

Owen, Wilfred. *Poems of Wilfred Owen*, ed. Siegfried Sassoon (London, 1920)

Packard, Vance. *The People Shapers* (London, 1978)

Parker, Peter. *The Old Lie: The Great War and the Public School Ethos* (London, 1987)

Parrinder, Geoffrey. *Sex in the World's Religions* (London, 1980)

Parrinder, Geoffrey. *What the World's Religions Teach* (London, 1958)

Pascal, Blaise. *Pensées*, tr. H.F. Stewart (Cambridge, 1942)

Pati, S. *Sex and Family Life in the Bible and the Middle East* (New York, 1959)

Pearson, Geoffrey. *Hooligan: A History of Respectable Fears* (London, 1983)

Pelagius. *Four Letters*, ed. R. Evans (London, 1968)

Perkins, Harold. *The Origins of Modern English Society* (London, 1965)

Perris, G.H. *History of War and Peace* (London, 1913)

Peters, R.S. *The Concept of Motivation* (London, 1958)

Plato. *The Republic*, tr. F. Cornford (Oxford, 1941)

Plutarch. *Lives*, tr. A.H. Clough (London, 1910)

Pollard, B.J. *Euthanasia: Should We Kill the Dying?* (Bedford, 1989)

Polo, Marco. *Travels*, tr. G. Marsden (London, 1854)

Porter, Roy. *English Social History in the 18th Century* (London, 1982)

Powell, Anton. *Classical Sparta* (London, 1989)

Power, Eileen. *Medieval People* (London, 1963)

Pratt, J.B. *The Pilgrimage of Buddhism* (London, 1928)

Prescott, W.H. *History of the Conquest of Mexico* (Boston, 1843)

Radishchev, Alexander. *Journey from St Petersburg to Moscow*, tr. R.P. Thaler (Cambridge, MA., 1958)

Radzinsky, E. *The Last Tsar*, tr. M. Schwarz (London, 1992)

Redfield, M. *Primitive World* (London, 1938)

Richards, Jeffrey. *Sex, Dissidence and Damnation* (London, 1989)

Riche, Pierre. *Daily Life in the Age of Charlemagne* (Liverpool, 1978)

Robertson, J. *The History of Morality* (London, 1920)

Robinson, J.A.T. *Honest to God* (London, 1963)

Rodzinski, W. *History of China* (London, 1977)

Roesdahl, Else. *The Vikings* (London, 1987)

Rokeach, M. *Beliefs, Attitudes and Values* (San Francisco, 1968)

Rolle, Renate. *The World of the Scythians* (London, 1989)

Romer, A.S. *Man and the Vertebrates* (London, 1954)

Rosa, Peter de. *Vicars of Christ* (London, 1988)

Rossiaud, J. *Medieval Prostitution*, tr. L. Cochrane (Oxford, 1984)

Rousseau, Jean Jacques. *Selections*, ed. M. Cranston (New York, 1983)

Rowan, John. *The Structured Crowd* (London, 1975)

Ruggiero, G. *Boundaries of Eros: Sexuality in Renaissance Venice* (New York, 1985)

Russell, Bertrand. *Human Society in Ethics and Politics* (London, 1952)

Ruthven, Malise. *Torture* (London, 1978)

Saggs, H.W.F. *The Might that was Assyria* (London, 1984)

Salmon, G. *Non-miraculous and Other Sermons* (London, 1887)

Sartre, Jean Paul. *Being and Nothingness*, tr. H.E. Barnes (London, 1969)

Schama, Simon. *The Embarrassment of Riches* (London, 1987)

Schweitzer, Albert. *Civilization and Ethics,* tr. C.T. Campion (London, 1923)

Scott, James C. *The Moral Economy of the Peasant* (London, 1976)

Sellin, J. Thorsten. *Slavery and the Penal System* (New York, 1976)

Sen, A.C., tr. *Ashoka's Edicts* (Calcutta, 1956)

Sen, K.M. *Hinduism* (London, 1961)

Sheils, W.J. *The Church and War* (Oxford, 1983)

Sherrington, Charles. *Man and his Nature* (London, 1955)

Smout, T.C. *History of the Scottish People* (London, 1969)

Smyth, A.P. *Warlords and Holy Men* (London, 1984)

Solzhenitsyn, Alexander. *Gulag Archipelago,* tr. T.P. Whitney (London, 1974)

Spinoza, Baruch. *Ethica,* tr. A. Boyle (London, 1959)

Ssu-yu Teng. *New Light on the Taiping Rebellion* (Harvard, 1950)

Stearns, Peter N. *European Society in Upheaval* (London, 1978)

Stevenson, C.L. *Ethics and Language* (London, 1944)

Stone, Lawrence. *Family, Sex and Marriage in England 1560–1800* (London, 1978)

Stone, Lawrence. *Past and Present Revisited* (London, 1987)

Stone, Lawrence. *The Road to Divorce 1500–1887* (London, 1990)

Storr, Anthony. *Human Destructiveness* (London, 1972)

Stubbes, Philip. *Anatomy of Abuses* (London, 1595)

Susuki, D.T. *Introduction to Zen Buddhism* (London, 1949)

Taga, Munchaya. *Eisai* (Tokyo, 1965)

Taipe, Victor L. *France in the Age of Louis XIII and Richlieu* (London, 1962)

Taseer, Salmaan. *Bhutto* (Ithaca, 1979)

Tawney, R.H. *Religion and the Rise of Capitalism* (London, 1961)

Tawney, R.H. *The Acquisitive Society* (Brighton, 1982)

Taylor, A.J.P. *English History 1914–45* (London, 1977)

Taylor, G. Rattray. *Sex in History* (London, 1963)

Taylor, William. *The Myceneans* (London, 1983)

Thapair, Romila. *History of India* (London, 1966)

Thompson, E.P. *The Making of the English Working Class* (London, 1980)

Thompson, F.M.L. *The Rise of Respectable Society* (London, 1988)

Thompson, F.M.L., ed. *Cambridge Social History* (Cambridge, 1990)

Thomson, Oliver. *Mass Persuasion in History* (Edinburgh, 1977)

Thoreau, Henry. *Correspondence,* ed. Harding and Bode (New York, 1959)

Thoreau, Henry. *Journal,* ed. J.C. Broderick (Princeton, 1981)

Tinbergen, Niko. *The Herring Gull's World* (London, 1972)

Tocqueville, Alexis de. *Ancien Regime,* tr. J. Bonnar (London, 1988)

Toynbee, Arnold. *A Study of History,* abr. D.C. Sommerville (Oxford, 1957)

Treitschke, H. von. *Politics,* tr. B. Dugdale (London, 1916)

Trelease, A.W. *White Terror: the Ku Klux Klan Conspiracy* (London, 1972)

Trudgill, Eric. *Madonnas and Magdalens* (New York, 1976)

Trumbach, R. *Rise of the Egalitarian Family* (London, 1978)

Turbeville, A.S. *The Spanish Inquisition* (London, 1932)

Turgenev, Ivan. *Fathers and Children,* tr. G. Garnett (London, 1920)

Ure, P.G. *Justinian and his Age* (London, 1957)

Usamah Ibn Munquidh. *An Arab Gentleman and Warrior,* tr. G.R. Potter (London, 1929)

Vahid, M. *Mohammed Iqbal* (London, 1959)

Vaillant, G.C. *The Aztecs of Mexico* (London, 1950)

Vale, Malcolm. *War and Chivalry* (London, 1981)

Valtierra, A. *Peter Claver* (London, 1960)

Vana, Z. *The World of the Ancient Slavs* (London, 1983)

Varley, Paul. *The Samurai* (London, 1970)

Voltaire. *Lettres Philosophiques*, ed. F.A. Taylor (Oxford, 1946)

Waley, A. *Three Ways of Thought in Ancient China* (London, 1939)

Waley, Arthur. *The Opium War through Chinese Eyes* (London, 1958)

Walzer, Michael. *Just and Unjust Wars* (London, 1978)

Warner, Marina. *Cult of Mary* (London, 1982)

Warner, Marina. *Joan of Arc* (London, 1987)

Warnock, G.J. *Contemporary Moral Philosophy* (London, 1995)

Washburn, S.L. *The Social Life of Early Man* (London, 1962)

Watt, W. Montgomery. *Muhammad: Prophet and Statesman* (London, 1961)

Webbe, William. *Discourse of English Poetrie*, ed. E. Arber (London, 1870)

Wedgewood, C.V. *The Thirty Years War* (London, 1938)

West D.J. *Homosexuality Reexamined* (London, 1977)

Westermarck, E. *Ethical Relativity* (London, 1908)

Westermarck, E. *The Origin and Development of Moral Ideas* (London, 1906)

Westrick, R. *Antisemitism* (London, 1990)

White, E.B. *Elements of Style* (New York, 1972)

Whitehead, A.N. *Concept of Nature* (Cambridge, 1920)

Whyte, R.H. *Organisation Man* (New York, 1955)

Williams, Bernard. *Morality* (Cambridge, 1976)

Williams, Eric. *British Historians and the West Indies* (London, 1966)

Wilson, Colin. *The Criminal History of Mankind* (London, 1985)

Wilson, Colin. *The Order of The Assassins* (London, 1983)

Wittek, P. *The Rise of the Ottoman Empire* (London, 1938)

Wolseley, Garnet. *Story of a Soldier's Life* (London, 1904)

Woods, William. *The History of the Devil* (London, 1973)

Wright, Derek. *The Psychology of Moral Behaviour* (London, 1971)

Yaffe, Mauria and Edward Nelson, eds. *The Influence of Pornography on Behaviour* (London, 1982)

Young, Arthur. *Autobiography*, ed. M. Betham Edwards (London, 1848)

Youngs, Joyce. *Sixteenth Century England* (London, 1984)

Zeldin, Theodore. *Ambition and Love in France 1848–1945* (London, 1973)

Zeldin, Theodore. *Taste and Corruption in France 1848–1945* (London, 1967)

Ziff, Larzer. *Puritanism in America* (New York, 1973)

Index